JUDY WILLIS, M.D.

Brain-Friendly
Strategies

D0461917

for the
Inclusion
Classroom

INSIGHTS FROM A NEUROLOGIST AND CLASSROOM TEACHER

Association for Supervision and Curriculum Development
Alexandria, Virginia USA

Association for Supervision and Curriculum Development
1703 N. Beauregard St. • Alexandria, VA 22311-1714 USA
Phone: 800-933-2723 or 703-578-9600 • Fax: 703-575-5400
Web site: www.ascd.org • E-mail: member@ascd.org
Author guidelines: www.ascd.org/write

Gene R. Carter, *Executive Director;* Nancy Modrak, *Director of Publishing;* Julie Houtz, *Director of Book Editing & Production;* Miriam Goldstein, *Project Manager;* Reece Quiñones, *Senior Graphic Designer;* Michael Rohani, *Typesetter;* Dina Murray Seamon, *Production Specialist/Team Lead*

All Web links in this book are correct as of the publication date below but may have become inactive or otherwise modified since that time. If you notice a deactivated or changed link, please e-mail books@ascd.org with the words "Link Update" in the subject line. In your message, please specify the Web link, the book title, and the page number on which the link appears.

ASCD Member Book, No. FY07-07 (May 2007, P). ASCD Member Books mail to Premium (P), Comprehensive (C), and Regular (R) members on this schedule: Jan., PC; Feb., P; Apr., PCR; May, P; July, PC; Aug., P; Sept., PCR; Nov., PC; Dec., P.

PAPERBACK ISBN-13: 978-1-4166-0539-3   ASCD product #107040
Also available as an e-book through ebrary, netLibrary, and many online booksellers (see Books in Print for the ISBNs).

Quantity discounts for the paperback edition only: 10–49 copies, 10%; 50+ copies, 15%; for 1,000 or more copies, call 800-933-2723, ext. 5634, or 703-575-5634. For desk copies: member@ascd.org.

Library of Congress Cataloging-in-Publication Data

Willis, Judy.
    Brain-friendly strategies for the inclusion classroom / Judy Willis.
        p.   cm.
    Includes bibliographical references and index.
        ISBN 978-1-4166-0539-3 (pbk. : alk. paper) 1. Learning, Psychology of. 2. Learning—
Physiological aspects. 3. Brain. 4. Cognitive styles. I. Title.

    LB1060.W544   2007
    370.15'23—dc22   2007001442

15 14 13 12 11 10 09 08 07 06   1 2 3 4 5 6 7 8 9 10 11 12

~

To Malana, the newest teacher in our family.
Your hundred hugs give me courage,
your sparkle and smiles make me soar,
and your intelligence, compassion, and integrity
will make all your classrooms magical kingdoms of joyful learning.

~

Why?

BY JUDY WILLIS

Dedicated to my students, past and present,
at Santa Barbara Middle School

Because you struggle and don't quit,
I use sincerity, not sarcasm.

Because you have a 70-minute math class looming ahead,
I put an optical illusion on the overhead projector
before the warm-up calculations.

Because you laugh at my corny jokes and ask
for my nostalgic stories,
I convince myself that it is not a ploy to shorten my lesson,
and I tell away.

Because in frustration you proclaimed, "I hate math,"
I gave you a calculator and you gave me a smile.

Because you wrote that for the first time you *think* you can do math,
I spend more time with you so you'll be *sure* that you can.

Because you get out of bed for school when it is still dark,
I give you a lollipop on your birthday.

Because getting a class of teenagers to sing is a delight,
I teach you the fat turkey song each November.

Because there are Monday mornings,
We always have Monday-Funday.

Because you tell me about your sisters, brothers, friends, and pets,
I speak of you as *my kids*.

Because your brains get worn out after writing three pages of notes,
I stop and give you syn-naps.

Because you remember to bring your books most of the time,
I give you my copy the day you forget.

Because you are whispering to your friend who is so sad,
I don't stand sternly and say, "I'm waiting for you to finish."

Because you care enough to ask to do corrections and take a retest,
I make up a new test so you can show what you learned.

Because you say hi to me in the halls years after you were in my class,
I come back every year to watch you grow.

Because you *might* be caregivers someday,
I want you to learn compassion with your algebra.

Because you *will* be the caretakers of the planet someday,
I teach you to care about yourselves every day.

Brain-Friendly
Strategies
for the Inclusion Classroom

Acknowledgments. ix

Introduction. 1

1. Success for All Students in Inclusion Classes. 11

2. Looking into Multiple Intelligence Brains. 51

3. Teaching Students with Attention Disorders. 62

4. Enriching the Inclusive Learning Environment. 108

5. Review and Test Preparation Strategies for
   Diverse Learners. 151

Afterword: What the Future Holds. 172

Appendix: Sample Lesson Plans for Inclusion
   Class Activities. 176

Glossary. 195

Bibliography. 205

Index. 215

About the Author. 229

ACKNOWLEDGMENTS

To Paul, my college sweetheart, for inspiring me to write books about the neurology of learning because you want all children to have the advantage of using their powerful brains to the max! I love you.

To my daughter, Alani Willis. You keep me grounded when I start floating away, and laughing when you tell it like it is. I am so proud of you.

To Norma Allerhand, my wise and beautiful mom, who without complaint or conditions sacrificed whatever was necessary to support my education and who continues to inspire me to be my best.

To Judy Gamboa, my best friend since 6th grade. As a resource specialist, you have enriched the lives of hundreds of children through your love, wisdom, and dedication. As a friend, you have taught me to be an active listener and have shown me that students who are cared about become people who care.

To Lynn Koegel, a brilliant proponent of inclusion classes, and to Pam Boswell, who lights the fires in her students' hearts.

With heartfelt gratitude to the encouragement and enthusiasm of ASCD's director of book acquisitions and development, Scott Willis, and to my ASCD editor, Miriam Goldstein, who deconstructed and reconstructed this book to make it worthy of readers' time.

As always, to my students, colleagues, staff, and parents of the Santa Barbara Middle School because you are all the diamonds in my wheels.

INTRODUCTION

Historically, teachers in regular classrooms have not felt prepared to teach exceptional students, preferring to leave the job to trained specialists. But times and laws have changed, and most classrooms today have at least some inclusive aspects to them. Brain research has provided educators with a better understanding of instructional practices that not only are essential for students with special needs, but also benefit their peers. These new tools will both help teachers face the challenges of teaching an inclusion class and make teaching more fruitful and rewarding.

THE LEARNING BRAIN

It is only relatively recently that cognitive neuroscientists have begun to study how our brain structures support mental functions. The late 1960s saw the conception of computerized axial tomography (also called CT or CAT scanning), which offered neuroscientists their first opportunity to look inside a living brain. The CT scan uses a narrow beam of X-rays to obtain multiple two-dimensional images of the brain in the form of a series of slices, or cross-sections. From these images, a computer can generate a three-dimensional image of the brain, thereby allowing for analysis of the brain's internal structures.

Today, the three most important tools used in brain research are the positron emission tomography (PET) scan, functional magnetic resonance imaging (fMRI), and the quantitative electroencephalogram (qEEG).

PET scanning produces a three-dimensional image of functional processes in the body based on the detection of radiation from the emission of *positrons* (tiny particles emitted from a radioactive substance administered to the subject in combination with glucose). As the subject engages in various cognitive activities, the scan records the rate at which specific regions of the brain use the glucose. These recordings are used to produce maps of areas of high brain activity with particular cognitive functions.

The fMRI measures the metabolic changes that take place in an active part of the brain. The technology behind fMRI makes use of the fact that oxygenated blood shows up better on MRI images than does nonoxygenated blood. Because active regions of the brain receive more blood and more oxygen, scientists can use fMRI images to determine which areas of the brain demonstrate more activity.

The qEEG uses digital technology to measure electrical patterns at the surface of the scalp, which primarily reflect cortical electrical activity, or brain waves. This brain wave monitoring provides brain-mapping data based on the precise localization and timing of brain wave patterns coming from the parts of the brain actively engaged in processing information.

All of these tools can help educators grasp the series of steps that occur when students learn. This information pathway begins when students take in sensory data. Their brains generate patterns by relating new material with previously learned material or by "chunking" material into pattern systems it has used before. The patterned data then pass from sensory response regions through the emotional limbic system filters. The limbic system—a group of interconnected deep brain structures involved in olfaction, emotion, motivation, behavior, and various autonomic functions—has a strong influence on the formation of memory. After passing through the limbic system, the data go to memory storage neurons (short-term, relational, and, ultimately, long-term). From the memory storage neurons throughout the cerebral cortex (the surface layer of gray matter of the cerebrum that coordinates sensory and motor information), information can be activated and sent to the executive function regions of the frontal lobes. These regions are where the highest levels of cognition and information manipulation—forming judgments, prioritizing, analyzing, organizing, and conceptualizing—take place.

GRAY MATTER

The basis of all memory is a chemical change that takes place in neurons. Most of the brain's neurons are located in the *cerebral cortex*, the outermost layer of the brain. This area is also known as *gray matter* because of the darker color of the neurons, compared with the lighter *white matter* made up primarily of the connecting and supporting cells, axons, and dendrites that bring information to and from the neurons. Every lobe of the brain is covered by its cerebral cortex packed with neurons. The lobe of the brain that the cortex surrounds determines which conscious activity the cortex's neurons will mediate, such as language, speech, perception, or voluntary motor activity. The neurons controlling such executive function processes as planning, problem solving, and analyzing are contained in the layer of cortex that covers the frontal lobes.

THE PROMISE OF BRAIN RESEARCH

Brain research has been a springboard for mind-blowing advances in teaching practices. We are learning to translate neuroimaging data into classroom strategies designed to stimulate parts of the brain that are metabolically activated during the stages of information processing, memory, and recall. My 25 years of experience in the field of child and adult neurology, as well as my background in education, have also helped me make connections between brain research and effective teaching practices.

We must, however, remain cautious about believing all claims made in the interpretation of functional brain imaging, especially those coming from special interest groups. In my medical practice, I often observe biased interpretations of medical research made by representatives of pharmaceutical companies. Similarly, vested interest groups in the education field, such as curriculum sales departments, brandish colorful brain scans as proof that their strategy, program, or educational therapy is the best, even though critical analysis of these scans does not support their inflated claims. Although high-quality peer-reviewed brain research can provide hard biological data, educators need to be able to sort spurious claims from valid information.

GRAY MATTER

Reevaluations of some early PET scan research interpretations have given us reason to be cautious about which research is valid enough to connect with actual learning.

During my chief residency at UCLA in 1979, one of my senior residents, John Mazziotta, now chair of the UCLA Department of Neurology, was working with the new PET scanner and conducting research with Michael Phelps and Harry Chugani to evaluate the brain metabolism in patients with seizures and other disorders affecting neural activity. In 1987, this group published the first research evaluating brain development in children. In a study of 29 epileptic children ranging in age from 5 days to 15 years old, the researchers determined that the highest rate of glucose metabolism occurred at age 3 or 4, when the rate was twice that of adults. This high metabolism remained relatively unchanged until age 9 or 10, when it began to drop down to the adult range. By age 16 or 17, the metabolism had leveled off (Chugani, Phelps, & Mazziotta, 1987).

The researchers did not intend their findings to be used as proof that the age of high brain metabolism was an especially opportune time for teaching interventions, and problems arose when people assumed that this information implied more than it actually did. For example, it turned out that there is a correlation between the age when synaptic density is greatest (Huttenlocher & Dabholkar, 1997) and the age when glucose metabolism is greatest. However, this finding does not prove that the reason for the greater metabolism is to maintain the greater density of synapses, or that either synaptic density or brain metabolic activity is the direct cause of any potential for greater learning during those years (Chugani, 1996).

In fact, Mazziotta and his colleagues never claimed that periods of high metabolic activity were the optimal periods for learning to take place. That may well be the case, but further cognitive research is necessary before we can make scientific claims linking brain synaptic density, metabolic activity, and potential for optimal learning.

What we can recognize is that scientific evidence from genetic research and neuroimaging studies has demonstrated the neurobiological basis of learning disabilities. Understanding the differences in how brains process information is helpful in understanding that students with learning disabilities are not incapable of learning or performing tasks. Rather, their brain processing in certain brain regions and networks is often merely less efficient—slower or less precise. In fact, it is possible for slower-developing brain regions to catch up to normal growth, changing students' learning strengths dramatically. Therefore, the label of *learning disabled* should not be considered permanent, but rather a guide for students' states of brain readiness at a point in time. Keeping this distinction in mind, we can best help these students by putting in place strategies, accommodations, and interventions that cognitive and functional imaging studies have shown meet their specific needs (Fiedorowicz, 1999).

At this early stage, we must rely on our best interpretations of neuroimaging research to guide our teaching practice. By using research conducted according to objective scientific criteria and interpreted by researchers without personal stakes in the outcomes, we can greatly increase our ability to align instructional goals with the brain functioning patterns of our students. It would be premature and against my training as a medical doctor to claim that any of the strategies I suggest in this book are as yet firmly validated by the complete meshing of cognitive studies, neuroimaging, and classroom research. For now, a combination of the art of teaching and the science of neuroimaging will best guide educators in finding the most neuro-*logical* ways to maximize learning.

BRAIN RESEARCH–BASED STRATEGIES IN THE CLASSROOM

As educators in inclusion classrooms, we want to support our exceptional students while not letting our focus on their learning differences diminish the quality of teaching for the rest of the class. Fortunately, brain research has confirmed that strategies benefiting learners with special challenges are suited for engaging and stimulating *all* learners. Each student is a unique learner with individual interests, talents, life experiences, and goals. Although standardized testing attempts to provide objective criteria for labeling students as special-needs, the designations remain arbitrary numbers on a grid. A more accurate picture is a continuum. Wherever students fall on this spectrum, they all differ from one another in various ways and to various degrees. Teachers who can engage and connect with the students at either end of this spectrum will be better prepared to connect with the students who fall in between.

For example, brain research has shown us the positive or negative effect that students' emotional states can have on the affective filter in their amygdalas (a part of the limbic system connected to the temporal lobe). Additional evidence now demonstrates the multiple benefits of the dopamine release that accompanies students' expectation of intrinsic reward. This research has given us techniques that, although originally designed for exceptional students, can be successfully adapted for all learners. It is becoming clear that special education students and general education students have more similarities than differences.

We can identify the practices that benefit all learners by looking at the skills most heavily emphasized in special education classes:

time management, studying, organization, judgment, prioritization, and decision making. Now that the brain imaging research supports the theory that students process these activities in their executive function brain regions, it appears that brain-compatible strategies targeting these skills will benefit all students.

Even high-achieving students do not appear to have equal strengths in all of the recognized executive functions. Many students at the top of the class academically may be using their superior intelligence or creativity to make the adaptations they need to compensate for a deficit in one or more of their executive functions. If these top students are so successful without instruction in the executive function strategies, consider how much more successful, more creative, and less stressed they might be if strategies to improve these skills were incorporated into the general curriculum. Research has borne this out: high achievers in inclusion classes that teach and practice executive function cognition strategies become even more successful in their academic, time management, analytical, and organizational skills (Stainback & Stainback, 1991).

In this book, I offer some background on the brain research examining how the "average" student learns, contrasted with exceptional students' unusual brain responses to sounds, numbers, emotions, people, external stimulation, and written and spoken words. Most of the strategies I suggest in this book are compatible with research showing how the brain seems to preferentially respond to the presentation of sensory stimuli. Understanding this brain learning research will increase educators' familiarity with which methods are most compatible with how students acquire, retain, retrieve, and use information.

CONTINUOUS GROWTH FOR ALL

Just as physicians are not specialists in all fields, general educators cannot become experts in all areas of exceptional student education. There will always be a need for specialists. Yet just as parents partner with their child's physician concerning medical care, teachers with an understanding of brain learning research will be in the best position to partner with education specialists, families, and students to make the classroom a comfortable place where all students experience the joy of learning. Just as scientists continually engage in self-questioning and revision, professional educators continue to examine, test, deconstruct, and reconstruct strategies to become better at the important job entrusted to us.

When my daughter Malana was in graduate school for education, she wrote to me, "Teaching is not meant to be a practice in perfection. Rather, it is an opportunity to continuously grow, learn, ask questions, be confused, and overcome challenges. Even more important, teaching, and especially the education of exceptional students, is a collaborative effort. It is the classroom teacher's responsibility to work with the student, the family, and a variety of professionals as part of a group to make inclusion a positive experience for all" (M. Willis, personal communication, March 15, 2006).

That continuous growth is what I hope to encourage with this book. With knowledge of how the brain learns, teachers will have the tools to determine which studies are valid and which are biased. They will have the information to go beyond the specific techniques described here to create their own brain research–based strategies. And valuable new neuroimaging research will continue to open more windows into the brain's learning processes. Educators will be able to interpret this future research and apply the results to keep their classroom instruction attuned to the needs of their students.

I predict that during the next few decades, the neuroscience of learning will continue to provide evidence supporting three core ideas:

- The instructional strategies reaping the most success are those that teach for meaning and understanding.
- The most learning-conducive classrooms are those that are low in threat yet high in reasonable challenge.
- Students who are actively engaged and motivated will devote more effort to strive for meaningful goals.

The strategies I describe throughout this book are firmly rooted in these ideas. When teachers use these strategies, they will reach the learners at the extremes of the continuum in their inclusion classes and prevent any from falling through the cracks.

We are fortunate to be educators during this period of illuminating brain research devoted to our field. The flipside is that we are teaching in a system that increasingly uses standardized testing as one of the most prominent measures of student, teacher, and school success. The resulting standardization of curriculum is a contradiction to serving students' unique needs. Our challenge and opportunity will be to incorporate the best teaching strategies—derived from valid scientific discovery and classroom implementation—not only to build test-taking and rote-memory competency in our students, but also to help them grow to their greatest potential as life-long learners.

CHAPTER 1

SUCCESS FOR ALL STUDENTS IN INCLUSION CLASSES

MORE INCLUSION FOR MORE STUDENTS

Most educators do not enter teaching with the expectation that they will be working with consistently well-behaved, enthusiastic, successful learners who enjoy sitting quietly in rows listening to teachers lecture at them. Nor do most teachers anticipate that all their students will dutifully use their highest cognitive processes to memorize, prioritize, analyze, and reflect on everything they hear. There may be some days when such a prospect is appealing, but for the most part, teachers and students have at least one thing in common: their brains are inspired and stimulated by challenge. Robotically attentive "Stepford" children, always ready for rote memorization and one-size-fits-all instruction, would not need teachers. Videotaped lectures and textbooks could serve their needs.

What makes teachers true educators is their acknowledgment, appreciation, and respect of students' differences. Students' diverse intelligences, talents, skills, interests, and backgrounds enrich our schools and our lives as teachers. Many of today's classrooms are more diverse than ever, including as they do students with LD.

Most of us know that the *L* in *LD* stands for *learning*, but the *D* can stand for a variety of terms: *disability, dysfunction, difficulty, diversity, dichotomy,* or *difference.* The fact that these two letters can represent more than one term is of value. The terms may not be clinically or diagnostically interchangeable, but my goal is to offer approaches to enrich the classroom experiences of students in all of the LD categories, as well as those of their classmates. No two students are the same, and no individual student has the same response to learning in every situation. What we consider a *disability* for a student in one situation may be a *difference* that enriches that student's learning experience in another situation. The generally accepted definition of the term *learning disability* is a cognitive, neurological, or psychological disorder that impedes the ability to learn, especially one that interferes with a person's communicative capacities and potential to be taught effectively. Some states require that students labeled *learning disabled* have normal or above-normal intelligence and difficulties in learning specific skills. Other states extend the definition to include people of below-normal intelligence who have such conditions as perceptual handicaps, minimal brain dysfunction, dyslexia, developmental aphasia, and AD/HD, but they do not include learning problems due to mental retardation, emotional disturbance, cultural or environmental disadvantage, or physical handicaps (for example, impaired sight or hearing or orthopedic disabilities).

Neither learning nor teaching is a single process. Neuroimaging studies show individuals' varying abilities to identify such sensory stimuli as color, shape, sound, and location. These variations correlate with individual students' different recognition capacities, learning styles, and responses to instructional materials and teaching techniques. Because each student is unique, teachers—especially those in inclusion classes—must use diverse strategies suited to students' broad array of abilities, intelligences, and learning styles. When we offer a variety of individually appropriate strategies, we enable all students to be true participants in a community of learners.

As teachers strive to meet the needs of all students, they will realize that there is no clear, consistent dichotomy between "special" and "regular" students. The same students will not always be at the top or the bottom when they are evaluated according to their intellectual, social, physical, and creative abilities. With the move from a divided general education/special education model to a unified inclusion system, the most successful educators will be those who work together and share resources and expertise to meet all students' needs in any way possible (Stainback, Stainback, & Forest, 1989).

As educators, we won't know what gifts are hidden in our students until we unwrap their packages. Most successful teachers of inclusion classes have found that when they teach basic skills within the context of meaningful lessons, all students can achieve higher-level learning. Such lessons stimulate critical thinking and motivate students to make personal connections with the material.

Students who are part of a community of learners tend to rise to higher levels of learning and joy, especially when they work cooperatively on in-depth, project-based units of discovery. In these supportive classroom communities, students acknowledge and appreciate one another's skills and talents. Stereotypical academic success no longer becomes the only standard for who is "smart." Students who learn about their own and their classmates' multiple intelligences and unique abilities begin to shed previous negative attitudes or preconceived notions about LD students. In addition, an education environment that values participation in cooperative activities can reduce LD students' academic anxieties and build their confidence as they receive positive recognition for what they bring to the community of learners.

THE LAW

The Individuals with Disabilities Education Act (IDEA) requires public schools in the United States to make available to all eligible children with disabilities a free education in the least restrictive environment appropriate to their individual needs. Under IDEA, public school systems must develop an appropriate individualized education program (IEP) for each of these students. The specific special education plan and related services outlined in each IEP should reflect the individual needs of the student. IDEA also mandates particular procedures that schools must follow in developing IEPs. Each student's IEP must be developed by a team of knowledgeable persons and be reviewed at least once annually. The team includes the student's teacher; the student's parents, subject to certain limited exceptions; the student, if determined appropriate; a state agency representative who is qualified to provide or supervise the provision of special education; and other individuals at the parents' or agency's discretion.

The decades since the initiation of IDEA in 1975 have seen the almost complete elimination of separate pullout classes for students with disabilities. Now students who were previously sent to "special" schools attend classes with their siblings and neighbors. Inclusion classes, when successfully planned and taught, become places where friendships are founded on the appreciation of similarities and differences.

The word *inclusion* carries positive connotations of belonging. Indeed, full inclusion of all students—even those with severe disabilities—in general education classrooms doesn't mean LD students work separately with their aide while the rest of the class does other work. Truly inclusive classrooms integrate and coordinate specialized school support programs within the general education program. This approach has replaced what was previously dubbed *mainstreaming*—nonacademic inclusion, in which LD students joined general classes for nonacademic work and were removed for academic special education.

BENEFITS OF INCLUSION

In the past, many students with severe disabilities were separated into special education classes and missed out on the benefits of having long-term social relationships with classmates who did not also have severe disabilities. As a result, when they left the supervised classrooms, they were not ready to join the larger, heterogeneous communities in which they would live and work for the rest of their lives. In contrast, a 10-year follow-up in one study found that LD students who had been taught in integrated classes demonstrated more independent functioning and social adjustment (Stainback et al., 1989).

Sometimes problems in separate special education classes arose because of insufficient teacher training. For example, teachers may have learned to identify and accommodate the needs of LD readers but lacked instruction in teaching higher-level reading. Also, because special education classes were not necessarily smaller than regular classes, many students with disabilities received no more individual attention in the segregated classes than they would have gotten in the integrated classes. In some such cases, teachers were obliged to teach the majority of the class to the level of the least common denominator—the most severely disabled students who needed the slowest pace and the least-challenging lessons (Affleck, Madge, Adams, & Lowenbraun, 1988).

Strategies derived from brain research enable LD students to learn according to their strengths and help them develop the characteristics found in successful students. In addition to promoting academic success, these strategies uncover such strengths as energy, curiosity, concentration, exceptional memory for details, empathy, openness, perceptiveness, and divergent thinking. Many students who struggle with LD become self-reliant at an early age, are good at expressing their feelings, are aware of their thinking and decision-making processes, and are tolerant of others' weaknesses (Goldberg, Higgins, & Herman, 2003).

Teachers who have used brain-compatible learning strategies to build on LD students' strengths report an additional long-term benefit over the course of 5 to 10 years. When I spoke with Judy Gamboa of the Learning Disabilities Association of Arizona, she noted that

> Children who practice the strategies successfully to compensate for limitations associated with their LD have become college and graduate students who stand out among classmates who never had to struggle with LD. The students who have incorporated the

adaptive strategies are standouts in their ability to express their feelings and exhibit tolerance and empathy for others. I have found that these former students who achieve success in later life have used the adaptive strategies they learned in school to enrich their lives once they leave the classroom. The discoveries they made about the correlation of practice with skill building and mastery stay with them and continue to empower them to work to achieve their goals. It is so satisfying to see these former LD students reach their goals and use the strategies we practiced to achieve competence. Joy of learning has taken the place of frustration and avoidance of challenge. There is nothing as rewarding as seeing my students years later with the confidence and perseverance to make their dreams become realities. (J. Gamboa, personal communication, Feb. 17, 2006)

Inclusive classes are also good for teachers. Whereas isolated special education teachers experience more burnout and attrition than regular teachers do, effective inclusion teachers tend to describe themselves as tolerant, flexible, and prepared to take responsibility for all their students (McGregor & Vogelsberg, 1998). These successful teachers' colleagues and administrators found them to be good collaborators who exuded warmth and sincerity in their interactions with students. Their most common concerns were insufficient time for collaboration and the challenges of managing students whose severe behavioral problems disrupted class. Evaluations have found that the most beneficial supports to successful inclusion teachers are strategic training, support from a team of professionals, and assistance personnel in their classrooms (Pryor, 2003).

THE ROAD TO SUCCESS

The principal goal for all students is to achieve their own highest level of success in supportive classrooms, taught by teachers who give them the tools to overcome obstacles and learn to their fullest potential. Although success means different things to different people, most people agree on certain common factors as important components of success, including positive family and peer relationships, self-approval, academic success, job satisfaction, physical and mental health, financial comfort, and a sense that one's life has meaning and value.

A study tracking LD students over the course of 20 years identified several specific attributes that seem to lead to such successful life outcomes. These attributes include a positive self-concept, a proactive approach to life, a tendency to set goals, perseverance, effective support systems, and effective emotional coping strategies. Although not every subject who achieved successful life outcomes had all of these attributes, the study found that their presence was more predictive of success than were such variables as school grades and IQ (Raskind, Goldberg, Higgins, & Herman, 1999).

FIVE CRITICAL CONDITIONS OF LEARNING SUCCESS

A sequence of five critical conditions of brain processing helps promote some of these attributes of success. I have defined the conditions according to the brain structures and functions that neuroimaging research has demonstrated are the basis of processing raw sensory data into retained and accessible memory. Most of the strategies I describe in this book help promote these five conditions. The strategies aim to empower students' brains to recognize which sensory data are worthy of focus; promote the passage of these data through alerting and affective filters; pattern the data into the coding of brain cell communication; and prepare the data to be successfully stored, maintained, and retrieved. The entire process turns information into the memories that become accumulated knowledge. The following five steps describe how the sequence of these necessary conditions of learning unfolds.

1. The brain responds to sensory input that engages the attention of sensory processing filters.

2. After the senses register the information, it passes along to the neurons in the amygdala, where it can be moved to memory storage.

At this point, the affective filter in the limbic system must be set to accept and not block incoming data. If high stress or negative emotions have overloaded the amygdala, the affective filter will block passage of the data into memory. On the other hand, pleasurable, positively reinforcing, and intrinsically motivating stimuli unlock the gates of the limbic system to facilitate active information processing. Such information has the best chance of entering long-term memory storage banks (Willis, 2006).

GRAY MATTER

The brain's emotional core is a connection of neural centers in and near the temporal lobes that together are called the *limbic system*. Composed of the *medial temporal lobe, thalamus, hippocampus, amygdala*, and parts of the frontal lobes, the limbic system is the core of emotional response, stress reactions, and fear patterns. All information enters the brain as sensory data from what we hear, see, smell, touch, or taste. This information must pass through the *reticular activating system* (RAS) and the limbic system to be acknowledged, recognized, connected with relational memories, patterned, and ultimately stored in long-term memory.

The amygdala is often referred to as the center of the limbic system because it is so responsive to threat and fear. fMRI and PET scans demonstrate that when the amygdala is in a hypermetabolic state in response to stress, the brain regions that process information show much lower metabolic activity (i.e., less oxygen or glucose use). This lower metabolic activity suggests that the information is not getting through the hyperactive amygdala's blockade and reaching the secondary processing areas (Introini-Collison et al., 1990; Introini-Collison, Miyazaki, & McGaugh, 1991).

The RAS is another critical brain entry pathway that is affected by emotion. A major attention-activation switching system located at the brainstem, the RAS receives input from the nerves that converge into the spinal cord from sensory receptors in the arms, legs, trunk, head, and neck. The spinal cord sends these sensory messages up through the RAS to gain entry to the brain. The RAS sets the state of arousal of the rest of the brain and affects the ability of the higher brain sensory recognition centers to receive and respond to incoming data (Eich, 1995).

3. Sensory data that pass through the brain's filters are coded into patterns that can be connected to existing neuronal pathways.

GRAY MATTER

Information travels along the nerve cell's axons and dendrites as electrical impulses. However, where these sprouting arms connect to the next neuron in the circuit, the information has to travel across a gap between the end of one nerve and the beginning of the next one. In these gaps, called *synapses*, there are no physical structures along which the electric impulses can travel. When crossing synapses, the information impulse must therefore be temporarily converted from an electrical one into a chemical one.

Neurotransmitters are the brain proteins that are released when the electrical impulse of transmitted data arrives on one side of the synapse. The released neurotransmitters then float across the synaptic gap, carrying the information with them to stimulate the next nerve ending in the neural circuit. Once the neurotransmitter is taken up by next nerve ending, it acts as an ignition to activate the electrical impulse once again so that the information can travel along to the next nerve cell.

4. Dendrites (neuron extensions that conduct electrical impulses to neighboring neurons) and the synaptic connections they form build neuronal pathways that cross-connect to multiple storage areas of the brain. These neuronal pathways are activated through relational, emotional, personally relevant, learner-participatory, and

experiential stimuli. The repeated activation of these new circuits by the variety of access stimuli will strengthen the new pathways, limit their susceptibility to *pruning* (a process of eliminating inactive brain cells), and increase the efficiency of memory retrieval.

5. Repeated multisensory stimulation brings new memories from the brain's data storage areas to its executive function processing centers. When the brain's highest cognitive levels use the facts, processes, sequences, and routines that it has acquired as memory, all learning comes together. At this stage, synapses are firing in brain centers of critical reasoning, prioritizing, judging, and pattern analyzing. This is the brain's electrical dance of original, creative discovery—the "aha" moments.

Teachers can best meet these critical conditions when they have access to professional development—inservice training or conferences, for example—that teaches them about the most valid brain-based teaching strategies. By using these techniques, teachers can successfully engage all students in appropriately challenging yet supported learning.

STRATEGIC ACHIEVEMENT OF INCLUSION GOALS

Although experienced teachers have learned how to structure lessons without having to plan every detailed component in advance, the additional complexities of teaching inclusion classes make planning a valuable procedure. In particular, the process of figuring out which strategies will engage and accommodate students' challenges, developmental levels, interests, gifts, and physical needs will help teachers achieve authentic inclusion for all their students.

I present the following strategies as a menu of options to empower all students to become more successful. Instead of attempting to match specific strategies to each category of LD, I developed most to be of general benefit to the diversity of learning styles and abilities found in inclusion classes. The goal of these strategies is to enable students in inclusion classrooms to enjoy the experience of school with optimism, motivation, confidence, and the desire to take on challenges while supporting one another in shared adventures in discovery and learning.

Start Slowly and Build

Individualizing instruction is a daunting task for a single teacher in a class containing up to 35 students. Instead of thinking of the task as all or nothing, the teacher should spend some time each day considering the individualized needs and interests of one or two students. Within a few weeks, the teacher will have a sense of which students might be responsive to a few specific strategies for one of their academic or social challenges. As time goes on, the teacher will begin to make connections between students' learning differences and the lessons and strategies that are best suited to them.

Watch Your Kids

Elementary teacher and Master of Education degree candidate Malana Willis observes that

> The dynamic process that individual students engage in as they interact with learning is happening all the time with all of our students. It will happen whether teachers notice or not. What we don't observe, we don't respond to, and those are missed opportunities to gain insight into our students' needs, strengths, and challenges. So as not to lose opportunities to support students' efforts to reach their potential, teachers should stay attuned to the important moments in their students' days. With as little as a few minutes devoted to individual "kidwatching" [see Olwocki & Goodman, 2002], teachers will be rewarded with keys to unlock the learning potential in all students. (Personal communication, April 12, 2006)

As teachers glean further information from subsequent observations, assessments, student interest inventories, IEPs, and resource specialists' input, the challenges of inclusion classes will become growth opportunities for teachers and students alike.

Make Physical Accommodations

There are several factors for teachers to consider when physically setting up their classrooms. Here are some ways to support students' individual physiologies, learning styles, and behavioral characteristics.

- If students' learning styles or visual limitations benefit from their drawing large graphic organizers, taking notes on big charts, using manipulatives, or using electronic devices for word processing, they may need to have access to larger work areas and electrical outlets.
- Students with attention difficulties or high attraction to the natural world may be distracted by sitting near a window.
- Students who are adjusting to medications that cause drowsiness may need a window's fresh breeze or a front-row seat to remain alert.
- Front-row seating can benefit withdrawn students who feel more comfortable experiencing what feels like a one-to-one relationship with the teacher at the front of the room.
- Interpersonal learners who are distracted by classmates with whom they enjoy conversing maintain better academic focus if they sit at the ends of tables or rows.

Make It Relevant and Meaningful

Neuroimaging confirms that the least-efficient memory strategy is rote memorization of facts and skills taught in isolation (Wagner et al., 1998). However, when information is embedded with personal relevance from prior experience, interests, goals, or real-world connections, the new data go beyond rote memory into long-term memory (Gardner, 1991; Poldrack et al., 2001). Whereas memorizing isolated facts and skills requires considerable practice and rehearsal, information that carries personal relevance links to existing neural networks and therefore is processed more efficiently, requires less practice, and is more likely to become part of the long-term memory bank (Brooks & Brooks, 1993).

Teachers should try to help all students relate to academic information through their experiences, goals, and interests. Students can find personal relevance in all kinds of events in the world around them, from sports to popular films. Creating or mimicking real-world experiences through demonstrations, projects, field trips, outside speakers, or student-centered discussions can instill personal relevance into academic content areas and show students why the information is, or could be, personally important to them. However teachers do it, making material authentically meaningful to each learner is crucial. If students can't relate to the new material, their neural networks will be less able to process it and retain it as memory, leading to frustration and discouraging classroom experiences. To maximize personal relevance, teachers should consider the following tools and tactics.

Realia. Many learners benefit from learning from real objects and experiences. When possible, teachers should include realia, objects of interest, and interactive experiences in unit introductions.

Stories. Children love hearing stories. Their favorites tend to contain tension and challenge and feature a protagonist who, with the support of older family members, magic, or superpowers, perseveres and succeeds in overcoming adversity and achieving goals. In class, teachers' support, encouragement, brain-compatible strategies, and knowledge of students' learning strengths provide the scaffolding that empowers students to discover their own "superpowers."

Narrative lessons. Lessons that present material in story or journalistic form make the same connections as stories do. When Mona Pinon, a high school teacher and curriculum supervisor, develops narrative lessons about the tough "Independent Clauses" who don't need commas and the wimpy "Dependent Clause" crowd that won't venture out without a comma, her students are pulled into the lesson. Then they are ready for the more expository material.

Teachers. Educators should never forget that they themselves are personally relevant to students. Teachers are probably the adults with whom elementary school students spend the most focused time every day. Even at the middle and high school levels, teachers are some of the most important people in students' lives. All parents who hear their children's daily stories about what this or that teacher did or said know how relevant teachers are. When teachers remain passionate about what they teach, students will remain motivated and engaged. If teachers have taught the material dozens of times before and reached the point of boredom, they should punch up the lessons by bringing in connections to their own interests or current world events. Teachers' enthusiasm will shape the emotional climate and interest level of their students.

Provide Realistic Challenge

It has been said that when we relieve students of their struggles, we rob them of opportunities to build self-confidence, along with knowledge. But when we value mistakes as learning opportunities and allow students to experience puzzlement, learning can increase. Imagine molecularly altering an orange by freezing it in liquid nitrogen. Now imagine dropping the orange on the floor and watching as it shatters into a dozen pieces. In a classroom, this demonstration would be beyond the realm of students' prior experience or understanding of the world. The phenomenon doesn't fit their understanding of the way things work. Phenomena like this one lead to a brain state of *disequilibrium*, and the curiosity it prompts can be a powerful motivator for learning.

When students are aroused by this curiosity, they will be on the lookout for information that can help them solve problems or understand the demonstrations that have piqued their interest. During this state of disequilibrium, the amygdala is stimulated (although not overly so), so it is able to transmit data efficiently from the sensory response centers to the patterning and memory regions of the brain. The hippocampus is primed to bring "online" any previously stored related information that may connect with the new data to bring a solution and restore equilibrium. When teachers foster disequilibrium-prompted curiosity, they will achieve the ideal brain state to engage the interest and focus of all students in inclusion classes.

The objective of this strategy is to provide experiences and develop student goals based on *individualized realistic challenge*, which connects students to knowledge by communicating to them high expectations while confirming that they have the capacity to reach these goals. Teachers can support this kind of challenge with clearly structured goals, frequent feedback, and positive intrinsic reinforcement, all geared to students' individual intelligences and learning styles. Students develop confidence when they know that they will have access to the tools and support they need to reach the expectations set for them.

Challenging students at reasonable, appropriate levels is one of the most powerful strategies for success, but teachers must carefully monitor the level of challenge. If goals do not provide sufficient challenge to engage students, or if the challenge exceeds students' levels of capability, frustration replaces motivation. A six-piece wooden puzzle would be as exasperating for an average 3rd grader as a 500-piece puzzle. Teachers should also keep in mind that LD students as well as gifted learners need to be challenged. Without reasonable challenge, LD students are at risk for learned helplessness, dependency, and feelings of inadequacy.

A study examining what makes computer games so captivating found that the key element is variable challenge based on player ability. The most popular computer games in the study took players through increasingly challenging levels as they became more and more skillful. As players' skill improved, the next challenge would stimulate new mastery to just the right extent that the player could succeed with practice and persistence (Malone, 1981). Extending that kind of incremental, responsive challenge in the classroom is motivating and imparts a sense of accomplishment.

Set Goals

Teachers must demonstrate to all students in inclusion classes that success is measured not only by standardized tests and grades, but also by the ability to set and reach appropriately challenging goals. Planning these personalized goals is time-consuming, but teachers' efforts will be rewarded by students' improved confidence, attitudes and behavior, and academic achievement. When students participate in setting reasonably challenging goals, they are also practicing the executive functions of planning, time management, and prioritization. They not only feel good but also have greater potential to reach their goals. The goal-setting process also has the brain benefit of lowering students' affective filters and stimulating the *dopamine reward system:* the brain's release of the pleasure chemical dopamine during naturally rewarding experiences.

Students are more willing to invest their time and energy in an area of study when they collaborate on setting goals that lead them in the right direction. When those goals are carefully planned to incorporate authentic use of the standards' required academic knowledge, students will be more engaged in the learning because it will help them reach their goals. Their increased investment in the outcome will also stimulate their interest in the tools teachers have to offer them. As students experience the connection between practice and progress in achieving their goals, they will appreciate their teachers for having provided them with the keys that unlock the doors to their aspirations.

Goal planners—scaffolding tools that teachers can call such fun names as *treasure charts, wizard plans,* or *trip planners*—can help empower students in setting and achieving their individualized goals. After teacher modeling and practice, students can reach varying levels of independence in creating their goal planners. Some students will develop their own wizard plans, and others will need preprinted treasure charts with spaces to write below column headings. These headings can also vary, but in general they will incorporate subject, activity, time allotted, predicted goal, and achievement.

Before the class starts on an activity, students predict how much of the activity they will be able to complete in the time allotted. They then write down their predictions, such as "4 of 8" for the prediction that they will be able to write sentences using four of the eight assigned vocabulary words during the allotted time. After the activity, students complete the chart by recording the amount of work they actually completed. Students may need teacher guidance when they first begin to make predictions, but as they progress they will learn how to predict more accurately. Charting their predictions and outcomes on separate pages once a week or so can provide additional useful feedback on their long-term progress. As students review their weekly progress charts, teachers should encourage them to make a note of particularly successful strategies.

When students reach or exceed their goals, they set new short- and long-term goals. If they find they are now completing all vocabulary sentences in the allotted time, for example, they may choose to add one of the bonus words, conduct a self- or partner review of previous vocabulary words, or create a puzzle or story using the vocabulary words.

Students who fail to reach their goals may need support to avoid falling into frustrated, self-defeating behaviors. These temporary setbacks can be opportunities for students to practice recognizing what strategies might have helped them succeed. When students build a backlog of strategies that work for them, these setbacks will become learning experiences. Writing down their plans will help them remember these strategies the next time they return to the subject or activity.

Offer Choice

Teachers can build choice into the classroom community in a manner that does not separate students based on intellect or ability. When it is time to do independent classwork, for example, students can choose which assigned work to do first. Having some students start their math homework while others conduct research for their reports combines choice with student activity variation. During this choice time, students will be doing work that needs varying amounts of teacher support. When more students are working at their independent levels or in cooperative groups, teachers have time to work with a few students who need more assistance, whether remedial or advanced. These classroom patterns become more effective as they become routine.

Most in-depth investigations and reports in history, language arts, or general science can follow curriculum guidelines and still be approached and presented in a variety of ways. Teachers may allow students to demonstrate their understanding through a broad array of projects, such as writing a report, making a board game or puzzle, or creating a book that includes questions and answers for students several grades below.

A note of caution: Problems can arise when choice takes precedence over learning objectives—for example, if certain students always choose to design book covers for their literature projects. These students are not striving for the *challenge* component of reasonable challenge. They are not extending their knowledge if they repeatedly choose the easiest or fastest activity. To avoid these situations, teachers should not give students responsibility for making all choices. Teachers who are comfortably familiar with their students' learning levels can provide choices that offer all students equal opportunities to learn the required material at appropriately challenging levels and make sure that all students are progressing and not stagnating.

Make Adaptations for Participation

Partial participation is a strategy that enables all students to follow a common curriculum at their own levels. This adaptation of the curriculum incorporates individual goals with appropriate levels of differentiated challenge within the same assignments that peers without LD perform. The assignments are age- and interest-appropriate but geared to each individual's level of ability at that time. For example, students whose faulty memory tracking slows their mastery of the multiplication tables may need to use calculators temporarily. Other students may initially need to write their notes about the new topic on outlines that are already partially filled in.

This strategy keeps students motivated because they are stimulated by suitable challenge while working within their own comfort zones. This ongoing process does require dedicated student observation so that teachers can make needed adjustments in the "right amount" of challenge and offer useful, specific feedback. This continual assessment creates opportunities for discovery learning within each student's *zone of proximal development*—the gap between the student's current or actual level of development and his or her emerging or potential level of development—while avoiding the frustration or resentment that activates the information-blocking power of the affective filter (Routman, 2000). Through practice and more familiarity with the new topic, students will gradually need less scaffolding, but in the meantime, they will not be shut out from the lesson.

Academic priming, or lesson previewing, can help students with disabilities prepare for the following day's lesson in advance, with an aide or with parents at home. For example, students who are easily confused early in a math lesson and become too frustrated to continue focusing will be more comfortable and confident if they preview the lesson's basics before class. Teachers can show parents how to help with this task and then gradually have students preview the material on their own. Usually after a few weeks, this process builds enough confidence that the cycle of early frustration breaks and students no longer need the preview. They begin to realize that they can keep up with new information in class if they stay attentive and don't give in to frustration the instant they feel the slightest confusion. It may also help lower students' affective filters to know that when a new subject is introduced, their classmates are experiencing similar ups and downs in comprehension. Also, as students learn that their teacher will reexplain the concept to suit multiple learning styles, they will become less stressed when they don't understand something immediately. They will learn to trust that within a few minutes the teacher will present the information in a way they can access it.

Teach Organizational Strategies

Students get bombarded with an awful lot of information and can easily feel overwhelmed. One way to help all students increase the amount of information they retain from their hours in the classroom is to have them keep personal learning logs. Learning logs allow students to choose how they wish to connect to the information, although students are still accountable for including the important nuggets from each lesson. For each new class or topic during the day, depending on student age and ability, students make new entries in their logs. Students can list, sketch, chart, or diagram three to five main points, new items they learned, or facts that were emphasized during the class. The ideal time to complete this summary activity is immediately after the lesson. The learning log can be used for all subjects and as an addendum to regular notes and assignments.

Because students have choice in how they log their new learning, the material becomes more personally meaningful. Using their preferred learning styles to record the material prompts students' most receptive brain centers when they review their logs. If certain topics interest them, they can investigate those outside class and add information to the logs. Adding material of personal interest to them will increase their connections to the lessons and reinforce their relational memories.

Another way to help students stay organized is to have them start homework, reports, and projects in class. Daily homework can be overwhelming once students leave the classroom, especially when that classroom includes a wide range of abilities. Information and instructions that seemed clear during class can become confusing when the scaffolding and security of teacher supervision is removed. Students with LD may be especially disturbed when they feel they have lost what they learned and can't do the work they are expected to do. Starting homework and long-term projects in class provides students with structure that they can build on at home.

Provide Feedback

Good feedback helps students examine their progress toward short- and long-term goals from an outside perspective or according to preset standards. As the unit of study advances, rubrics and formative assessment can help students monitor their progress and adjust their strategies and actions responsively.

Rubrics. Teachers can provide *pre-feedback* even before students begin a project, using rubrics or examples of student work from previous years. These work samples are especially helpful if teachers include examples of *A-*, *B-*, and *C*-level papers that match the high, medium, and low criteria included on the rubric. In inclusion classes, teachers can use the same rubric for all students and set individual goals at the appropriately challenging level for each student. Rubrics generally include several categories of measurement, such as quality of work; organization; effectiveness in following assignment instructions; artwork, charts, or graphs; cooperation in group work; grammar and punctuation; and any other categories appropriate to the project.

Rubric-based grading can keep the bar high in inclusion classes. Most students will feel capable of achieving the highest level in at least one rubric category. Even when they perform at the lowest level of another category, the high and low scores tend to balance out, and students could still end up with a fairly good grade. Because rubrics prompt students to acknowledge their academic progress, they contribute to a sense of accomplishment and intrinsic motivation. Specific teacher comments along with rubric ratings can add to students' awareness of their successes and the areas in which they can improve. Teachers can find sample rubrics and online programs to create their own rubrics at http://rubistar.4teachers.org/index.php and http://janeconstant.tripod.com/Rubrics.htm.

Formative assessment. Ongoing assessment is necessary to keep all students in inclusion classes actively connected to the lessons.

Teachers can implement many creative and effective assessment strategies during lessons, often with the help of students themselves.

One quick way in which teachers can provide individual assessment and feedback during whole-class activities is to distribute whiteboards to students. When the teacher asks a question, each student writes his or her answer on the whiteboard and holds it up for the teacher to see. More simply, teachers can have students give the thumbs-up or thumbs-down sign in response to a yes-or-no question. Written teacher responses on papers and tests can also give students timely feedback on their work. To ensure that students actually read these comments, teachers can require them to return their papers with their written responses to the comments and a few ideas about what they will do next time to reach their goals and avoid the same errors.

Teachers should keep students in mind as potentially valuable partners in ongoing assessment (while keeping in mind that they first need to model and have students practice feedback and assessment strategies). During independent work time, for example, students who already understand the lesson's content can explain it to and then gently quiz partners who need more practice. Teachers can also give three student volunteers short response forms to complete after a classmate gives a presentation. These forms could be simple rubrics with a few categories, such as completeness of presentation, speaking voice, eye contact, and familiarity with material, and perhaps only three ratings for each. Or teachers could ask for oral responses to student presentations, requiring that classmates be specific in their comments, don't repeat what someone else has already said, always start and end with a positive comment, and don't make comments about things a classmate has no control over, such as tics or speech disorders. Finally, teachers could have students exchange papers for peer editing, using checklists that provide space for specific comments.

Plan Developmentally Appropriate Lessons

Just as children mature physically at different rates, chronological age may not reflect students' readiness to learn. Jean Piaget set forth guidelines for average stages of development in multiple aspects of thinking. He noted that the average 7- or 8-year-old is in the *pre-operational stage*, able to think symbolically to the extent that he or she can represent concrete objects and experiences with symbols in his or her mind. By age 10 or 11, the average child is in the *concrete operational stage* and able to think in abstract terms, generalize, and make connections (Piaget, 1971).

Developmental variation is much greater in inclusion classes than in noninclusion classes, and teachers may find it useful to assess struggling students' developmental stages so that they can direct instruction to their appropriate levels. If LD students in 5th grade are having difficulty grasping such abstract principles as warfare, taxation, property rights, sound waves, and light reflection, they might need more concrete material and structured, sequential instruction and practice to prepare them at their developmental level. When they have reached the concrete operational stage, they will have the background they need to perform executive function reasoning tasks.

Children cannot be pushed through a developmental stage. They need time to assimilate information before passing to a higher cognitive level. The confusion and frustration caused by developmentally inappropriate lessons can lead to withdrawal from active learning, disruptive behavior, and decreased motivation and confidence. As long as teachers provide a safe, supportive environment for learning, students will reach the higher developmental stages at the time appropriate for them. Giving them opportunities to practice and build on the cognitive skills they have and are learning will ensure their successful experiences as learners.

Lower the Barriers, Not the Bar

The students entering inclusion classes may have had years of unproductive and painful school experiences, but teachers do not need to lower the bar or eliminate challenge in the name of access. It does require patience and persistence to undo students' discouragement and frustration and help them regain the willingness to challenge themselves again. At first they will need more support and encouragement and smaller, more reachable goals so that they can recognize their successes. Teachers should help them set challenging but realistic and achievable goals, then model and scaffold the strategies that are compatible with how their brains learn most successfully. Teachers can acquire this information through observation and formal and informal assessments of students' learning styles and strengths. Through miniconferences and progress charting, teachers can help students see the connection between their efforts and their improvement.

Eventually, students will build the resilience that comes with knowing that their own efforts are powerful enough to overcome obstacles and attain meaningful goals. Teachers can then turn students' newfound confidence and self-esteem toward other academic, social, and behavioral goals that seemed unreachable when these students felt discouraged and disparaged.

COMMUNITY BUILDING IN INCLUSION CLASSES

In my neurology practice, I was initially astonished to see my patients respond with relief when I told them that their symptoms were due to a pinched nerve from a bulging disc in their spine or a blockage in the outflow of spinal fluid. I had thought that such news would be disturbing. What I discovered was that people who experience abnormal sensations, weakness, pain, or mental states often begin to think they have the worst possible disease or malignancy. So the news that they have serious but treatable conditions comes as a relief.

Similarly, when students experience learning problems without understanding the reason, they also may imagine the worst: that they are inferior students who will never succeed in school. When parents first hear that their child has a type of LD, they may share that reaction. General education students new to inclusion classes may also have misconceptions about new classmates with LD. It is helpful for all students and parents to know that everyone is unique—physically, emotionally, in the rate at which their brains develop, and in the way their brains learn.

To help students understand that having different ways of thinking does not limit LD students in all areas, teachers can introduce the concept of a band that needs a variety of musical instruments, or a team that benefits from a diversity of specialized skills. Non-LD students in inclusion classes will learn about the talents and interests that make their new peers interesting and worth knowing. They may find that the classmates they help with a math problem are giving them tips on the basketball court or in a computer class. Here are some strategies to foster students' recognition and appreciation of their classmates' unique attributes.

Peer interviews. Peer interviews are a beginning-of-the-year activity designed to build connections. Pairs of students who did not know each other previously interview each other to discover interests, talents, travel experiences, and various "favorites," from foods to films. Students then use the interview results to introduce their partners to the rest of the class. The interview process is a class bonding exercise that can also provide first buddies for new students.

Class interest graphs. Students place dot stickers next to the appropriate items on a prepared chart listing interests and hobbies, types of pets, number of siblings, sporting activities, favorite subjects, and other grade-appropriate topics. The teacher can then tabulate the data and list names under each topic. This information will give students an idea of what they have in common with classmates and can become a springboard for conversations and friendships.

Class expert or resident expert charts. Similar to class interest graphs, expert charts go a step further, listing not only students' interests and hobbies but also their areas of expertise, whether academic, artistic, physical, dramatic, or social. Students can make these posters more compelling by adding photos or sketches of themselves engaged in favorite activities or even pictures from magazines or the Internet that represent their talents. Through these charts, students gain an awareness of the degree of talent and know-how in their own classroom. The charts increase the inclusion and raise the self-esteem of students who may not have the same academic strengths as their classmates, but who have unique talents that are acknowledged and respected by classmates.

Teacher modeling. It is especially important in inclusion classes that teachers demonstrate their own appreciation of differences and remain open to teachable moments that unite the class as a community. Modeling by a teacher who "shows instead of tells" sets a standard that students want to emulate.

Academically, when teachers ask evocative questions and stimulate curiosity and problem solving, more learners can participate in class discussions at their individual comfort and interest levels. The goal is to attract students to ideas and encourage them to follow the ones that lead to "aha" moments. Especially at the beginning of the year, holding class meetings on topics that engage all students at all ability levels can set a tone of safe participation. These topics should be high in interest and open-ended so that all opinions are valid. Examples could include

- Should we have mixed-grade classes?
- What class trips might be fun and connect with the topics we'll study this year?
- Whom would you like to invite to be a class speaker?
- What famous person, living or dead, would you like to meet, and why?

Once the community builds and students have experienced cooperative, respectful, and active listening, the topics can address bigger issues. Eventually, academic discussions will be safe opportunities for all students to participate.

Another effective tactic teachers can try is exploring tangents. In *Teacher Man*, a memoir about his 30 years as an English teacher in a vocational high school in New York City, Frank McCourt (2005) describes his community-building strategies of getting off subject and following student leads. McCourt's students appreciated the stories he told them about his own life because he spoke to them as peers, not as inferiors. As a result, they opened up to him and showed a desire to work with him and one another. McCourt also remained open to their leads. After a long stretch of reaping only dismal results from his formal writing assignments, he realized that students' forged excuse notes from their parents contained creative and dramatic prose. He seized the opportunity to have students write essays and letters in the form of excuse notes, such as one from Adam and Eve to God, or from Lee Harvey Oswald to the Kennedy family.

Another way in which teachers can model community building is to use language of inclusiveness. Teachers should refer to special accommodations with terms that have no negative connotations and that can apply to any student who at one time or another needs assistance—for example, *one-on-one time*, *homework help*, or *study skills assistance*.

The most powerful thing teachers can do to model inclusiveness in their classrooms is to emphasize the value of a community of unique individuals. All students have strengths and weaknesses. Students with LD may have long believed that they were destined for failure in all academic endeavors. Even with the encouragement of a positive community in an inclusion class, they may still generalize any difficulty in math to mean that they will "never be able to do math." They may interpret their incorrect pronunciation of certain words in group reading as an indication that they are bound to underachieve in all aspects of language arts. To prevent these misconceptions in LD students and their classmates, teachers should avoid such generalizations as, "Because of your learning disability, I will give you different assignments in all your subjects." Instead, a teacher should explicitly tell students that the fact that they have trouble understanding the words in a math problem doesn't mean they can't do the math—and then show them practice activities that will help them improve their reading comprehension. The teacher should assure students that while they practice this reading skill, the teacher will help by giving them word problems with important words and numbers underlined so that they will know what to focus on. When students understand that their difficulties are specific and not global, they can be more confident about their potential to reach achievable goals. They will begin to embrace learning because they will no longer fear being doomed to a future of academic failure and permanent dependency on special accommodations.

When a student does an outstanding job in any subject, whether computer science or poetry writing, the teacher should acknowledge the student specifically for that success without giving the impression that his or her standards are lower because of the student's LD classification. For teachers' private record keeping, it is appropriate to record accommodations and student progress toward individualized goals and to tell most students of appropriate age when there are modifications. This process does not need to involve the whole class. If students ask why they can't have the "easier work," one response, in private, is to ask them if they think they need special assistance or if they prefer to be challenged to their highest potential. Given that choice, most students appreciate their abilities and would not trade them for what seems like an easier assignment.

GRADE-RELATED CONSIDERATIONS
Grades K–3

Even in the primary grades, students begin to self-identify with their status relative to their classmates' and to know what they are good at and what challenges them. This is the time when teacher intervention and support can break the destructive cycle that starts with LD students' decision that "I'm not good in math so I'll never be good at it, so I'll just decide that math is stupid and I hate it."

I frequently allude to the powerful positive expectations that most children have when they enter kindergarten. They are excited to learn, to be with peers, and to enjoy some independent adventures in the exciting grownup world of school. During this critical time, teachers can use brain research–based strategies to keep students' brains open, stimulated, and motivated. Positive teacher intervention during these early elementary years will reduce the stress, frustration, anxiety, and disappointment that can close the doors of LD students' affective filters and inhibit learning.

It is likely that LD students will respond to the teaching strategies that have long served to engage the "average" student. However, from the start of the first school year, LD students need special attention, or they risk losing their joy, motivation, and confidence (Kohn, 2004). Young children have limited coping skills. Without appropriate teacher intervention, LD students will soon feel the anxiety of not being as successful or efficient as their classmates. In addition, parents don't usually suspect a learning disability this early, so they think their child just isn't trying hard enough, or that the school or the teacher is the problem (Raskind et al., 1999).

Grades 4–6

During the intermediate grades, peer pressure becomes more intense, and parents may still not have a clear understanding of their children's struggles. Students not yet evaluated as LD may not be receiving the interventions they need. To keep confusion and frustration from limiting school success and motivation in LD students, this is the time to help them identify their learning strengths through direct and specific praise. This modeling and feedback demonstrates to LD students and their peers that all students are unique. They will realize that students who have problems in reading circle may make valuable contributions to cooperative response-to-reading projects that welcome multiple learning styles.

By the time they reach the intermediate years, students are not fooled by homogeneous reading or math groups designated by color, shape, or animal name. They know who is in the "smart" group and who is not. If community-building strategies have been set in place, students will recognize that some classmates need specific strategies to help them in certain subjects and that other gifted classmates are given opportunities to do advanced work. Students in a positive classroom community will see the benefit of working toward reachable yet challenging personalized goals, and they will experience the rewards of mutual support. What they won't respect or tolerate is dishonesty, so being forthright is key to their success and resilience.

Fourth, 5th, and 6th graders are ready to discover and use the strategies that promote their success. They are willing to work toward their goals (such as behaving appropriately in class and completing homework before watching television) when they feel that they have been treated as partners in working out their individualized plans and recognized for their positive efforts toward achieving them. Students will also work hard when teachers incorporate choice and learning style preferences into their instruction.

Most students in these grades, along with their parents, are capable of understanding that specific learning difficulties do not correlate with general lack of intelligence or ability. A student who is limited by short stature and a lack of upper-body strength in basketball may be the most agile soccer player or a whiz at creating computer graphics for group projects.

Middle School

If students with learning differences have not been brought into the class and school community or developed social and academic coping strategies by middle school, they will be particularly vulnerable to the loneliness and isolation that can mark this developmental period. During the tumultuous changes of adolescence, students without peer support may be overwhelmed by memories of earlier school frustrations and embarrassments. If they don't have the social skills to gain the support of a peer group, they can fall farther behind in all areas of their lives.

In an article on resilience and hope theory, special education expert Malka Margalit observed LD students who were less likely to view themselves as lonely or socially distressed than were their non-LD peers. These students had age-appropriate social skills and what Margalit called a strong sense of coherence: they viewed the world both within and outside themselves as ordered and predictable because their strong repertoire of social strategies led to positive social interactions.

From classroom interactions and cooperative activities, these resilient students had learned about their classmates and were able to recognize those with similar interests or complementary talents. They were able to act on this knowledge to connect with classmates in class, at recess, and during after-school activities (Margalit & Idan, 2004).

By nurturing friendships in an inclusion classroom, students develop attitudes that do more than just protect them from isolation and low motivation. The confidence built through collaborative partnerships in middle school helps all students develop empathy and problem-solving experience. This is the time when students must realize that passively observing bullying or social exclusion makes them part of the problem. Proactive educators promote discussion through video presentations, guest speakers, or life-skills class discussions on such topics as bullying and cliques.

Teachers can implement several successful interventions to empower middle school students who have not gained the resilience and skills to form positive relationships with peers.

Interest discovery. Interest inventories and direct questioning may not be as fruitful with middle school students as they are with younger students, who are more apt to confide in teachers, but anything teachers find out about students' interests can serve to prompt friendships and connect them to academic work.

Students as resources. The class inventory of students' talents and interests comes in handy here. The list can connect LD students with academic partners who seek them out for their artistic, dramatic, computer, musical, or interpersonal skills. Through these experiences, the LD students gain confidence and class acceptance of their strengths, and gifted students feel appreciated for their intelligence rather than isolated or envied for it.

Planning. By carefully planning partnerships and cooperative groups, teachers can ensure that excluded students receive opportunities to offer input that their group partners will acknowledge and appreciate. It is not unusual during the middle school years for a single peer connection to bring an excluded student into a larger social and academic support group.

Modeling. This powerful activity has students reenact scenarios of bullying or social exclusion after viewing a film on the topic. Teachers can ask students to exaggerate what they saw as the inappropriate behavior of the bullies or "queen bees" in the film. By performing these over-the-top exaggerations, the perpetrators might recognize some of their own behaviors. If the class community is one that honors respect and tolerance, that self-recognition can motivate students to adopt more inclusive behaviors. Post-film discussions can also enlighten more withdrawn students about how they may be perpetuating their learned helplessness or playing into the victim role. Role-playing activities in which each student portrays both the socially and academically dominant role and the excluded role are also powerful opportunities for enlightenment. Here's one example of a role-playing scenario:

> You are selected to be captain of one of the class basketball or kickball teams and are selecting players for your team. You know Bonnie is always picked last, and you are wise enough to know that her feelings are hurt. You recall how she shared her lunch with you when you forgot yours, and you also care about your class community. Some of the kids you already picked for the team are pointing to the more athletic students waiting to be chosen, and one points at Bonnie and laughs. What will you do?

Even if this exact situation does not really play out on the field, most students participating in this role-play will feel the social consciousness to make the right choice. Sometimes just practicing this role-play and having their decision acknowledged and sincerely praised by a teacher will promote similar behavior when the real situation comes up.

High School and Beyond

Hopefully, by the time students at the extremes of the social and academic spectrums reach high school, they have had teachers who challenged them to reach their highest potential, helped them build confidence, and showed them that individuality is more empowering than trying to fit in.

If LD students entering high school have never had that support, they will be unprepared for the stress of joining inclusion classes, where they will see classmates confidently participate in discussions, focus on their work, receive higher grades, and be sought after as project partners. They are unlikely to have the strategies and resilience to avoid feeling inadequate and self-conscious in their new classes. At this stage, it is much more challenging for teachers to help them, but also more important. If these students are unable to make social connections or gain confidence, they may drop out, self-medicate, or lose any possibility of believing that it is worth their effort to try. Without attuned teachers, individualized strategies, and supportive class communities, these students may come to believe that acting out in class or dropping out of school is preferable to academic embarrassment and social rejection.

STRESS REDUCTION IN INCLUSION CLASSES

Before information can reach the relational, patterning, and memory storage areas of the brain, it must pass through the reticular activating system (RAS). The RAS filters all incoming stimuli and decides which data a person attends to or ignores. The most powerful stimulus for the RAS is physical need; the brain will not be able to engage in the task of learning unless basic survival needs are first met. If students associate their classrooms with a visceral sense of fear, the RAS will filter out all but life-sustaining sensory information. This survival response to the stress of the classroom will greatly limit brain access to incoming information, and the students will fall farther behind (Cooper, Bloom, & Roth, 1996).

When we take into account the information-blocking potential of both the RAS and the affective filter in the amygdala, it becomes clear how important it is for teachers to create environments low in destructive anxiety and high in appropriate challenge (Introini-Collison et al., 1991). Several indicators can clue teachers in to excessive student stress. For example, students may broadcast the stress of confusion by looking bored or acting out. Shortened attention spans are the brain's way of shutting out anxiety-producing confusion about material that is not being presented in an engaging and comprehensible manner (Meece, Wigfield, & Eccles, 1990). Low participation, as demonstrated by a sudden drop in the usual number of questions or comments during a difficult lesson, can also signal confusion and anxiety. When students stop asking questions— especially LD students who often do ask them—teachers should consider the need for assessment.

It's important to make sure that students are not emotionally and intellectually dropping out of a lesson because they don't have the foundation to keep up. When it's not feasible to interrupt the lesson's flow by working with the students who are not keeping up, the teacher can offer a few words of assurance that he or she will work with the students individually as soon as there is a break. That reassurance will help students at least remain passively receptive to some of the sensory input of the lesson, rather than shutting down the information flow at the affective filter. Teachers need to tell students that they should try not to worry about what they don't understand and just absorb what they can. This message will be most reassuring if teachers always follow through with their promise to meet with these students as soon as the others are doing independent work. Once students see that their teachers are reliable in meeting their needs, they will lower their affective filters, even when confused, and absorb some of the data as they listen. It may not be active learning, but comfortable passive listening does build familiarity and keep motivation up. When teachers teach in a patient, positive manner and offer clear explanations and frequent, varied forms of repetition, students will gain confidence in their abilities to understand even the lessons that seem confusing at first.

When stress is getting high from a lesson that is overly abstract, not relevant to students' lives, or too simplistic, the teacher should make the lesson more personally interesting. Neuroimaging research has demonstrated that pleasurably challenging lessons moderately stimulate the amygdala's metabolism and thus facilitate the brain's processing of information (Introini-Collison et al., 1991). Lessons and activities that arouse the brain's search for meaning will penetrate the RAS and reach the higher cognitive centers because of humans' natural survival instinct—the need to understand their environment and make meaning of what they see, hear, smell, and touch. Connecting the lesson to students' lives and interests therefore reduces stress and increases motivation (Kumar, 1991). Teachers can try the following stress-reducing strategies.

Bring lessons to life. The Internet is a great resource for finding strategies to bring fact-heavy, cold-data lessons to life. Sample lesson plans from other teachers abound, and even state Web sites listing standards often provide sources for student activities and links to information databases.

Give students a three-minute vacation. Teachers should occasionally give students a break by relating a personal anecdote, asking about films that students have recently seen, or telling a joke. A brief mental vacation takes the RAS out of its basic survival response to stress, allows the amygdala to cool down, and provides time for neurotransmitter supplies to rebuild.

Reward students' efforts. When a lesson is heavy on dry facts and memorization, teachers can offer an authentic reward for students' mental efforts, such as letting them participate in a stimulating experiment, watch a film version of the book they've been assigned, or use geometry to calculate the height of buildings outside. The anticipation of an engaging activity will increase students' receptiveness to the lessons (Wiersma, 1992). As an added bonus, students' enjoyment of the associated activity will ensure that the information they learned will have more relational connections (neuronal links) to hold it in long-term memory storage.

To motivate students to put effort into homework, teachers should consider planning homework that is clearly connected to the class activities, enabling students to see its importance and motivating them to complete it so that they can participate fully in the follow-up activity. For example, if the assignment is to read a chapter in their social studies book, the teacher can give a short quiz of fairly simple questions directly related to the reading (so that LD students who completed the assignment won't miss out due to lower reading comprehension). Students who score high enough to demonstrate that they completed their reading will get to perform group skits reenacting the events in the reading, while the students who did not do their homework sit quietly and read. When students realize that their homework is relevant and not just busywork, they will be more motivated to complete it with appropriate focus.

DE-STRESSING TESTING SITUATIONS

In subsequent chapters, I provide strategies for making assessments positive learning experiences. At this point, I offer a few suggestions for reducing the stress that often accompanies formalized, especially standardized, test taking. These "de-stressors" can be crucial for students who have had only negative testing experiences.

Students in inclusion classrooms will already have an advantage because they have learned according to their individual intelligences, interests, and learning styles. So one of the best things teachers can do is remind them about how prepared they are, pointing out the presentations or projects they made that demonstrated their strengths and having students take a few moments to recall and focus on these strengths. Teachers can also lead students through a body relaxation or breathing technique, which will help take students' reticular activating systems out of survival mode and reduce the blockade in the affective filter built by test anxiety.

Teachers can take students' brains out of the fight-or-flight mode by reminding them that this test is just one assessment of their knowledge. Putting the test in perspective will free students to do their best and not be frozen by anxiety. It's helpful to remind students that many standardized tests include questions about things they have not been taught and are not expected to know—that some questions are included as trial questions to see if they are valid to use the next year (Bangert-Drowns, Kulik, Kulik, & Morgan, 1991). This reminder will prevent students from becoming fixated on what they don't know and thereby block neuronal access to what they *do* know.

INVOLVING PARENTS

Teachers are experiencing increased pressure from parents to keep up with the influx of information on how the brain learns. Parents read about new brain research–based strategies in parenting books and magazines and naturally want to know if their children's teachers are using them in class. Parents of children with learning differences in particular don't hesitate to express their expectations that their children's teachers be at the forefront of strategic teaching.

Rightfully so. No parent of a child with epilepsy has ever come to my neurology office and said, "Just do what you think is best without explaining my child's condition or your interventions to me. Whatever happens to my child is all in your hands, because you are the expert. I'm just the parent." Similarly, teachers can and should expect parents to be advocates for their children, especially when their children have learning differences. Here are some ways in which teachers can include parents in their children's education.

Contact parents. Teachers can help parents understand and appreciate their children's learning styles by sharing good news about their children, such as personality traits or behaviors that contribute positively to the class. This contact will increase parental support, because parents will trust teachers to recognize their children's positive attributes. Teachers should also assure parents of gifted students that their children's gifts will be nurtured—through independent projects with outside consultants or special conceptual math projects, for example.

Give homework advice. Teachers should guide parents on how to help their children with homework, individualizing their recommendations according to students' learning styles. It's also helpful to provide information on brain research–based learning that supports their suggestions and instructional strategies. For example, parents may be skeptical of a teacher's suggestion that music can help their child focus.

But if the teacher accompanies his or her recommendation with an explanation of how music enhances some students' brain patterning, the parents may be more willing to try what seems counterintuitive.

In response to requests for homework assistance, parents' best policy is to help their children understand directions or to suggest a possible solution to a comparable problem. Parents should not be homework tutors, however. Excessive parent involvement in homework can impair teachers' insight into students' understanding.

Parents can collaborate in more helpful ways. For example, rather than assign a set amount of homework each night, teachers in inclusion classes may require a certain amount of daily on-task "focus time" for homework—say, an hour and a half. Some students may spend this period dawdling and daydreaming as they watch the clock. But they're much less likely to undermine the system if parents send in notes indicating how much focused time their children actually spent on specific homework assignments. Most parents want to work with the teacher to increase their child's success with homework and will honestly indicate if their child focused for only 45 minutes. The teacher would then deduct points for incomplete work.

Other students may rush through assignments so that they can have more free time. In these cases, parents can intervene by asking, "Did you do your best work? Are you proud of what you're putting your name on and handing in?" If students are not doing their best, their parents should be encouraged to require them to use the full allotment of homework time to further their academic knowledge and study skills by reading, practicing typing, working on long-term assignments and projects, or reviewing their class notes.

Parents of gifted children can let teachers know if their children are completing homework in less time than students at their grade level should spend on homework. That feedback can let teachers know which students would benefit from a higher level of challenge appropriate to their learning strengths.

Explain assessments. Teachers should let parents know that they will be using various styles of instruction and assessment to help their children learn according to their individual strengths as well as incorporating assignments aimed at strengthening students' weaker learning styles. Teachers should assure parents and students that they will vary assessments and offer choice whenever possible so that tests become opportunities for students to demonstrate what they have learned, not just what they have failed to learn. It's important for parents to know that these assessments help teachers fill in gaps in students' knowledge so that the students can enjoy future success in the subject. When standardized tests come up, parents can ally with teachers in confirming to their children that the tests are just one parameter on which they'll be assessed, and not necessarily the most valid one.

Discuss rewards. Parents often ask about motivating their children with rewards for achieving academic goals. Often, the best reward parents can give their elementary or early middle school children is to spend quality time together doing an activity the children enjoy. For older adolescents who are less interested in together time with parents, a positive reward could be more free time to play their video games, watch a favorite television show, listen to music, play sports, or socialize with friends.

When parents know that teachers share their desire to provide their children with safe, positive, and successful school experiences, they will support teachers in their efforts to help students develop to their highest potential and achieve success in and out of the classroom.

WHAT ARE TEACHERS DOING RIGHT?

The initial learning curve of discovering students' key needs and individualizing lessons to reach each learner is steep. Some of this information will come from independent observations and authentic assessments; more-personal feedback will come from teachers' work with students on goal modifications and guided metacognition. A strong, collegial faculty community will encourage teachers to pair up for peer observations and receive professional feedback on which strategies appear to be most successful in engaging students' attention.

It is important for teachers of inclusion classes to stay motivated and to acknowledge what they are doing right. Instead of assessing themselves solely on the basis of students' performance on standardized tests, educators should consider what they achieve each time they stimulate a student's curiosity, observe students applying strategies they taught them, or watch students working cooperatively with classmates. Just as students are more successful with positive feedback, so are their teachers. So let's take the time to acknowledge our own successes!

CHAPTER 2

LOOKING
INTO MULTIPLE
INTELLIGENCE BRAINS

Neurological research confirms the value of connecting students to academic material by engaging their interests, fostering positive emotions, and making real-world connections (Caine & Caine, 1994). In addition, research on individual learning styles abounds, and textbooks often include suggestions on how teachers can vary their approach to make information accessible to each of their students.

Unfortunately, many schools are reacting to the current era of accountability with factory-style test prep. Teachers are pressured to produce students whose standardized test scores will maintain their schools' rating and funding. Because these tests are predominantly a measure of rote learning rather than critical thinking, the curriculum can easily become dominated by rote instruction. It is frustrating that just as brain-compatible teaching strategies to increase authentic, long-term learning are coming to light, teachers are following formulas in pursuit of higher test scores.

But the challenge for today's teachers goes beyond finding ways to access students' diverse abilities in the face of accountability pressures. Because of the increased external stressors in today's society, it is crucial that we build supportive classroom communities in which our students retain (or regain) the excitement they felt when they entered kindergarten. Now more than ever, we need to make our classrooms safe, magical realms of fun, friends, discovery, and learning.

We know that students with special education needs are not necessarily less intelligent or capable than their classmates. Accordingly, inclusion teachers shouldn't view the integration of LD students into their classes as a mandate to simplify assignments and lower expectations. Instead, they should increase their repertoires of research-validated teaching strategies and incorporate students' diverse learning styles and intelligences into their lessons. Presenting information in ways that all students can process will promote the academic success of LD students and increase the breadth of all students' learning skills.

I indicated in Chapter 1 that I like the abbreviation *LD* because it can stand for so many different terms. Throughout this book, I also use the *LD* initials for students who do not strictly fulfill the criteria for LD. Some inclusion classes contain students with below-average intelligence or students who have severe physical limitations and a spectrum of intelligence levels. These students do not technically fall under the *LD* label—which refers to students with average or above-average intelligence who have learning difficulties that prevent them from achieving the academic success commensurate with their level of intelligence—but they will be incorporated under that term when the strategies I describe apply to a variety of students with different learning needs.

IDENTIFYING STUDENTS' LEARNING STYLES

The first step of successfully teaching an inclusion class is to identify students' individual learning styles, abilities, and developmental levels. The term *learning styles* refers to the way the brain perceives and processes what it needs to learn. When teachers tailor their teaching strategies to students' learning styles, students will respond with the optimism they had when they first entered kindergarten. Students will enter learning experiences with more confidence and connectedness and will become active participants in their learning.

There are so many classifications of learning difficulties, differences, and disabilities that classroom teachers cannot be held responsible for identifying the specific category into which a struggling or underchallenged student fits. Crossover between categories and behavior problems that may be part of (or could be obscuring) underlying LD further complicate specific diagnoses.

Are students acting out, withdrawing, losing focus, or being defiant because they are frightened, stressed, physically ill, confused, or bored? Is the behavior disorder the primary problem, and the academic difficulties the result of the psychological or biochemical dysfunctions causing the aberrant behavior? We know that some students who struggle to learn have average or above-average intelligence and display inappropriate behaviors out of frustration, fear, or anxiety. Other students have not yet developed the neural circuitry to sit attentively for traditional direct instruction. All of these are important factors to consider.

Determining the cause of students' school problems is a job for a team of professionals. In my neurology practice, I need input from teachers, parents, test results, resource specialists, and students themselves to diagnose neurological learning disorders. As a teacher, I know that my role in the process is to provide information to the professional team and respond to their guidance. Once they are armed with information about individual students' learning styles and abilities, teachers can provide the classroom experiences that will change frustration to motivation.

MULTIPLE INTELLIGENCES

Howard Gardner developed the theory that intelligence, rather than being an all-or-nothing entity, is made up of distinct learning proficiencies that can work individually or together. In 1983, Gardner reported seven such learning strengths or styles, which he called *intelligences*: verbal-linguistic, logical-mathematical, visual-spatial, musical-rhythmic, bodily-kinesthetic, interpersonal, and intrapersonal. In 1996, he added an eighth to the list: naturalist intelligence (Gardner, 1999). In addition, some have proposed a ninth: emotional intelligence, characterized by self-awareness, self-regulation, self-motivation, empathy, hope, and optimism (Goleman, 1995).

Keeping in mind that students rarely fit into only one intelligence category—and that students who match a given intelligence won't necessarily demonstrate all its associated responses or characteristics—here are descriptions of the eight intelligence categories recognized by most educators (Checkley, 1997).

Verbal-linguistic intelligence. This intelligence encompasses the ability to use language to convey information well and to analyze language use. Verbal-linguistic learners' high auditory skills make them sensitive to the nuances, order, and rhythm of words, and they are likely to enjoy rhymes, verbal word games, storytelling, reading, writing, and talking. They tend to be strong in vocabulary building, memorization, and foreign language acquisition.

Logical-mathematical intelligence. Students with logical-mathematical intelligence have a strong grasp of abstractions, cause and effect, code and pattern recognition, logic problems, and equations. These students often excel at using unique approaches to solve problems, but they may not be able to show their work or explain how they arrived at their solutions. They often enjoy science, puzzles, computer activities, and higher mathematics, and they tend to perform well on multiple-choice or standardized tests.

Visual-spatial intelligence. Visual-spatial learners understand the relationships of objects, concepts, or images in different fields or dimensions. These students are often capable of diagramming or artistically representing what they perceive. They may enjoy taking things apart and reassembling them, playing board games, following maps, building models, conceptualizing in three dimensions, and engaging in hands-on science projects. Visual-spatial learners often respond well to graphic organizers and to visualization memory strategies.

Musical-rhythmic intelligence. This intelligence includes sensitivity to pitch and rhythm of sounds and responsiveness to listening to or performing music. Musical-rhythmic learners may be able to remember a song or tune after hearing it only once or twice, and to play or sing its melody without printed music. Students with this intelligence often benefit from strategies that connect learning to rhythmic dance, songs, raps, or jingles. They can also engage in units of study through music—for example, they may learn about a period of U.S. history through the regional music of the time, or compare wave forms in science or parabolas in calculus with sound waves in music.

Bodily-kinesthetic intelligence. This intelligence category includes the ability to use fine and gross motor skills in visual or performing arts, sports, and scientific manipulative experimentation (electronics, dissection). Bodily-kinesthetic learners can use body movement to connect with information, solve problems, and convey ideas. These students benefit from teaching that incorporates dramatizations, crafts, and models.

Interpersonal intelligence. This intelligence is evident in students who work well with others and in group learning activities. They are perceptive of and responsive to others' moods, feelings, and behaviors, and their ability to interact with others with understanding makes them well suited for cooperative and peer leadership roles.

Intrapersonal intelligence. This intelligence is apparent in students who understand and are dedicated to their own beliefs and goals. Intrapersonal learners tend to be independent and are unlikely to be influenced by what others think of them. These students can form successful relational memories by linking learning to personal experiences or positive emotions. They enjoy working independently at goals they help establish and may prefer making written rather than oral responses to information they learn in class.

Naturalist intelligence. This intelligence involves knowledge of the features of the natural world, including plants and animals. Naturalist learners, who are often skilled at categorization, tend to be detail-oriented observers who can recognize patterns in nature. These students learn well through strategies that call their attention to differences and similarities, such as metaphors and Venn diagrams.

Using these multiple intelligences as a guide, teachers can vary their approaches to units of study to allow students opportunities to stimulate all of their brain regions. When students learn in an environment rich in varied intellectual and sensory stimuli, they are better able to engage and develop both their dominant and their secondary intelligences. Given the choice, most students will initially select study modes and activities that match their intelligences and learning styles. For example, when teachers allow students to decide on their final product for a unit, verbal-linguistic learners will likely choose to write news articles or press releases or to make oral presentations incorporating talk, song, dramatic performance, interview, or debate. Logical-mathematical learners lean toward presentations using PowerPoint, the overhead projector, video, illustrated posters, or charts and graphs. Bodily-kinesthetic learners may choose to create models, dioramas, or mobiles or to reenact scenes, conduct scientific experiments, or invent games to teach the class. Because students enjoy variety, after initial engagement in a new topic of study through their preferred learning styles, they will later participate in activities that relate to other styles of learning.

The top three dominant intelligence styles—verbal-linguistic, visual-spatial, and bodily-kinesthetic—are the same for students today as they were for students 25 years ago, although the percentage of students in each category has shifted considerably. In the United States, we have seen a dramatic increase in visual-spatial learners (accounting for 50 percent of learners) and a drop in the proportion of verbal-linguistic or auditory learners (accounting for 15 percent of learners), with bodily-kinesthetic learners representing the other 35 percent (Gardner, 1999). Some attribute this change to students' increased exposure to technology. The theory is that children no longer grow up visualizing images to accompany stories they hear or read because computers, television, and video games visualize everything for them (Sousa, 2000).

To better serve the changing learning dynamics of the student population, teachers and curriculum specialists are stepping out of the more traditional verbal-linguistic comfort zone of directed lectures and including more visual-spatial and bodily-kinesthetic instruction. For teachers of inclusion classes, this shift in student learning styles is further evidence that instruction and review geared toward multiple intelligences are valuable for engaging all students in successful learning.

THE BROADER CATEGORIES

Once educators have an idea of their students' dominant intelligences, they can begin to tailor their instruction to those strengths. But with eight different categories, that task is easier said than done. A more practical starting point is to look at three broader categories that each encompass several of Gardner's multiple intelligences. Here, I describe the optimal learning styles of students in each of the broader categories and the teaching strategies that I believe to be consistent with brain research and have found most effective in helping students in each category achieve success.

Sequential learners. Also called *analytical learners*, these students tend to process information in a "parts-to-whole" manner and are usually verbal-linguistic, visual-spatial, or logical-mathematical learners. They respond to logic, order, and sequence and work best with information that is presented methodically, with learning activities broken down into sequenced steps. Lessons that progress sequentially can actually benefit all students because they offer frequent opportunities for assessment and feedback, enabling students to build on knowledge and skills they have mastered with more complex concepts or processes.

For example, students can begin a lesson on adding fractions by building a circle out of plastic wedges and figuring out what fraction of the "pie" each wedge constitutes. Students then practice writing out their findings as sentences ("Four blue pieces equals one whole") and as an equation using fractions ($\frac{1}{4} + \frac{1}{4} + \frac{1}{4} + \frac{1}{4} = 1$), and drawing diagrams showing how these four pieces create a circle. Next, students work in pairs to see what other combinations of different-sized pieces can be used together to fill a whole circle, drawing sketches of their models and writing equations (for example, $\frac{1}{2} + \frac{1}{4} + \frac{1}{4} = 1$ or $\frac{1}{8} + \frac{1}{8} + \frac{1}{4} + \frac{1}{2} = 1$). Whole-class discussions follow in which students explain how fractions can be combined to equal a whole. After sufficient practice in writing equations and adding fractions to build a whole object, students can progress to manipulating fractions to create parts of a circle instead of an entire circle (for example, $\frac{1}{8} + \frac{1}{8} = \frac{1}{4}$).

Global learners. These learners process information best when instruction starts with the whole and breaks the content down into parts. Students who fall into this category have predominantly musical-rhythmic, naturalist, and bodily-kinesthetic learning strengths (and possibly some visual-spatial strengths). They are apt to perform well in activities that involve recognizable patterns, and they may be creative problem solvers and innovators.

Because global learners tend to work from the broad to the specific, teachers should help students connect a new general topic to something concrete or familiar before they start to process the information. At the beginning of a unit of study, teachers may want to present the big picture of a topic to stimulate multiple regions of students' brains. This "preheating" of the brain prepares more neural networks to process the data and helps students see the relationship between themselves and what they are about to study. Students' brains are more receptive to the information because they are drawn in through connections to their prior knowledge, personal experiences, or individual interests (Van Overwalle & De Metsenaere, 1990). For example, one good way to introduce a unit to global learners is to invite speakers who have experience using the knowledge in their careers or hobbies. Models of finished products or manipulatives for students to examine are engaging aids, and videos or bulletin boards with pictures are better introductions than are formal lectures or assigned readings.

Teachers can also stimulate global learners by engaging their abilities to respond to major events in history and broad themes in literature, to grasp graphs and charts, and to create graphic organizers with whole-to-part patterns. It may be beneficial for these students to write down what they need to learn in personal goal charts, create individual work schedules, and respond to what they hear and read with sketches or diagrams.

Exploratory learners. These learners enjoy discovery learning that frees them to experiment, create, construct, and explore their environments rather than be restricted by overly structured lessons. These students tend to be bodily-kinesthetic, interpersonal, or visual-spatial learners. The introductory activities that best draw them into units of study incorporate movement, tactile experiences, construction, dramatic representations, and other participatory learning experiences.

Although not all exploratory learners have attention or focusing difficulties, they may benefit from some of the strategies that are helpful for students with attention deficit/hyperactivity disorder (AD/HD). These include squeezing a Koosh ball during class, using a word processor to record notes, using manipulatives or calculators to get through math stumbling blocks, creating graphic organizers, and learning through rhymes, raps, songs, dramatizations, and visualizations (Kagan & Kagan, 1998).

The task of teaching to suit students' individual learning styles is not as complex as teaching every lesson eight times, each focusing on a different intelligence category. Because nearly all students fall into one of these three broader categories, educators can tailor instruction quite manageably to diverse abilities and styles and help all students in inclusion classes succeed (Campbell, Campbell, & Dickinson, 1998).

THE IMPORTANCE OF DIFFERENTIATION

Although standardized tests may be the enemy of authentic learning, most national and state standards do recognize the importance of using strategies that are compatible with students' individual learning styles or intelligences. For example, *California Standards for the Teaching Profession*, adopted in 1997, organizes content standards into six categories of teaching practice, four of which emphasize individualized access to learning: Engaging and Supporting All Students in Learning, Creating and Maintaining Effective Environments for Student Learning, Understanding and Organizing Subject Matter for Student Learning, and Planning Instruction and Designing Learning Experiences for All Students.

The contradiction between *standards* and *standardized tests* arises when teachers lack the resources to plan and carry out lessons offering multiple entry points for students with diverse learning styles. Brain-compatible strategies for individualized learning include experiential learning, experimentation, exploration, movement, and the arts—areas in which time and funding have been cut to allow for more highly structured lessons geared to rote memorization. Because such lessons limit many students' capacity to access the information through their learning strengths, the information may not efficiently reach their hippocampi and relational memory centers. Thus, students' ability to process the information is impaired, and memory retention is less likely to occur.

In contrast, instruction geared toward students' preferred learning styles is more likely to evoke positive emotional responses, enabling affective filters to open access to the brain's processing centers. When lessons are adapted for multiple intelligences, the content is more likely to be personally meaningful to students and to connect to their relational memories for successful patterning and long-term retention. As a result, students will be better able to access the material at test time. Most important, the information will reach the frontal lobe regions where the highest levels of cognitive processing take place—where learned information becomes wisdom.

It is neuro-*logical* to employ a variety of brain research–based teaching strategies suited to multiple intelligences, but more and more often, teachers are being asked to defend their chosen instructional strategies with "supporting research." On one hand, we could view this trend as validation that education is a profession, just like such other research-based occupations as chemistry and medicine, and that classroom instruction is not just a matter of personal whimsy or robotic obedience of a cookbook curriculum. On the other hand, these demands for documentation of supporting research are coming with the same inadequate planning as has the legislation specifying required standardized test performance.

Administrators, curriculum consultants, and teachers have not been granted adequate resources to attend conferences or independently study the neuroscientific literature pertaining to education. Educators have received only limited opportunities to gain the background knowledge they need to devise, practice, revise, and academically defend the instructional strategies needed for students to receive developmentally appropriate instruction geared to multiple intelligences.

It will take a period of catch-up for teachers to become expert in interpreting neuroscientific education research and for this research to be reviewed for bias or misinterpretation. But when the horse catches up with the cart and curriculum and instruction begin to honor multiple learning styles, learning will be revitalized in classrooms that have been deflated by almost a decade of pressure to teach to the test.

CHAPTER 3

TEACHING STUDENTS WITH ATTENTION DISORDERS

In 2002, the National Center for Health Statistics reported that from 1997 to 1998, more than 2.6 million U.S. children ages 6–11 had been diagnosed with an attention disorder or a learning disability (Pastor & Reuben, 2002). This prevalence of attention disorders, coupled with the increasing inclusiveness of U.S. classrooms, means that most educators, at one time or another, will teach students with attention challenges.

GRAY MATTER

Attention deficit disorder (ADD) refers to a condition that interferes with a person's ability to concentrate and control impulses and behavior. A student who has ADD is not hyperactive but will often experience difficulty sustaining a functional level of attention in performing (and completing) tasks or play activities. Attention deficit/hyperactivity disorder (AD/HD) describes a disability that interferes with a person's ability to regulate activity level, inhibit behavior, and attend to tasks in developmentally appropriate ways. Common characteristics of AD/HD include difficulty sustaining attention and concentration, developmentally inappropriate levels of activity, distractibility, and impulsivity.

As a neurologist and classroom teacher, I have worked with patients and students of all ages who have disorders affecting focus and attention, including AD/HD (both the hyperactive-impulsive type and the inattentive type) and OCD (obsessive-compulsive disorder). For the purpose of simplicity, I refer to the various attention disorders under the umbrella of AD/HD. Although each disorder has its own distinct characteristics, the strategies I suggest in this chapter are appropriate for almost any condition involving difficulty in focusing and maintaining attention. As a bonus, these strategies can increase the focus of *all* students in inclusion classes, especially those with exploratory learning styles and bodily-kinesthetic intelligence.

Functional brain imaging conducted while test subjects are actively learning reveal the brain's processes of capturing and maintaining attention and can help determine which teaching strategies are most effective for students with AD/HD. Initial brain imaging and mapping studies revealed which areas of the brain are active in the areas of attention, memory, learning, and information retrieval, and subsequent studies have built on that information by evaluating how these brain learning centers respond to varied teaching strategies and learning environments (Gabriel, 2001). It turns out that the strategies that are common sense to successful teachers—offering students choice, providing lessons and tools structured to support their learning strengths, and helping them recognize the progress they make toward their goals—are those now supported by neurological learning research.

GRAY MATTER

Neuroimaging and brain-mapping research are increasing rapidly in the study of attention disorders. So far, research seems to have found a correlation between many AD/HD subjects and a lower quantity of neurotransmitters (especially dopamine and norepinepherine), a lower level of brain metabolism, and a lower quantity and complexity of interconnecting brain cell networks. These variations from the norm are most prominent in the frontal lobes, the limbic system, and the reticular activating system (RAS).

GRAY MATTER
(CONTINUED)

When activated by emotion, the RAS sends messages to the frontal lobes' executive function and memory centers. When the RAS is below normal activity levels, the decreased stimulation of these frontal lobe centers can result in learning and memory difficulties and impaired self-control. Too much stimulation of the frontal lobes from an overactive RAS may result in hyperactivity and hyperkinetic behavior (Kinomura, Larsson, Gulyas, & Roland, 1996).

Some theories associate AD/HD symptoms with a deficiency of the neurotransmitter norepinepherine in the RAS, which would account for focusing difficulties and the decreased efficiency with which some students process information. One theory behind the use of stimulant medications, such as Ritalin, is that they increase the levels of norepinepherine (and probably dopamine) in the RAS and frontal lobes and therefore promote more activity in the frontal lobe centers of executive control (Pawlak, Magarinos, Melchor, McEwen, & Strickland, 2003).

But the first and perhaps most important strategy is not a direct result of brain scan studies: it is simply the demonstration of respect for students and their families. As we saw in Chapters 1 and 2, when students' perceptions of school are linked with negative emotions, their brains' affective filters block sensory input from entering memory storage. Thus, it's crucial to maintain a supportive classroom community built on respect.

AD/HD students crave approval from their peers, parents, and teachers. To help them gain respect, teachers' first step should be to show them and their parents that they will not be prejudged according to past performance. Acknowledging students' challenges and recognizing their progress sets them up for success. Students will thrive when they trust that their teachers are evaluating them according to the progress they're making toward their goals rather than just handing out a grade for the final product. By communicating their respect for students with attention difficulties, teachers will be able to gain their trust while also modeling tolerance to their classmates.

The letter below is one that I shared with Cody, a 5th grader with AD/HD, before sending it to his parents. With Cody's permission, I also read it aloud to the class.

Dear Carla and Dan,

   I know you wrote to me that during his last school year Cody did not reach his potential in school. The Cody I have come to know in the first weeks of school is astonishing. I have nothing but sincere praise for him in every aspect of student success. He is kind, appreciative, sensitive, very responsible, and, at this point, the most diligent of all of his classmates (he handed in two personal interest surveys before anyone else). He has done beautifully on every assignment, but more important, he is respectful and resourceful. He thinks out his questions carefully, and when he asks me a question it is very appropriate and often something the whole class benefits from. He has done advanced conceptual math independently and checks his work. When he needs help, he first uses all the resources available to him and then asks questions that are to the point and insightful. His class behavior is exemplary. He is helpful, never refuses a request, and often sees a need and steps in without being asked. I could go on, but I have to save something for parent conference day.

   Thank you for allowing me the pleasure of spending this time with your wonderful son!

In that short note home, I acknowledged Cody's efforts and made sure to include specific examples of what he was doing right. Sure, there were times when he jumped out of his chair because he wrongly assumed that the class had been dismissed for recess. Yes, his notebook had loose papers, and his cubby was in disarray. But he was trying, and his efforts in the right direction warranted positive reinforcement. Once I established mutual respect, I could work with Cody and his parents on the details. His parents' response follows.

Dear Judy,

Thank you. Not just for the kind words, but also for the specifics you gave us. Cody actually comes home with a smile on his face. He is beaming! He actually sits down and does his homework on his own without our prodding him to do it. He is happy, inspired, and actually talks about school! He is excited to be there and excited to learn for the first time in his life! He can't wait to tell us about the extra credit points you can earn, or how you can study what you want. Every day he asks us a million times to test him on the states.

Thank you for allowing him room to be him, for the inspiration, and for the support he will need to push past even his own limitations.

With relief and appreciation,
Dan and Carla

THE LEVELS OF ATTENTION

For students to learn to the best of their abilities, they must be able to achieve appropriately high levels of attention to process and retain lesson information. Many AD/HD students have not reached the elevated level of focus that stimulates the brain's executive functions and allows learning to take hold. Here I offer an explanation of the three levels of attention, from lowest to highest: survival mode, attention mode, and selective mode.

Level 1: Survival mode. The capacity to attend to one's environment is a basic survival skill. Whether watching for food to gather, prey to hunt, or danger to avoid, higher animals depend on their brains to respond selectively to the multitude of data continually barraging their senses. Every waking second, 400 billion bits of information approach the brain through sensory input channels, but the brain processes "only" 2,000 of these bits per second. This large volume of input, along with the high speed at which it's processed, requires the brain to admit information largely according to unconscious judgment based on previous knowledge and experience. This selection process demonstrates why attention is as much about what our brains do not attend to as it is about what we do focus on.

Ideally, students are beyond the basic survival mode and can direct their attention to more than just securing safety. However, too much stress can push students into this survival mode. Excessive stress commonly arises in AD/HD students when they feel confused and overwhelmed by a lesson or separated from classmates because of their inability to connect with, focus on, or create meaning from the lesson's information. From this state of tension and agitation, it is difficult to get back on track, make sense of the data, and know what to focus on.

This stress-induced survival mode, like the adrenalin fight-or-flight response, blocks students' abilities to select the meaningful input from their sensory environment. What little information they can separate out as important cannot readily pass through the over-stressed amygdala and limbic system into the brain's relating and memory centers (Dozier, 1998).

Level 2: Interest mode. Students in this mode pay attention to things that are of interest to them. When students are engaged through novelty, pleasant surprise, creative play, or enjoyable videos or stories, they are emotionally comfortable and are able and willing to work to block out extraneous sensory stimuli and focus on the compelling stimuli provided (Malone, 1981). Teachers can foster this state by balancing novelty with the security of familiarity—by including some predictable, purposeful rituals throughout the lesson, for example.

Teachers can prime students' attention by bringing student interests and talents into their lessons. If students are interested in baseball, for example, asking how batting averages are calculated could prompt their interest in a probability lesson. For students interested in computers, asking about how hard disk storage capacities compare is a good lead-in to a discussion of the powers of 10. This strategy enables students to see how the information in the lesson is relevant to them or to the world they know (Reeve, 1996). Recognizing students' areas of interest also provides avenues for connecting them to the rest of their academic studies. The attention-focusing skills they develop in their areas of interest become behavior patterns that promote success and attentiveness in other academic areas.

Level 3: Selective mode. Students who have reached the highest level of selective attention can focus on the sensory input they need to understand the lesson. This state is most likely to occur when students link their own ideas to a topic of study and raise questions to which they want answers or embark on paths they want to follow. During this state, they will be motivated to work through interesting problems that puzzle and challenge them.

When students are tuned in to and care about the activity or process, they will want to acquire the academic tools they need to solve their problems. Students at the level of selective attention don't perceive lessons as random, isolated bits of dry information. They want the tools that the lessons have to offer so that they can apply the knowledge to their areas of interest. The academic material they *need* to learn for the required curriculum becomes the tool they *want* to acquire to reach their own goals.

During this elevated state of selective focus, the frontal lobe executive functions are stimulated. Just as with any repeatedly used and stimulated brain circuitry, the more students use these brain regions, the stronger the circuits will get. More dendrites and synapses will grow, and presumably this brain region will increase its efficiency. By maintaining positive emotional states, using challenging and engaging material, and applying strategies that focus attention, teachers can help students with AD/HD reach this most productive state of attention and gain the confidence and skills they need to develop goal-oriented behaviors. With each success they experience in reaching their individualized goals, AD/HD students will become more confident, motivated, and capable of thinking at these higher levels.

PATTERNING FOR BRAIN NETWORK ALIGNMENT

As we know, the brain filters sensory input before processing it, selectively focusing attention on the information that it recognizes as having survival or interest value. Beyond those selective responses, the brain is most attuned to information that it recognizes as patterns or categories it has already formed (Coward, 1990). When sensory information does not match any known pattern, the brain may reject, misinterpret, or ignore it. The film *What the Bleep Do We Know!?* (Arntz, Chasse, & Vicente, 2004) provides a theoretical example of this phenomenon in its discussion of the Caribbean natives who had never seen ocean-crossing vessels before Christopher Columbus's ships sailed in. According to the legend, when the shaman and natives saw the ships and the ripples in their wakes, they did not initially perceive the vessels as ships because the concept did not fit any preconceived patterns in their brains. After days of watching the ripples, the shaman reportedly interpreted that they must be made by objects moving in the water. Only then could the natives interpret what their eyes saw as ships traveling along the water.

For students with attention deficits, it is as difficult to separate the multisensory stimuli around them into individual components as it would be for you to pick out one specific voice in a chorus. These students have difficulty seeing the patterns in the information they are reading, seeing, or hearing, and, as a result, their brains may not be able to follow one new idea before another intrudes (Jeffries, Fritz, & Braun, 2003). When they cannot select out the patterns in mathematical concepts, songs, spelling rules, or puzzles as effectively as their classmates can, they may be not only confused but also frustrated by the stress of feeling different. This high stress level increases their difficulties in following the stream of information being delivered.

Certain interventions can help students with AD/HD develop brain-patterning skills that enable them to categorize the multitude of sensory inputs they receive. Neuroimaging conducted on the learning brain suggests that patterns or templates that connect new sensory data to neuronal networks increase success at converting short-term or working memories into long-term memories (Calvin & Bickerton, 2000). Students' attention and learning appear to improve when strategies help them focus on stimuli. For example, some students with AD/HD tap their pencils on their desks or their feet on the floor, creating external patterning rhythms that may help their brains' attention networks converge on a single predominant sensory input. This input then becomes the structure on which they coordinate other incoming data, analogous to the way the pull of a magnet lines up iron filings in an orderly direction (Schneider, 1993).

Some theories grounded in this research suggest that music can increase the attentive focus of students with AD/HD, enabling them to link new information with preexisting brain networks. The external pattern from the beat of the music or the ticking of a metronome can act as a guiding pattern, or "landing strip," a structure onto which students can organize incoming academic information, connect ideas, and align their thoughts.

When I tell parents how their children with AD/HD improved their math performance when they listened to music, most are willing to try the technique at home, as counterintuitive as it seems to some of them. I first show parents the individualized analysis of their children's work with and without the music. The computerized math program I use, ALEKS, keeps detailed records of time spent and concepts mastered. During conferences, students who are clear responders to music add their own descriptions to the computer analysis of their increased mental efficiency. They tend to write variations of "Now I can see how this math problem fits together. It is as if the music makes my mind able to concentrate on the math." Once their brains are aligned by the patterns established by music, they are able to hone their conceptual or abstract learning. The music seems to work like a graphic organizer that helps students catalog newly learned material.

It is possible that with time, these students will need less external patterning as their frontal lobes mature and they develop more-advanced patterning skills. If they don't receive some assistance with focus and patterning while they are in school, however, these students may fall farther and farther behind.

DOPAMINE: A VITAL INGREDIENT

Reinforcement learning theory is based on the assumption that the brain finds some states of stimulation to be more desirable than others and therefore seeks them out. The brain is believed to make associations between specific cues and these desirable states or goals (Brembs, Lorenzetti, Reyes, Baxter, & Byrne, 2002). A vital key to this theory is the neurotransmitter *dopamine.*

Neuroimaging scans reveal that the brain increases its release of dopamine in response to rewards and positive experiences, such as play, laughter, exercise, and acknowledgment for achievement (Black et al., 2002). Dopamine release is also stimulated when subjects merely *anticipate* pleasure or reward (Nader et al., 2002). Because dopamine is a major chemical neurotransmitter associated with attention, decision making, and executive function, it follows that the brain's release of dopamine in connection with pleasurable experiences has the benefit of increasing the efficiency of the synapses controlling attention and executive function. An additional bonus is that dopamine released in expectation of reward triggers the release of acetylcholine, a neurotransmitter that in turn directly stimulates the hippocampus, the modulating center for consolidating new learning to related stored memory (Ashby et al., 1999).

GRAY MATTER

fMRI blood oxygenation signal imaging enables researchers to study how the human brain senses, predicts, and acts to acquire rewards. Rewarding stimuli increase brain activity in the frontal cortex (executive function center); the amygdala; and the *nucleus accumbens*, a center deep in the brain above the brainstem. These are the brain regions where dopamine is found in the highest quantities. Because these dopamine centers are activated by reward and by unexpected events, it's neuro-*logical* to incorporate surprise, novelty, and student-centered

GRAY MATTER
(CONTINUED)

activities in the learning environment, as well as to link knowledge with students' positive memories and experiences.

When the amygdala is moderately and pleasurably stimulated, information passes more easily into the brain, first reaching the nucleus accumbens for the pleasure/dopamine response, then being transmitted to the frontal lobes for processing, and finally being successfully sorted into long-term memory storage (Anderson & Sobel, 2003). Dopamine not only affects the opening or closing of networks into the working memory but also encodes predictions and adjusts behavior to achieve the rewards it predicts (Montague, Hyman, & Cohen, 2004).

When learning activities are repeatedly linked to enjoyable experiences, students' brains learn to seek out those activities. When students perceive a cue that the pleasure-linked learning activity will begin, their brains release dopamine in expectation of the experience (Nader et al., 2002). For example, if teachers integrate fun and physical activities into their vocabulary lessons, such as acting out or illustrating the meaning of the words, students' brains will learn to associate the cue of the announced vocabulary lesson with the expectation of pleasant stimulation. The dopamine released will then enhance their brains' focus and executive function during the lesson.

In addition, once students are in the dopamine-reward state, they are open to prompting, so their cognitive focus can be incorporated into other academic learning. For example, when working on projects in cooperative groups, students can act as experts in their fields of interest by building a model or writing the script for a skit. The sense of accomplishment they get from their contribution will promote their brains' dopamine-reward state, which will in turn increase the efficiency of their executive functions, making their brains more receptive to learning the other aspects of the subject being investigated by their groups.

In the dopamine-reward state, students will be eager to practice and improve so that they can continue to experience the intrinsic rewards of successfully connecting to school. As their brains continue to release dopamine, their nerve cell connections will grow and existing neural circuits will grow stronger. The following strategies make the classroom a more pleasurable place to learn, thus promoting dopamine-reward brain states and enhancing learning.

Strategies to Promote Dopamine Release

Provide choice. Giving students some degree of choice—even as small as deciding how they wish to investigate vocabulary words—stimulates a positive emotional response. Although standardized testing and overly structured curricula do not permit students to study only what interests them, teachers can still offer choice and variety in work areas, partners, and scheduling time. The sense of empowerment derived from knowing they have some choice in *how* they study the material affects students' ultimate engagement and success (Patrick, Skinner, & Connell, 1993). Teachers should make sure to avoid too little structure in assignment requirements and deadlines, however. Students need appropriate structure so that they don't lose direction.

Engage students in discovery. Discovery learning and hands-on/minds-on explorations motivate and stimulate dopamine release because making discoveries is so rewarding. Students can make new connections to previously learned information, which makes them feel good about themselves. They grow to connect that pleasurable reward state with learning, and gradually the frustrations they have associated with school in the past will diminish.

Let students take ownership. Before introducing a new unit, teachers can build positive anticipation by involving students in the preparations for the unit. Students can help rearrange the classroom, gather background material for bulletin boards and classroom displays, or write questions on note cards in anticipation of a visit from a guest speaker. This degree of involvement heightens students' subsequent attentiveness to the event or unit of study because they have already established a brain category or relational memory with which to connect the coming lessons.

Give students time. Teachers should allow for the fact that students with attention difficulties sometimes need more time to learn new material. Teachers may want to prime students for an upcoming lesson or chapter or pair them up with a partner or aide to gain some familiarity with new or challenging material. These preview strategies help nip frustration in the bud and increase attention and receptivity. Teachers should also make sure to expose students to new material multiple times before assessing their retention of the information. Finally, because students with AD/HD tend to experience a continual onslaught of stimuli running through their brains, they may have difficulty prioritizing. Teachers can help students manage their time by helping them sort out what they think is the most important work to do first.

Plan frequent "syn-naps." The best time to give students "syn-naps," or brain rests, is before synaptic overload causes them to tune out and act out. Teachers can avoid the cycle of "rewarding" attention-challenged students' negative behavior with a break by planning brain rests for times when students are still feeling good. Students should get a few minutes notice before the actual syn-naps, however, so they can bring their activities to a close without feeling frustrated by the interruption.

Reinforce positive behaviors. Teachers should be sure to give praise and encouragement when students stay on task, not just when they master a topic or complete a final product. As student compliance increases, teachers can acknowledge their cooperation by giving them greater responsibility. When students experience this sincere response to their concentration, they begin to see the connection between practice and success and will respond with increased compliance.

Make use of cues. When teachers are about to cover the most important information in a lesson, it's helpful to have a consistent cue prompting AD/HD students to pay special attention *now*.

Teachers can use such prearranged signals as putting on a special cap or wizard's cape, writing in a certain color, or announcing, "Here comes some dendrite food."

These strategies will lead students to discover that the more effort they invest, the higher they will achieve. The learned expectation that effort has its own intrinsic reward will have major benefits. Students will experience the dopamine reward state first when they anticipate pleasurable activities and again when they are actually engaged in the activities, increasing their mental clarity and executive function skills. Engaging lessons will also open and activate the brain pathways and neural circuits that carry information from superficial awareness into working and relational memory. Bottom line: if teachers enhance lessons with activities that students find pleasurable, students' brains will respond by adjusting their behaviors to achieve the rewards that their dopamine reward systems predict.

Teens and Dopamine

Although attention disorders are lifelong conditions, they have certain age-related characteristics. For example, the hyperactivity component of AD/HD, manifested in children as excessive physical activity, chair tilting, impulsivity, and other large muscle movements, becomes more refined in adults. These are the adults who doodle during meetings, chew pencils, fidget with their keys, and frequently reposition their bodies in their chairs. With age, social conditioning, practice with patterning, and increased selectiveness in responding to sensory input, most adults tend to reduce the outward signs of hyperactivity.

Unlike hyperactivity, attentive filtering challenges may persist as older students struggle to maintain mental focus and resist distractions. The more strategies students develop throughout their school years to manage their hyperactivity and direct their focus, the more successful they will be at redirecting their spontaneity into productivity and creativity.

The time between childhood and adulthood is when it can be most challenging for teachers to recognize and respond to students who appear to have attention deficits. Teenagers are, by virtue of their hormonal changes and ongoing brain development and pruning, prone to be emotionally volatile, unpredictable, self-absorbed, and hypersensitive. The last parts of the brain to fully develop during the teen years are the frontal lobes—the centers of emotional stability as well as executive function, concentration, value and moral judgment, planning, and consequence prediction. Until this maturation is complete and hormonal balance is achieved, events or changes that most adults think inconsequential may seem huge to young teens. Conversely, things that adults consider obvious and important may not be interpreted that way by the still-incomplete frontal lobes of teenagers. What may appear to be bad judgment or selfishness may really be a failure of teens' brains to see and interpret the sensory stimuli bombarding their immature brains.

GRAY MATTER

MRI scans distinguish gray matter, which is high in neurons, from white matter, which is mostly made up of axons and dendrites covered in myelin (fat-protein layers of insulation). At age 5, and continuing for the next 15 years, gray matter begins to thin and be replaced by white matter. As the gray matter thins, the myelin coating of the connecting fibers in the white matter thickens. Myelin increases the speed of connections between brain regions, resulting in more efficient information access and retrieval. This is one reason that adults are better able than teens to analyze information and make logical decisions (Bartzokis et al., 2001).

The regions that are last to myelinate control executive function and emotional regulatory areas associated with planning, judgment, attentive focus, prioritizing, critical analysis, emotional self-control, and empathy (Bennett & Baird, 2005). This delay in pruning and myelination in the frontal lobes of teenagers correlates with their tendencies toward lapses in judgment. One-third to one-half of adolescents with substance abuse disorders have AD/HD. In addition, teenagers are three to four times more likely to die than children past infancy, largely because they take more risks and thus have more accidents (Hoyert, Heron, Murphy, & Kung, 2006).

Similarly, the problem some middle school students have with sustained academic focus is not just a matter of hormones or adolescent "acting out." To focus attention appropriately, the centers in the frontal lobes must sift multiple environmental stimuli from moment to moment and prioritize the input determined most relevant to the task. Again, these frontal lobe centers are the last to be pruned of the unnecessary gray matter neurons that delay information acquisition, processing, and retrieval.

When small, tangible rewards were given for simple tasks, the nucleus accumbens of young children and adults showed a strong response, whereas the response for teens was much lower. However, when teens received medium or large rewards for the same task, their nucleus accumbens had the strongest response of any group. A possible implication of this exaggeratedly positive response to reward is that teens may be motivated to engage in risk-taking behaviors (fast driving, drugs and alcohol use, binge eating, or sexual activity) to feel the pleasure surge associated with instant gratification (Galvan et al., 2006).

Considering these findings, it seems unlikely that even teenagers who do not engage in high-risk behaviors will eagerly sit to study vocabulary words when there is little intrinsic reward and lots of required focus and delayed gratification. It is therefore vital that teachers are aware of the changes in adolescents' developing brains and use strategies that promote the stimulation of the reward-response centers and release of dopamine so that students experience pleasurable reactions to things that will benefit them academically, emotionally, and physically.

It helps to separate developmentally appropriate behavior from a multitude of authentic psychological and physical conditions, such as AD/HD, bipolar disorder, and oppositional defiance disorder.

By the teenage years, many students with LD or AD/HD have been turned off from school. For some, these negative feelings are reactions to teachers who have embarrassed or disciplined them for their inattentive behaviors. Other students may have had such difficulty focusing on lessons that did not relate to their interests or connect with their creativity that they developed negative expectations about school.

Winston Churchill is described as having hated school, especially reading. He was even considered "backward" by his teachers. His turning point was said to have taken place at age 10, when his father gave him the book *Treasure Island*. Churchill loved the book and extended that positive experience into a passion for reading. When his teachers saw him reading books beyond his years but still not producing work that they felt merited good grades, they were offended by what they labeled his laziness. According to Churchill biographers, he acknowledged that when his teachers did not engage his imagination or interests, he would not or could not learn (Jenkins, 2001). Nowadays, teachers can apply some teen-specific strategies to activate students' dopamine-reward systems and increase their learning.

Play. Teens may sometimes appear to disdain the type of imaginative play that delights younger children, such as skits, songs, and games. That façade is part of their trying on the adult image. Nevertheless, finding ways to use play and physical activity will stimulate their dopamine-reward systems. Helping them connect to these positive activities will also reduce their tendency to resort to high-risk behaviors (drugs, alcohol, overeating, violence, dangerous physical activities, or sexual promiscuity) to produce their dopamine and adrenaline boosts.

Sincere and specific praise. When teachers provide praise, it should be immediate and specific to the tasks or goals that students achieve. Expressing expectations for future performance along with praise makes students' success a burden and limits the benefit of the feedback. For example, comments like "You have done so well in math this month, I'm sure you will get an *A* on the next test" can cause anxiety and stress. Sincere praise is also more constructive than extrinsic rewards, which can reduce intrinsic motivation and interfere with the development of a true joy of learning. Each success that students recognize as personal achievement helps them develop the strategies that help them control their attention and focus. Finally, one of the most powerful forms of praise comes from classmates who acknowledge their peers' success and express appreciation for their contributions to cooperative work.

Metacognition. By middle school and beyond, students with AD/HD are at a prime teachable age to practice metacognition. With guidance and support, they can learn which strategies to use to best direct their focus, avoid distractions, organize their schedules, persevere even when confronted by setbacks and frustration, and make reasonable decisions.

BUILDING GOAL-DIRECTED BEHAVIOR

Readers may recall hearing about the Marshmallow Test, part of a longitudinal study beginning in the 1960s carried out by Stanford University psychology researcher Walter Mischel (Sethi & Mischel, 2000). The study evaluated the predictive value of self-discipline as measured by the ability to delay immediate gratification in exchange for long term goal achievement. The test was simple: the researcher sat a 4-year-old down in a room in front of a marshmallow and informed the child that he could eat it at any time. But if the child waited while the researcher ran an errand, he would get two marshmallows when the researcher returned. About one-third of the children tested grabbed the single marshmallow right away. Another third waited a little longer before eating it, and the final third were able to wait the 15 or 20 minutes for the researcher to return.

Years later, the differences between the group that delayed gratification and the group that gave in to it immediately were dramatic: the "resisters" who controlled their impulses were identified as more positive, self-motivating, and persistent in the face of difficulties. They were still able to delay gratification in pursuit of their goals and had also developed other characteristics associated with successful adults, including long-term marriages, higher incomes, greater career satisfaction, better health, and more self-described fulfilling lives than most of the population. On the other hand, those who as 4-year-olds had grabbed the marshmallow were more troubled, stubborn, indecisive, and mistrustful, and they were still not able to put off gratification. During their later education years, they had trouble achieving long-range goals and were easily distracted by more pleasurable activities when they knew they needed to study for a test or write a report. As adults, they reported less successful marriages, lower job satisfaction and income, poorer health, and higher frustration in their lives.

It turned out that the Marshmallow Test was two times more accurate a predictor of later SAT scores than the subjects' IQ scores. The one-marshmallow kids scored, on average, 210 points lower on SAT tests than did the two-marshmallow kids (Sethi & Mischel, 2000).

The ability to envision the future and understand that effort over time pays off allows all students to tolerate occasional failures in their pursuit of their goals. This ability is especially important for AD/HD and LD students in inclusion classes, who often feel frustrated by the fact that their progress is slower than their classmates'. When students are helped to clarify their goals and the steps they need to take to achieve them, they are able to persevere and overcome the confusion that can occur when learning new material.

GRAY MATTER

Research shows that the brain is surprisingly *plastic*, or capable of change. When I was in medical school, I was shocked to see the extraordinary lifesaving measures extended to infants born three months prematurely and weighing less than two pounds. I figured that the lives they would lead, if they survived, would be ones of severe retardation and physical pain. Yet as I watched these infants grow over the years, I was repeatedly astonished by their physical and intellectual abilities. Thanks to the plasticity of the newborns' brains, the reorganizing of brain pathways that can follow injury allowed portions of healthy brain to take over the work of damaged brain.

This plasticity is not something we often see in older adults who suffer similar regional brain destruction from strokes. As brains become more specialized, they lose much of their plasticity and cannot use as much undamaged brain to pick up what was lost. Yet research is revealing that brain plasticity can be stimulated beyond infancy, in children and even in some adults, with such techniques as computer programs, music and art therapy, and innovative teaching methodology that can rewire the brain to improve or restore memory and learning skills. As we discover more about the brain's plasticity, we will be able to enhance learning efficiency and treat attention deficits and other learning disorders more successfully.

Engage Through Interests, Empower Through Success

The behaviors that build such executive functions as focus, prioritization, organization, critical analysis, and judgment are also those that build skills in self-monitoring and self-discipline (goal-directed behaviors). When the frontal lobes are not functioning optimally, students have more difficulty sustaining attention, particularly on tasks that don't capture their interest. It's therefore crucial to set up conditions that do capture students' interest and stimulate their creativity.

For students with AD/HD, who have difficulty delaying immediate gratification, stronger intrinsic attraction to goals will increase their self-discipline to achieve those goals. Helping students explore their interests can uncover potential goals they will want to work toward. Teachers may want to administer formal interest inventories or give creative prompts in class, such as having students fill out a personal "coat of arms" with sketches or words that represent their interests. Or students could engage in peer interviews, filling out their partners' interest inventories through Q&A and then introducing their partners to the class. Even if students don't use all the information they've gathered, teachers can collect the completed peer inventories to add to their student interest files. These files can be a go-to resource for teachers who want to incorporate students' personal interests into units of study. For example, if a teacher knows that one of her students collects baseball cards, she can use baseball averages to connect the student to the math of probability, prompt him to investigate the concepts of acceleration and deceleration through the perspective of hit balls, or encourage him to read about Willie Mays during Black History Month.

I was able to help one 10-year-old student who had AD/HD set and reach goals that she found worthy and engaging. Her attention span was very low if she was not doing something she loved—for example, she approached all writing assignments with anxiety and frustration—but if she was working on art, watching a science technology video, or playing computer games, she could remain on task and in her seat for extended periods. When I discovered her interest in underwater exploration technology and saw the homemade submarine she made for her science class, I knew I had found a passion of hers that I could channel into writing.

For the next book report I assigned, I gave her the choice of writing about the further adventures of one of the characters in her book. After discussing various possibilities, we decided that her protagonist would design and test submarines for deep ocean exploration. I helped her find suitable books at her independent reading level to provide scientific and mathematical background to make her new chapter more authentic. She kept a sea log of facts and definitions (with correct spellings) of the vocabulary of underwater technology and oceanography. I modified some of her regular math textbook problems to relate to sea exploration and had her design her report cover using a new computer art program.

Throughout this process, authentic problems came up for which she needed mathematical, grammatical, and computer skills. She would have previously avoided these academic investigations, but because she was in an emotionally positive state of engagement, her need for the skill was important to her intrinsically. Her own interests and purpose prompted the problems she was trying to solve and the questions she needed to answer. The solutions had personal meaning for her. As she worked to find these answers, her attention and ability to plan, prioritize, and work toward long-term goals increased.

As students build up their abilities to focus on and persist in academic tasks, they will experience increased success and self-confidence. This sense of competence will drive them to persevere when obstacles arise in subsequent learning activities. With each success, students will set higher goals for themselves and build patience, resilience, and tolerance of setbacks. Students will also increasingly correlate effort with achievement. Van Overwalle and De Metsenaere (1990) found that students who made this correlation attained their goals more readily than did students who were taught techniques for time management and comprehension of new material.

GRAY MATTER

Students can increase their confidence in their ability to face challenges by visualizing their own success. The visualization can increase their sense of emotional well-being and can also prime the neuronal circuits needed for the academic activity they are about to attempt (Eliassen, Souza, & Sanes, 2003). What the brain actually hears, smells, and sees and what the brain *imagines* when it thinks of those sounds, smells, and sights stimulate the same areas of the brain. When athletes visualize their ideal physical movement, or when students visualize their academic success on a history test, they are stimulating the same neural circuits that are activated when that physical movement or academic thinking actually takes place. This visualization-stimulation increases the probability of success because it's priming the neural circuits that will be used in the activity. Helping students develop their skills of metacognition will further increase the benefits of this strategy and others. Recalling the strategy that helped them attain success will prompt them to use it again and to integrate that strategy into their executive functioning.

Of course, that's not to say that certain strategies won't also help students pursue goals and build self-discipline. In addition to engaging students through their interests, teachers can foster goal-directed behavior by

- Showing students how to identify, name, and monitor the emotions that either help or hinder goal-directed behavior.
- Introducing rubrics that help students see the steps leading to their goals.
- Displaying charts that give students visual feedback on their progress.
- Teaching students metacognitive skills to help them assess when they are making progress and when they are backsliding—for example, students may ask themselves, "What did I do right, and what can I do that worked before that I'm not doing now?"

Students in inclusion classes may never have experienced the positive effects of delaying gratification. Yet that experience is crucial for them if they are to become successful students and, later, fulfilled adults. When students work toward a self-selected goal that they are interested in, they can see the connection between their practice and their progress. This learned association helps them achieve the self-awareness, proactivity, perseverance, and emotional stability that will serve them in the classroom and throughout their lives (Raskind et al., 1999).

Extending Students' Goal-Directed Success

After the first few weeks or months of working with students on goal-directed behavior, teachers can review students' strategies. If students' interests lend themselves to advanced or independent work where practice results in greater mastery (for example, typing, math calculations, or matching states and capitals), teachers should acknowledge and encourage that strategy. Each time these students acknowledge that their greater success resulted from practice, they feel more capable and self-confident. With these confidence boosters, students with attention difficulties will be more likely to put in the extra work in other subject areas because they have experienced the rewards of practicing to achieve goals.

Sandy, a 12-year-old student, speaks to these points: "I hated math because I didn't know my multiplication and division. That took so much time that I'd never finish the practice problems we were given in class. I'd still be doing the long division part of the problem when the other kids would have finished the whole problem. They were able to do fun calculator and computer activities, and I was still feeling stupid doing little-kid division."

What changed for Sandy? "Once I was allowed to use the calculator to do the multiplication parts of long division, I really could listen to the math lesson and do the problems with the rest of the class, because I wasn't slowed down by the multiplication and division. I got so good at the calculator that the teacher asked me to demonstrate a calculator activity on television screen for the whole class. I was so proud. What I also discovered was that I was really good in math. It was just the arithmetic of the multiplication that was slowing me down. Since that day, three months ago, math has become my favorite subject. I still had to go back and learn those multiplication tables, but I didn't mind practicing them because I knew that the more I practiced the better I got, and there was a reason to learn them because I am a smart math girl. I finally saw a reason to make all the practice worth my time."

For some students with AD/HD, the challenge lies in selecting individual thoughts from the multitude of ideas passing through their consciousness. Sometimes a more formal approach is needed to help students structure their thoughts, put them into words, and write them down. An adult partner can provide this structure by listening to the students express their ideas and then repeating them back so that the students can hear them and use auditory processing to organize their "reflected" thoughts. Adult structuring may also be needed as students work on planning and prioritizing their work schedules. James, age 12, who has the predominantly hyperactive-impulsive type of AD/HD, states that "I got tired and gave up during the last few weeks. I needed to focus more and not be so distracted. It was so frustrating to see all the homework I had and realize that it might take my friends an hour, and I'll probably mess around and not even finish by bedtime. Then I'd be even further behind, and everyone would be mad at me." His mom confirmed his difficulties, saying, "James has great intentions and big plans, but landing long enough to do them is too hard for him. He has no ulterior motive to beat the system, but ours is a busy house with active siblings. He's overwhelmed at home."

What changed for James? After two months of working on organizational techniques with the school's learning specialist and participating in a small homework club, James developed his planning skills. To build his accountability skills, James, his parents, and his teachers developed and committed to such rules as "No books, no entry to class." With this increased structure and supervision, James became more successful at avoiding distractions and completing most of his homework in study hall or homework club. He helped create a routine in which he completed the more challenging homework at school and left the homework he was interested in—such as computer interactive math, typing practice, and Internet research—for home. James was pleased because he caught up with his work and began making his own weekly schedules. His parents were delighted because he did not need prodding to do his work at home, and he had more time for family activities.

FINDING SUCCESS IN GROUPS

One of the most successful ways teachers can use information gathered about student interests is to form cooperative work groups. Cooperative group work can incorporate students' artistic creativity, computer skills, model making, or dramatic talent because it's designed to value a diverse range of skills. For example, including a poster in a group's presentation on the water cycle or the causes of World War II will not only engage an art enthusiast's interest in the project but also increase the value placed on her by the group, facilitating behavior management as well as enhancing learning. Group work involving skits or dramatizations appeals to the bodily-kinesthetic, verbal-linguistic, and interpersonal intelligences of many students with AD/HD. When these students observe modeling and then practice the skills needed for successful group work, they are able to develop their self-control, manage their emotions, and learn to cooperate and resolve conflicts with others. Finally, the process of working with a group reduces stress and builds confidence because students do not feel the familiar sense of failure often associated with individual formal assessments.

To assess group work, teachers can use clearly defined rubrics that separately assess individual and group achievements and attitudes. After participating in several cooperative activities, students can take more responsibility in their own assessments. For example, they can fill out rubrics evaluating their own strengths and weaknesses both in their individual contributions to the group and in their cooperative behavior as members of the group.

One spring, a 2nd grade inclusion class primarily made up of English language learners of varying proficiencies and students with AD/HD participated in an extended cross-curriculum cooperative learning unit investigating the extinction of the dinosaurs. It took more planning than most lessons, but students' resulting sense of accomplishment carried into their academic and social interactions for the remainder of the school year.

The cross-curricular unit, which I created, incorporated science, literature, and mathematics. Students used the process of *group consensus* to decide which theory of dinosaur extinction their groups would defend. Group projects included creating a poster and performing a dramatization depicting their chosen theory of dinosaur extinction. In creating their posters, students used addition and subtraction to represent the growing numbers of dinosaurs before the occurrence of the crucial event contributing to extinction, and the diminishing numbers of dinosaurs after the event. To assess the goal of balanced participation, each member of a group was designated a different color marker to use when adding words, calculations, and drawings to the group poster. After each day of work, the groups had time to see which colors were underrepresented on their posters and discussed how the students using those colors could have more opportunities to add to the project the next day.

These cooperative-group techniques also apply to middle and high school classes, where students of mixed abilities can participate through their strengths. In middle and high school, groups could use their individual skills and interests to launch advertising presentations or political campaigns. For example, a class divided into groups supporting one of two candidates could create posters and political cartoons, stage oral debates and skits, and produce computer or video ads. Engaging the sometimes-marginalized AD/HD students through their talents will put them at peak attention levels. Their group partners, who might be used to thinking of them as disruptive, will probably acknowledge their increased focus and valuable contributions.

BUILDING COMMUNITY AND RAISING AWARENESS

Another way to integrate AD/HD students into the classroom community is to raise class awareness and empathy. As we know, the brain focusing centers in students with AD/HD often have difficulty distinguishing which sensory input is the most important. These students are likely to feel anxious about looking foolish during class discussions, making homework errors, or not being able to understand lessons that classmates seem to have no problem with. In that state of anxiety, students' brains are receiving limited information because their reticular activating systems are in survival mode and their affective filters are raised.

Feeling a part of the community increases marginalized students' positive attitudes about school and lowers their affective filters, allowing information to pass more successfully through the emotion centers of their brains into the processing and memory storage regions. In other words, when students with AD/HD feel comfortable, they can become more successful learners. This success in turn reduces their defensive, distracting behaviors and increases their focus, benefiting the whole class.

The following activity uses brain research–based strategies to build empathy in an inclusion class where some students have been marginalized because of attention differences. This strategy is particularly useful when preparing students for cooperative group work.

> Stupid is what she called me, and that is what I am because I never know the answer the teacher wants, even though all the other kids know and put their answers on their papers or raise their hands, sometimes waving them so violently that even if I have a spark of an answer, the tornados their hands make blow out my spark before it can ever take hold and become a flame that would become an idea that might be worthy of being added to their conversation, which by now has already gone on to some other subject and passed me by, with my extinguished spark now only a cold ash that proves to me how stupid I am for even believing that I could think of something to say when every teacher has told my parents that I'm either stupid or lazy, and they know how much I try, even if it keeps me up past their bedtime, to write an essay or poem that no lazy person would work so long at, leaving me no choice, because she said I was either lazy or stupid, and although I wish I could say I'm lazy, if that is my only other choice, I guess I have to agree that I am stupid

Does this read as if it could have been written by one of your students challenged with a different way of relating to his or her world? I wrote it as I imagined what it might feel like to be a student with LD or AD/HD in an inclusion classroom. Writing the paragraph from this perspective increased my empathy for these students.

The following similar activity could raise students' compassion for and understanding of their classmates with AD/HD. The activity begins by simulating what it feels like to try to focus when one has an attention deficit.

Consider what *attention deficit* really means. It is not truly inattention, but rather attention in many different places simultaneously. Students with AD/HD are not lazy, zoned out, or "empty-headed." Neuroimaging scans of AD/HD brains do not resemble those of people who are drowsy, mentally retarded, or sedated by medication. The AD/HD brain's metabolism is often normal or high because it is responding to an excess of inadequately filtered sensory input. Their minds may be distracted, but they are not oblivious.

To reproduce a similar brain state, teachers can bring multiple sensory stimuli into the classroom. For example, they can tune two radios to different stations; play a tape of the sounds of street construction or the playground at recess; light candles in several places around the room; randomly turn the lights on and off; and bring in a bird in a cage right at the beginning of the exercise as a new classroom attraction (or distraction).

When I have carried out this exercise in my classroom, students at first tend to be excited with the changes in the classroom. They are not anxious because we have already established a sense of community and safety, and students are familiar with my tendency to use elements of novelty and surprise in my lessons. They call out questions and make guesses about the activity, but I stand silently and don't respond. After one minute, I give them the signal to sit quietly, and they quiet down enough to hear my instructions.

I explain that the students are to do their best to ignore these distractions and focus their attention on the math lesson I am about to teach. There are usually more questions, but I tell them I won't answer any until the lesson is over. I then present a new lesson about a math concept they have never studied and that is not in their textbooks. (The lesson does not have to be on math, but it does need to be one where the students are on even ground so that no one can use previous knowledge to comprehend the material. For example, the distraction-filled lesson could teach words and phrases in a language that none of the students know, or teachers could read aloud a page from an unfamiliar book and ask students to write as much of it from memory as they can.)

The lesson I use demonstrates that any integer raised to the exponent of zero equals one. I show students the mathematical proof and then lead a hands-on demonstration in which they see how many times they can fold a piece of paper. They see that each fold increases the number of divided sections exponentially, but when they unfold it there is only the single sheet of paper. Thus, no matter how many folds there are to begin with (i.e., no matter how big the original integer is), when you raise it to the zero power (no folds) you have one paper.

At the conclusion of the lesson, with the distractions still present, I ask students to write a summary of what they have learned. They are to put in their own words how the paper-folding activity demonstrated that any integer raised to the exponent of zero equals one. To simulate the discomfort that students with AD/HD often have about asking for clarification, I don't permit the students to ask questions about the assignment, nor will I repeat the instructions. The restriction against questions causes considerable agitation. Students initially call out the expected, "That's not fair!"; "But I don't understand!"; "You always explain, why not now?"; and "Will we be graded on this?" The students with AD/HD tend not to complain about the no-questions policy.

After students complete their summaries, I remove the distractions and have them write for 5 to 10 minutes about how they felt during the distraction-filled math lesson, noting especially their feelings about not having the opportunity to ask for help. I also give them an optional prompt to reflect about a time when they were different from friends or classmates (for example, in terms of clothes, accent, family structure, illness, physical challenge, or finances) and how it felt. Stacy wrote, "I thought we were going to have some fun game with all the crazy things going on, so I didn't really try to listen very hard to the math lesson. When I saw that it was a real lesson and Dr. Willis wasn't fooling around, I tried to pay attention, but I just didn't get it. I felt frantic and hated it." Ray noted that "I didn't know if this was for real or not. Especially with the bird and candles and stuff. When you got serious with the lesson, I could hardly hear you, and I really wanted to just turn off the noise. I felt dizzy. I finally put my fingers in my ears and just tried to watch what you were doing and see what you wrote on the board. It's a good thing you wrote on the board so I could at least see the numbers that I could write about. I still didn't really get the math, and I don't want to feel like that ever again."

I conclude the demonstration by explaining to the class that the exercise's purpose was to show them how it feels to be so distracted by sights, sounds, and feelings that it is difficult to focus on a lesson. I tell the class that each person's brain has a different information filter and that some brain filters don't limit much of the information that competes for the brain's attention. To demonstrate this concept in a tangible way, I pour a mixture of stones, pebbles, marbles, and sand (representing all the sights and sounds of the distracting class-room) through an open tube (representing an AD/HD brain) and ask whether the tube filtered out any of the mixture. Next, I pour the mixture into a strainer (representing a non-AD/HD brain's filter), which filters everything but the sand. I then lead the class in a discussion, starting with the following prompt:

> Today you felt what it would be like if your brain didn't have a very helpful filter, and all the distracting pebbles and marbles came in along with the sand you needed to focus on. What would it be like for you to feel like that in class all the time? Imagine if the sound of the clock ticking or the birds outside captured so much of your attention that you couldn't focus on the lesson and missed important information.

The discussion eventually gets around to one of understanding and empathy for people who have filtering systems that don't work as well as others', and students begin asking how they can help. Most of the AD/HD students don't participate in the discussion at first, but after hearing the supportive comments of their classmates, they usually offer to read their own reflections.

One AD/HD student read, "It was news to me that so many kids got nervous when we couldn't ask questions. I know I'm not big on asking questions because I think you might have already answered the question, and I wasn't listening so it was my fault. Now I know that there are times that everyone has questions even when you did explain it, so I won't be so afraid to ask questions." He then spoke these words to the class: "I feel good about you guys, and it sure sounds like you understand what it is like for me to focus. You have never been mean to me about it, but some other kids have. Just now you can know that I'm not trying to be bad and sometimes everything just gets all jumbled."

Another AD/HD student wrote, "You probably all know that I go to the office for medicine and that I'm a hyper kid. I'm not embarrassed, because you are my friends. Dr. Willis told me before class what we'd be doing, and I thought it would be pretty cool to have this whole math class time given to showing things about my mind. I'm working on my focusing, and I think I will feel better about asking questions now if I'm really confused."

This lesson is a bonding experience for the class. After the demonstration and discussion, students become more allied in helping their attention-challenged classmates and are even proactive in asking if they need help. It becomes easier to pair AD/HD students with non–AD/HD classmates for partner work. Students come to understand the special challenges of students with attention difficulties and become more patient and considerate.

Students with AD/HD often have fears about what is wrong with them. These fears are usually much worse than the reality. This activity—planned carefully, perhaps in consultation with the school's learning specialist—can powerfully improve their self-concept.

ADAPTING WHOLE-CLASS LESSONS TO STUDENTS WITH AD/HD

Educators can make all kinds of creative adaptations to fully integrate AD/HD students into their classes. It's important to keep in mind that techniques that bring more enjoyment and positive emotion to the learning activity are not crutches but adaptive facilitators that are appropriate and valuable—especially for students with attention deficits, who have so many pulls on their attention. The following practices will benefit the entire class.

Physical Movement

Physical movement appeals to the kinesthetic style of many AD/HD students and has the added benefit of linking the material to be learned with sensory input, thereby increasing access to the brain's memory banks. Brain imaging has revealed that almost half the brain's neurons are in the cerebellum, an area at the back of the brain just above the spinal cord, and that many of these cerebellar neurons have connecting pathways to neurons in the frontal lobes—the areas responsible for the executive functions of focusing, prioritizing, analyzing, and organizing. Adding movement to learning therefore helps activate these important frontal lobe regions, which tend to be underdeveloped in AD/HD students. The following are some movement activities that teachers can implement in their classrooms.

Class games. Simon Says or Prime Number Buzz are both good learning games involving movement. For the latter, students take turns naming numbers in sequence, starting with 1. If the number is a prime number, students say "Buzz." If it is not prime, students say the number. Students sit down when they make an error, but even then they remain engaged by trying to catch errors made by students still standing.

Thumbs up or down. Holding their thumbs up or down is an easy physical way for students to communicate whether they agree or disagree with an answer to a question the teacher asks.

Height check. Students are measured in inches by the teacher or by a partner and then convert their heights into centimeters. Next, students go to the front of the room and line up, from shortest to tallest. If a student sees that a shorter neighbor's card shows a height that's taller than his or hers, or that a taller neighbor's card shows a shorter height, then the pair of students knows that at least one calculation is an error. The students can then recalculate and try again.

Narrative sequencing. This activity combines group work with movement. Each member of a group of four or five students gets an index card with a line of text summarizing an event in a timeline from history or from a story they read. Group members read their cards and sort themselves into what they believe is the correct order. The group then stands in front of the class in their selected order, holding their cards for the class to see. The class can vote on whether to change the order or leave the students and their cards in their original placement.

Choosing sides. Students are read an opinion question related to the topic of study, such as, "Did the British have any good reasons for expecting the colonists to pay taxes after England spent money defending the colonial territories in the French and Indian War?" Students who agree with one side of the argument walk to the left side of the room, while those who disagree walk to the right side of the room. As the teacher provides more facts about the theory or policy, students can change sides. When there are roughly equal numbers of students on each side, they pair up with partners from the opposite side and engage in mini-debates about why they chose the side they did. This activity prompts students to think and move simultaneously, combining movement with information input.

Students as science models. Students can physically demonstrate how electrons move around a nucleus; the relationship between sun, moon, and tides (students stand close together in a small cluster as the tidal surge); and echolocation in bats (students designated as "stationary objects" beep to prevent collisions when the blindfolded "bat" approaches).

Simple Simon and Follow the Leader. In these activities, students take turns acting as the leader. The leader points to different parts of his or her body, and the class responds by naming that body part (or the bone or muscle). In a foreign language class, the leader can point to objects in the room, which students then name in the language they are studying.

Surprise and Novelty

The element of surprise is a useful tool to engage students with AD/HD when introducing a new lesson or topic. The brain is designed to attend to surprise, a survival instinct that was of critical importance in the early stages of human evolution. The reticular activating system continually monitors incoming sensory data and alerts the brain when it senses a change in the environment. Because the brain is still wired to be alert to novelty, teachers can prime students with attention deficits to focus on lessons by introducing material in novel ways. For example, they could put up a poster relating to a topic that they will soon introduce; invite a surprise guest speaker to class; or wear a costume appropriate to a new lesson (such as a wizard's hat to introduce a science experiment).

Continually changing the classroom environment, without making it overly distracting, also helps retain student interest. Classroom walls should not be papered with an excess of posters, artifacts, quotes, photos, and charts. Instead, teachers should keep these areas stimulating, putting up fresh content to complement new topics of instruction. To keep from overwhelming students' brains with too much newness, teachers can periodically rotate the placement of displays during the several weeks of the unit of study. This rotation will give all students a view of the displays at some time during the unit and allow students to see them from different perspectives.

Bring in All Students from the Beginning

As we know, it is important to connect students to lessons through their interests and learning strengths. In particular, if students with attention difficulties don't see an immediate use for new data, it will be harder for them to internalize, remember, and apply the information later. Incorporating individual interests and intelligences early in the unit, even briefly, will keep students engaged until teachers can address their strengths and interests more fully.

To promote early engagement for AD/HD learners, teachers can show short videos depicting a given historical period or geographical region, read rich passages from a novel, tell a story, display a compelling piece of artwork, or present a curiosity-inspiring artifact. The goal is to provide an inclusive experience that will resonate with each student. Teachers can also bring in all students from the beginning by presenting the big picture through a comprehensive experience that will connect to some area of interest or personal experience for all students.

Certain general themes will connect with most students in a class. For example, an initial presentation of a new unit in a middle school class incorporating sports, popular music, and audiovisual technology will engage most students through at least one of their primary or secondary learning strengths or interests.

Another way to engage all students is to start with an innovative presentation. Teachers could read aloud a recent newspaper report, invite a guest speaker to the class, or pose a thought-provoking question through a demonstration. An example of the last comes from Ron Koch, a professor of education at the University of California, Santa Barbara, who provided a provocative introduction to a biology unit. He first posed a general question, prompting multiple responses that were recorded on an overhead screen. He then lit a candle and asked the class, "If this flame can consume oxygen, reproduce, and react, and has a beginning and a termination, it fits with the list of characteristics we came up with for living things. Does that mean this flame is alive?"

Teachers will know students are authentically engaged when they start making personal connections and asking questions that relate the initial experience to concrete references or abstract connections. Students will be motivated to share their responses because they are personally touched in some way. These introductions are valuable just for that reason.

Linking information to a strong sensory stimulus optimizes AD/HD students' ability to focus. Connecting information to students' preferred sensory-receptive styles—visual, tactile, or auditory—enhances the brain's alerting process, responsiveness, and data patterning. The sensory stimulus must be strong enough to stand out from the barrage of input that AD/HD students must filter. When the tactic succeeds and the stimulus becomes a focal point for students' attention, the information can be processed in their higher cortical functions and stored in memory.

Once students are responsive to the sensory-linked information, the class is in the ideal state for learning. The next step is to encourage all students to remain engaged in the lesson. Teachers can facilitate this step by asking student-centered and open-ended questions that offer all students the opportunity to express opinions and receive positive feedback. Because the introduction engaged their focus with sensory connections, AD/HD students will be more likely to share their reactions in class discussions. For an example of such a lesson, see "Sample Lesson: Early Engagement of Attention Through Sensory Experiences."

SAMPLE LESSON

Early Engagement of Attention Through Sensory Experiences

Subject: American Colonial Settlements   GRADE RANGE: **4–7**

A 5th grade unit on early American Colonial settlements that I taught kicked off with a guest speaker from the community who was a food stylist and the director of the local farmers markets. Without any advance notice, she entered the classroom in Colonial attire with a large basket of produce indigenous to the early New England colonies. She first gave the students several unfamiliar vegetables to taste and then told them, "You have been told not to play with your food, but today we will." Right off the bat, the lesson used strategies aimed at engaging AD/HD students, along with their non–AD/HD peers. First, because the class hadn't been prepared for a speaker, the lesson incorporated surprise and novelty. Second, distributing food to the students let them know the presentation would be an interactive experience and prevented them from focusing on hunger prompted by looking at the food. Finally, the promise of playing with food alerted the interest of the bodily-kinesthetic learners and AD/HD students, and the speaker's use of humor and surprise won students' trust and attention.

Her presentation continued with demonstrations of how to cut and display foods to make them look more appealing while she explained which foods were the first ones available for gathering or planting by the colonists. She finished her presentation by constructing a cornucopia, first assuring students that they would have an opportunity to make their own cornucopias as soon as she finished. This promise of a desirable activity to come after a passive demonstration is an important strategy to keep the focus of AD/HD students, because they know that the attention they give now will help them successfully engage in the connected activity immediately following.

After the food stylist left, the students were excited to start building their own cornucopias. After a brief reminder about cooperative group behavior, fair division of activities, and decision by consensus, the class broke into small groups to construct cornucopias out of cardboard, filling them with fruits and vegetables left by the guest speaker. Each group decided its members' roles. One or two students in each group drew a picture of their cornucopia, one student photographed it, and another student listed the foods they used on a chart. Whichever group finished first had the option of labeling the more unusual fruits and vegetables with identification tags or finding out more about them in books or on the Internet.

After each group shared its project with the class, the class held a culminating discussion to connect the morning's speaker and group cornucopia activity to the Colonial unit that would follow. The experience had generated interest in the Colonial period, and students prepared a list of questions they would still like to ask the speaker. I compiled their questions on a chart and added questions based on their suggestions about other facets of Colonial life that they believed might be interesting to investigate. Before the next history lesson, I added questions incorporating the curriculum standards for the unit to the question list.

When I took attendance the next day, I asked students to respond to their names not by saying "Here" but by recalling one thing they had learned from the previous day's cornucopia activity. This strategy is a good, quick way to increase focus and recall.

We then reviewed the formalized list of questions on an overhead projector and arranged them into five main topics. Next, students wrote on note cards their first and second choices of which of these five topics they would like to investigate further. I then formed small groups based

SAMPLE LESSON (CONTINUED)

on students' interests, compatibility, and learning strengths. The last consideration enabled students with AD/HD and LD to participate in groups in which their creative strengths and intelligences would be acknowledged as valued contributions to the group project.

Starting the Colonial social studies topic with the guest speaker and the novel, artifact-centered cornucopia experience prompted students' curiosity and motivated them to learn the research skills required to satisfy their curiosity about the questions they had raised. Instead of being passive recipients of the unit's content, they became co-creators of an investigation that emerged from their own interests and goals.

Dramatization

Dramatization can involve movement, such as acting out the role of an author or historical figure, or it can be as stationary as having students demonstrate their knowledge of vocabulary words through facial expressions—showing what a *haughty* person might look like or how someone might respond to a *noxious* odor. These types of dramatization appeal to the bodily-kinesthetic, intrapersonal, and visual-spatial learning styles of many students with AD/HD. In terms of brain-based techniques, dramatizations have the added benefit of activating regions of the brain where prior relational memories are stored. The personal meaning inherent in dramatization provides opportunities for new information to be connected by the relational memory hook-ups that enhance patterning and retention.

Personalize Through Visualization

Any strategy that helps AD/HD students personalize academic material will give it immediate interest value. Visualization—creating vivid mental pictures of important points in a lesson—is one way of personalizing information and raising engagement.

Teachers can introduce this strategy by prompting students to close their eyes and recall with all their senses what their last Thanksgiving dinner brings to mind. Teachers can then model the technique of visualizing an event that students did *not* personally experience but can imagine in detail—such as what sounds, sights, smells, and tastes might have been present at the first Thanksgiving dinner shared by American colonists.

After demonstrating the technique, teachers can suggest that students visualize their images of factual information either described in a lesson or read to them from a textbook or novel. To help students practice the visualization strategy during a lesson, teachers should start by describing a multisensory event, such as the big bang theory of the universe, or by reading a captivating and detailed description of a literary character from a novel. After giving students' imaginations free reign for a silent wait period, teachers can ask them to visualize the event or character they just heard about. Students may describe their visualizations to partners, write about them, or sketch what they imagined. These visualizations will help pattern new information by connecting it to multiple relational memories in more than one memory storage area (visual, auditory, olfactory). In addition, when students interact with (actively process) the information, it will have more personal emotional emphasis (increased release of such neurotransmitters as dopamine and serotonin) to stimulate and reinforce synaptic connections in their neural pathways (Kumar, 1991).

ASSESSING LESSON SUCCESS

Developing curriculum and strategies to create a brain-friendly learning environment for AD/HD students and their peers can be challenging. Which techniques are best for which students? Can teachers give additional attention to one or two students without reducing the quality of teaching for the rest of the class? In evaluating lessons, it helps to recall that good teaching is good for all students and that the strategies that are *critical* to AD/HD students are also *valuable* to all students. The following self-survey can help educators examine the effectiveness of their practice.

1. Is your classroom a place where students feel welcome, connected, safe, and confident that they will be treated fairly?

2. Do your lessons have enough surprise, novelty, and variation to inspire curiosity and to capture and hold attention?

3. Do you provide enough structure to help students pattern the information they receive and respond selectively to the sensory input that carries the most valuable information?

4. Are there opportunities for students to explore a multitude of skills, abilities, and interests so that they can discover one or more that engage them? Will they be motivated to repeat these activities and pursue them as challenging goals they want to achieve?

5. After you have identified students' strengths, have you given students opportunities to practice so that they will learn that practice promotes goal achievement, and mastery feels good?

6. When your students with attention deficits need to learn complex or conceptual information, such as writing powerful opening sentences, do you strive to "show not tell"?

7. Do you have a cue to alert students that the next item you're teaching is especially important?

8. Do you use experiential learning, hands-on/minds-on science, multisensory demonstrations, and cooperative activities to reach students who have the most difficulty directing attention, seeing patterns, or building relational memories?

9. Do you plan lessons that allow students to *own* the knowledge by creating personal meaning and making connections with interests and previous experience? Those are the lessons that stimulate their brains' release of dopamine and increase their focus.

10. Once you have students' attention, do you stimulate them to stay connected and on task by offering choice and engaging their learning strengths and creativity?

11. Are you giving recognition for progress, not just for final goal achievement?

ATTENTION DISORDER
THERAPIES BEYOND THE CLASSROOM

Parents sometimes ask teachers about treatment recommendations for their children with attention disorders. As a neurologist, I am not yet convinced that any one of the treatments in use today is the answer for all types of attention disorders—which is not to say that one or more interventions are not successful for some. Until more long-term clinical research trials become available, all I am comfortable doing is reporting on several of the more common interventions.

Cerebellar stimulation. Proponents of this intervention posit that because many neurons in the cerebellum (the balance/coordination control center in the back of the brain) are connected to neurons in the frontal lobes, increased cerebellar stimulation will strengthen underdeveloped frontal lobe regions responsible for vital executive functions. This intervention involves a regimen of physical balancing exercises, such as standing on a wobble board, juggling, and standing on one leg with eyes closed. Proponents reason that because children with AD/HD are often the ones who enjoy tilting back on their chairs, balancing on fences, drumming, surfing, snowboarding, and skateboarding, they will actually enjoy these targeted exercises for the balance-oriented cerebellum. But the question remains: does stimulating the neurons in the cerebellum actually accelerate the maturation of neurons in the frontal lobe?

Exercise and diet. People with AD/HD are at higher risk for self-medicating with drugs and alcohol (Cardinal, Winstanley, Robbins, & Everitt, 2004). This tendency may result from less-developed frontal-lobe executive functions or from decreased dopamine release due to a lack of rewarding experiences at school and elsewhere. One potential intervention is to increase activities that are associated with increased dopamine-reward responses, such as play and exercise. There are no definitive studies connecting exercise and AD/HD, but it makes sense that physical exercise would be beneficial because it increases levels of the dopamine and norepinepherine involved in the mental processes of focus and memory storage. In particular, the complexities of team sports, with their structured schedules and warm-up drills, can help students practice concentration and organizational thinking, while the physical activity increases their focusing neurotransmitters.

Adjusting AD/HD children's diet is another possible intervention, but caution is warranted. It is a commonly held belief that sugary snacks, artificial colors or flavors, and preservatives aggravate or provoke hyperactivity, but a recent extensive controlled study by the *Journal of the American Dietetic Association* (Marcason, 2005) found that these substances have no effect on AD/HD. There is also a lack of convincing data showing that giving children caffeinated beverages with breakfast or high doses of omega-3 fatty acids in the form of fish oil will reduce symptoms of AD/HD. Because many parents are dedicated to learning all they can about how they can help their children cope with AD/HD, they may be vulnerable to early data that have not yet been confirmed by large-scale, double-blind controlled studies. For example, soon after small preliminary studies suggested that very high doses of omega-3 fatty acids might be a remedy for AD/HD, several larger studies indicated that doses of Vitamin E greater than 200 milligrams per day could carry a risk of higher incidence of cancer (Virtamo et al., 2003).

EEG biofeedback therapy. EEG biofeedback is based on the assumption that if AD/HD is characterized by disruption or lack of formation in the frontal lobes' executive function centers, then the stimulation of the frontal lobes will reduce AD/HD symptoms. Common AD/HD traits include short attention span, distractibility, procrastination, disorganization, underachievement, impulsiveness, hyperactivity, and slower-than-average brain wave activity in the frontal lobes. The theory of EEG biofeedback for AD/HD is that when people learn to alter their brain wave patterns through practice, they are able to change their frontal lobe brain function. This biofeedback is profitable to some doctors, who charge about $500 for the EEG topographic brain mapping and thousands more for the 30 to 50 sessions required to train their clients to alter their brain waves. However, I am not convinced that the benefit of this treatment has been confirmed in double-blind, multicentered academic research analysis.

Other therapists use quantitative EEG (qEEG) to help predict which medications might be most helpful for a particular patient's AD/HD. Therapists assess the patient's category of brain wave disturbance, then match the pattern to a data bank of other patients with similar patterns. They look at how others with similar brain wave patterns responded to various medications and then select the type of medication they believe will best suit the patient's type of AD/HD. Again, these theories are not yet confirmed in the academic neurological literature. There are abundant references for qEEG analysis on the Internet, but these are predominantly in "secondary" journals that do not have the same high level of objective peer review found in the academic medical literature.

Medication for attention disorders. I have heard it said that AD/HD is the waterfall of the mind, and medication is the hydroelectric plant that harnesses it and turns it into useful power. When brain chemistry is out of sync, appropriately prescribed medication can restore balance. In my neurological practice, prescription medications have been of considerable benefit to many of my patients. But not all children do well with medication, and there are significant side effects to be considered on an individual basis. The ideal medication is one that doesn't just mask the symptoms of AD/HD, but permits the central nervous system to function optimally. The right medication should enable the affected students to more easily control their symptoms of distractibility with minimal alteration of their personalities and sleep or eating patterns.

The ultimate decision about prescribing medication belongs to parents. Educators can provide information about students' classroom behaviors and academic performances and, if medication is used, report any positive or negative changes. However, as teachers, we don't really know what happens at home—how irritable our students become in the evening, how poorly they eat, or how little they sleep. Sometimes parents decide to stop a medication that seemed to have been beneficial in the school setting. When a medication is discontinued, teachers and resource specialists need to stick with the student and see what can be done during school hours to help him or her return to that state of stability or improvement. Frustrating? Indeed, but achievable. That is why teachers who are flexible and resilient—and who model these qualities for their students every day—are such valuable assets for these children.

TEACHERS MAKE THE DIFFERENCE

Students can turn their lives around when they are encouraged and supported by teachers. They may start the school year unable to sustain attention, filter sensory input, or pattern data into memory. They may have been losing self-confidence with each year of school, as lessons were increasingly built on previous lessons that their brains didn't have the organizational structure to support. Informed educators make the difference, especially when the brain research–based strategies used help students reach their emotional comfort zones and rebuild their self-confidence. Helping students build their focusing skills through pursuits in their areas of interest and talent lets them develop the life skills of practice, patience, and perseverance. Their status will grow, not only in their own minds, but also in the opinions of their classmates, family members, and future teachers.

Here is a final reflection about Cody, whom I wrote about earlier in this chapter. I wrote this near the end of the school year.

> Cody smiles not only with his face, but with his entire being, and hugs me with the might of each of his 11 years, multiplied by the factor of love. Like reflecting mirrors, each sincere compliment I give him about his classwork and homework bounces back as more love for school—more love for himself.
>
> Today, I called him over for a miniconference. He had long since lost the fear that weighted him down when he started 5th grade—that when a teacher beckons, it is to chastise. I congratulate Cody on his detailed social studies notes, creative cover for our class Ethical Dilemma essay book, and his accurate and legible

math homework. I tell him I'll be sending a note about these successes to his parents.

Cody's smile becomes impossibly brighter as his sense of scholarly success grows. Another hug, and he bounds out the door for recess—finally believing he is a worthy student.

As with Cody, all children have gateways through which teachers can access their gifts or interests and guide them into effective learning channels. Evaluating and engaging students as individuals with brain research–based strategies will help them reach their maximum potential with joy and confidence.

CHAPTER 4

ENRICHING THE INCLUSIVE LEARNING ENVIRONMENT

NEUROLOGICAL RESEARCH BASIS FOR BRAIN ENRICHMENT THEORIES

Only recently have we begun to understand that the human brain is plastic—that it can change structurally and functionally as a result of learning and experience. Neuroimaging research suggests that this brain plasticity results in increased neuronal growth associated with enriched, stimulating environments and activities.

For example, one study examining the PET scans of Rumanian orphans who lived from infancy with little human interaction and no toys or other environmental stimuli found that by age 3, these children had 25 percent less brain development than normal (Perry, Pollard, Blakley, Baker, & Vigilante, 1995). And in the United States, the Abecedarian Project correlated academic cognitive outcomes with the amount of enrichment in children's environments. The study followed the cognitive development of children of poor, borderline–mentally retarded mothers. The children ranged in age from 4 months to 8 years old and were followed through age 15. The children in the control group received good health care and nutrition but no other intervention, whereas the experimental group of children spent five days a week in enriched environments and experienced frequent interaction with caregivers, who conversed with them, told stories, played games, and responded to their emotional behaviors. The control group of children remained low-functioning, but the experimental group developed what was determined to be average intelligence. By the age of 15, half of the children in the control group had failed one or more grades in school, but only 13 percent of those in the experimental group had failed any grades. In addition, children in the enriched-environment group who entered the program before age 5 scored higher in math and reading at age 15 than did children in the control group (Ramey, 1996).

For many years, enrichment programs in U.S. schools were offered only to students selected for their high level of academic performance. However, data from neuroimaging studies now suggest that enriching the learning environment of all students in inclusion classes may maximize their cognitive, emotional, and social development. Classroom strategies I have used based on my interpretation of the research include offering multisensory, personally relevant, and thought-provoking lessons that motivate students to acquire knowledge and master skills. Such enriched environments generally provide

- A variety of approaches and activities geared to diverse learning styles.
- A variety of culminating projects (art, writing, or model-building, for example).
- Student-centered, open-ended discussions and explorations.
- Opportunities for individual, peer, and group learning experiences.
- Active learning or discovery opportunities.
- Multisensory stimulation.
- Alternating activities at work stations throughout the room.
- Changing classroom displays and posters.
- Lesson-appropriate manipulatives.
- Varied seating configurations (for example, chairs arranged in a horseshoe, in rows, or in groups, or floor activities with no desks or chairs).

- Developmentally and academically appropriate challenges to suit the needs, gifts, and goals of each student.
- Structure and planning to support students' increasing responsibility for their own learning and goal achievement.

In an enriched, stimulating classroom, students should also receive individualized opportunities to verbalize, write, or otherwise create something using the lesson's material. My theory behind this strategy is that the more opportunities students have to receive and consciously manipulate new information, the greater the brain stimulation, and thus the greater retention of information. Such manipulation could include verbal or written response to the information, visualization, or use of the information in an activity requiring executive function (for example, comparing and contrasting or making a judgment or an analysis based on the information) (Wagner et al., 1998).

Because manipulation and application of new information correlates with increased brain stimulation, direct lecturing and rote memorization alone are inadequate. These passive transfers of information will not equip students to use and think about what they have learned in the productive, meaningful ways associated with long-term memory formation. Multisensory exposure to information, student-centered activities, and discovery and hands-on learning experiences are the strategies most likely to build strong neuronal circuits and sustained memory storage (Reeve & Bolt, 1999).

MULTISENSORY LEARNING

In inclusion classes where intelligences, learning-style preferences, and developmental levels span a wide spectrum, lessons that engage multiple senses could offer the greatest access to knowledge for the most students. Teaching information in a variety of contexts gives students greater equality in access to knowledge and more opportunities to be challenged to their highest potential.

Experts have long believed that students remember what they receive through multiple senses more successfully than what they receive through only one of the senses. Indeed, neuroimaging studies have observed a greater amount of activity in the brain's information-processing areas following multisensory input than following single-sense input (Eliassen et al., 2003). Lessons incorporating cross-curricular studies, discovery science, role-play, games, physical activity, art, music, or drama have the advantage of stimulating more regions of the brain (Thesen, Jonas, Calvert, & Österbauer, 2004). Of course, multisensory learning does not require teachers to stimulate every sense simultaneously, which would just lead to confusing sensory overload. Rather, teachers should engage various senses sequentially and incorporate stimuli that engage all learning styles, thus drawing all students into the topic.

One study supporting the theory of multisensory input examined how learning to juggle affected subjects' brains (Draganski, Gaser, Busch, & Schuierer, 2004). After several weeks of practice, subjects' brain scans showed increased numbers of synapses and dendrites in the brain regions stimulated during the juggling sessions. The implications are powerful: if greater brain stimulation promotes the growth of synapses and dendrites, and more areas of the brain are stimulated when information is presented through multiple senses, then multisensory presentation of lesson material could stimulate the growth of more brain connections and lead to better information storage.

Linking new information to more than one sensory experience (visual, auditory, tactile, and so on) connects multiple brain regions to the lesson because each sensory system has a separate storage area in the brain. Multisensory input travels to memory storage along more than one pathway, resulting in enriched, reinforced information transit. This redundancy of pathways and storage regions leads to better memory retention, faster and more accurate recall, and increased ability to retrieve stored memories through a variety of stimuli. Multisensory strategies may increase subsequent access of the cross-referenced memories for use on tests; build future relational memories; and, most important, connect with the frontal lobe executive functions to enable higher-order thinking.

GRAY MATTER

Is there still a place for brain hemisphere–differentiated lessons? Early interpretations of psychological investigations in the 1960s and 1970s, before the existence of neuroimaging and qEEG data, often made sharp distinctions between left- and right-brain functions. Although current evidence does show that certain brain function centers are more developed on the right or left side of the brain for specific processes, the newer studies do not support the theory of one-sided brain dominance (Katz & Smith, 1974; Marshall, Caplan, & Holmes, 1975).

For example, someone who responds to light touch sensation with elevated activity in the right parietal lobe might show more activity in the left frontal lobe when working on word puzzles. Complex mental processes, such as reading and comprehending, do not take place all in one brain hemisphere but are the result of networks of cross-connecting neuronal paths throughout the brain (Stein & Talcott, 1999).

Using manipulatives or hands-on experiments to introduce a lesson often results in greater activity in the right hemisphere, due to its greater concentration of neurons responsive to data received by sensory receptors (touch, sight, pressure, temperature). But if the lesson progresses to more analytical, verbal discussion, there will be increased activation in the executive function–processing cortex of the left frontal lobe.

Multisensory lessons do not work because they are designated right-brain or left-brain. Rather, the multisensory input stimulates more than one specific sensory receptor region in the brain. When multiple brain regions are activated and form neural connections to the new content, the information is more likely to be successfully coded, patterned, and stored in multiple sites. For example, a lesson that uses both manipulatives as concrete representations of a math concept and formulas to represent the concept in abstract form will stimulate both hemispheres. The opportunities for comprehension and retention will increase because of that stimulation of multiple brain sites.

Most students have some ability to process information through all the sensory learning modalities, although they tend to rely on their strongest learning preference when the activity or information is particularly challenging. The more a lesson connects to students' most-developed neural pathways, the more their dominant sensory processing strengths will engage them in the lesson. Once students are engaged, they can be exposed to the information through their less-developed intelligences. For example, students with a strong preference for visual learning will have more initial activity in their occipital lobe's visual cortex during a multisensory lesson. But as the lesson continues, their other associated brain areas will be brought online to process the new information. If students with a strong preference for auditory processing are presented with the same multisensory lesson, they will first show increased metabolic activity in their temporal lobe's auditory processing centers before the brain activation spreads to other areas of their brains (Baynes, Eliassen, Lutsep, & Gazzaniga, 1998).

THE MEMORY SYSTEMS

One of the primary goals of education is for students to retain information in—and retrieve it from—their long-term memories. A hundred billion neurons connect with one another in complex ways to enable students to think, learn, understand, problem-solve, create, and remember. Multisensory lessons that key into students' learning strengths help them connect their sensory response systems and brain activity and storage centers to the new learning. These connections allow the new information to be patterned into relational memories that can then be stored in the brain's memory banks. A review of the roles of the brain's various memory systems can provide insight into how to incorporate multisensory stimulation in inclusion classes.

Working memory. After information passes through the amygdala's affective filter and the reticular activating system, it goes into the prefrontal cortex, which serves as another information filter. Information that reaches this cortex can be either retained and encoded or discarded. Unless the new information makes a meaningful connection, it remains in working, or short-term, memory for about 20 seconds and is then discarded. On average, by ages 4–6 the brain can retain seven pieces of new information at one time, so it is important to make connections to as many previously stored relational memories as possible. This enables the brain to pattern the new information into long-term memory before it is lost (Schneider & Chein, 2003).

Semantic memory. Semantic memory is the most difficult to remember and retrieve. It consists of facts obtained through rote and drill activities and is stored in the hippocampus of the temporal lobe. Because these facts and their presentation are isolated from meaningful or emotional content, they have limited connections to relational memory or positive emotions, and are therefore less likely to be patterned for storage in long-term memory. If teachers must present information in static list format students will need more help remembering those listed facts. Helpful strategies include frequent reviews, mnemonic devices, graphic organizers, rhymes, outlines, and any activity that promotes mental manipulation of the information, such as visualizations or metaphors (Baddeley & Andrade, 2000).

Episodic memory. Like semantic memory, episodic memory (also called *event memory*) is stored in the neurons of the hippocampus rather than in the brain cortex, where most long-term memories are stored (Bliss & Collingridge, 1993). Episodic memories are recollections of events, along with the times, places, and emotions associated with the events. In episodic memories, people see themselves as actors in the events they remember and therefore memorize not only the events but also the context surrounding them. The emotional charge experienced at the time of the event influences the quality of its memorization, so connecting important event memories to positive emotions can increase retention. For example, if a teacher makes a funny (or corny) joke about rain in the classroom during a demonstration of how steam condenses into water when it cools, the additional emotional hook of the humor may help imprint on students' brains the visual and auditory memories of the event. If students act out the changing states of water with hand or whole-body gestures, they will have an added bodily-kinesthetic connection to the event.

Episodic memories can also include visual details related to the location where the event took place—a good reason to have students change seats regularly, to hold classes outside the usual four walls of the classroom (on a field trip or in the athletic field, for example), and to periodically switch the placement of material posted on bulletin boards. Students can more successfully retrieve episodic memories when they associate the memories with a variety of physical settings.

Procedural memory. The cerebellum is the brain region that controls coordinated movement and balance. It also stores procedural memories, such as physical routines (patterns) for driving a car, riding a bike, or typing. Teachers in inclusion classes can access procedural memory by integrating movement into their lessons—for example, having students perform skits of historical events or pantomimes of the meanings of vocabulary words; physically demonstrate the location of U.S. states on giant floor maps; or use manipulatives in math. Another way to increase procedural memory is to have students get up and move to specified areas of the room to "vote" for their opinions on a given question or problem. For example, when asked who should have had control of grazing land in the development of the western territory in the United States, students can stand in the corner of the room that aligns with their answer: cattle ranchers, sheep ranchers, American Indians, or townspeople.

Automatic memory. Conditioned-response automatic memories are stored in the cerebellum and include information that needs to be automatically activated because it is used frequently or as a base on which other actions depend. When teaching this kind of material, teachers can show students keys to quickly unlock it. Examples include the alphabet song, which helps students access the order of letters; mnemonics for the order of mathematical operations; and rhymes like "*I* before *E* except after *C*, or when sounding like *A* as in *neighbor* and *weigh*."

Emotional memory. All learning is affected by accompanying emotions because information gains access to the brain through the affective filter in the amygdala. When a student associates a lesson with positive emotions, the information will not only pass more rapidly through the amygdala's filter but also be linked to the student's positive emotional state during the lesson. Information taught while students are embarrassed, frightened, stressed, sad, or angry, however, is less likely to become accessible long-term memory. The passage of sensory data into the brain's cortical information-processing regions is optimized when students feel safe, supported, and reasonably challenged in a classroom community that encourages creative thinking and turns mistakes into opportunities for learning.

Relational memory. Relational memories engage or expand on neuronal circuits and maps already present in the brain. As we know, information enters the brain as sensory input and must be patterned into a format that is recognizable by the neuronal circuits. When new information is related to existing memories, the brain links it to the content that has already been mastered. The brain process of searching stored memory banks for categories to link to new information stimulates executive functions, and subsequent review that reactivates the newly formed relational memories strengthens the connections between the neurons in the new circuits.

STIMULATING MULTIPLE MEMORY SYSTEMS THROUGH MULTISENSORY LESSONS

Experiential learning activities are by definition multisensory because they stimulate two or more memory systems in separate brain regions. PET scans show these systems as networked (cross-referenced) together (Iidaka, Anderson, Kapur, Cabeza, & Craik,

2000). The most common kinds of experiential lessons link factual information (semantic memory) to sensory input (episodic memory). The stimulation of these parallel memory systems results in greater memory retention through relational connections and personalization, both of which are associated with greater metabolic activity in the frontal-lobe areas of cognition and memory (Wunderlich, Bell, & Ford, 2005).

Stimulating more than one memory system with more than one type of sensory input significantly increases the likelihood of creating a long-term memory of the information. In addition, varying the sensory style of information delivery increases access to the variety of intelligences and learning-style preferences that are especially prevalent in inclusion classes.

To maximize individual student success, teachers should begin with pre-assessments and advance planning: what do the students know, what do they need to know to accomplish mastery, what are effective methods to reach all students, and how will they be assessed? The lesson plans can then continue with strategies that engage students through the learning styles and intelligences that will best stimulate and enhance their various memory systems. These strategies generally include the following characteristics.

Diverse methods of information delivery. Curriculum materials and teaching resources are available in multiple media, including text, graphics, graphic organizers, audiotapes or CDs, videos, models, computer programs, and manipulatives. For the initial presentation, teachers can choose some of these to include the majority of students while keeping track of other strategies that will help connect all students to the unit in subsequent study and review sessions.

Multiple options for interaction with the information. Teachers should offer choice in the format and materials that students use to connect with the information. The methods of interaction should be adapted to the needs of diverse learners and allow students to express themselves in their preferred learning styles. Experimenting with multiple styles of expression can also develop students' less-used learning intelligences. For example, teachers can let students pick the ways they will interact with the week's vocabulary words. Students could choose to use the words in a story, draw a diagram for each word, create a word puzzle, make flashcards, or cut the words out of a newspaper. The catch? Students can repeat word-study choices only after they have explored at least three different ones. Most students will initially choose the methods that best match their learning preferences, but gradually they will become ready to branch out to less-familiar learning styles. Keeping notes in their language arts books about their responses to each approach—how it felt and how they succeeded—will help them make future strategy selections.

Student engagement. Materials and activities should engage the interest and emotional comfort of a wide range of learners, setting the stage for focus and motivation. Emotional comfort allows the reticular activating system to admit data to the thinking brain that extends beyond survival needs. In addition, when students' interests are stimulated by positive emotions and the expectation of enjoyable experiences, their affective filters facilitate the passage of new information through the limbic system into the memory circuits.

GRAY MATTER

PET scans of students at different levels of engagement reveal the relationship between student interest and brain activity. Students experienced the lowest level of metabolic brain activity while engaged in passive independent reading. As the testers added multisensory stimuli by letting subjects hear the story read aloud as they followed the words visually, their brain information-response centers experienced increased activation. When students were asked to make connections between their lives and the story, the activation grew in intensity (relational memory patterning). Greatest yet was the amount of brain activation when students were told that they would soon be telling the story they were hearing and reading to someone else (Sousa, 2000).

Ongoing, multiple forms of assessment. Formative assessment gives students the best chance to access and demonstrate what they know will put them in the mental state to do their best. Teachers can use these assessments to provide specific feedback so that students can see the progress they made toward their individual goals and what information they still need to master.

Review and reinforcement. Even after an engaging multisensory lesson, students need opportunities to reflect on, review, and mentally manipulate their newly acquired knowledge to build relational memories and then to reactivate (and thereby strengthen) their brains' newly formed neuronal circuits and dendritic connections. One review strategy is to create graphic organizers the day after the lesson and share them with partners, groups, or the whole class. For example, working in pairs, students can conceal certain segments of the graphic organizer with Post-it notes and quiz their partners about what information has been hidden. Students retrieve the hidden words through their visual memory or by making deductions based on the surrounding clues. K-W-L charts are another great tool for review. Students can reexamine or add to the charts during review sessions, or they can use the charts to compare and contrast aspects of related topics. Finally, summarizing units of study through such culminating projects as models, PowerPoint presentations, posters, interviews, or murals provides opportunities for LD students to review material using their learning strengths while pushing other students to use a less-practiced learning style to develop further insight into the topic. Using a different sensory modality or learning style for their culminating activity also enables students to build memory links to additional regions of their brains. These cross-referencing neural circuits result in greater opportunity for subsequent memory prompts to retrieve the stored memory.

Specific activities that can stimulate multiple intelligences and promote neural transmission of information through multiple memory circuits include brainstorming sessions in which students share and record ideas; unit-specific thematic learning centers in the classroom; cross-curricular units; interactive note taking, with one side of the page used for factual note taking and the other side for note making (personal thoughts, relationships to previous knowledge, real-world connections, questions); and physical movement, which keeps students active, engaged, and alert. Another activity is the card party, in which small groups each read about and discuss a different aspect of the lesson's general topic. After each group member becomes an "expert" on that subtopic of the unit of study, new groups form. One representative from each original group presents his or her section of the material to the new group and then listens as the others in the new group present their segments. This technique is valuable for inclusion classes because students are responsible for only a small amount of material, and they have the chance to engage in the content through multiple senses: by reading about it, hearing about it, and then teaching it to others. For all students, the need to communicate content to others increases their attention in learning it the first time, and verbalizing the material to their new group helps cement it into permanent memory.

Like these strategies, the following two sample lessons engage students through their optimal learning styles and intelligences, thus stimulating their senses and activating their various memory systems.

Magnetism (Grades 4–7)

This lesson on magnetism connects semantic, episodic, and relational memories and engages verbal-linguistic, logical-mathematical, visual-spatial, bodily-kinesthetic, interpersonal, and intrapersonal intelligences. To kick off the lesson, students explore a variety of magnets and assorted magnetic and nonmagnetic substances to develop theories of magnetism. Which materials respond to or move toward the magnet, and which do not? What does each set of materials have in common? This activity, which engages kinesthetic learners, builds episodic memory and involves discovery learning, analysis, prediction, and deduction.

Students continue their investigations either individually (intrapersonal learners) or in groups (interpersonal learners). They have the option of reporting their discoveries or hypotheses about what makes a substance respond to a magnet by writing observation notes, drawing sketches, or summarizing their hypotheses orally. This choice is a motivator that links students to material through their learning strengths and lowers the barrier of the affective filter. The various options engage multiple intelligences and activate the episodic, emotional, procedural, and relational memory systems.

Next, a more structured period of demonstration and direct lecture from the teacher activates semantic memory and engages verbal-linguistic, logical-mathematical, and visual-spatial learners. During this time, teachers can also make real-world connections that give the topic of magnetism personal value and help students activate their relational memory by linking new sensory input with past experiences, such as using a compass, an Etch A Sketch board, or refrigerator magnets.

After this segment, students conduct individual research investigations on magnetism using sources that align with their learning styles. For example, visual learners could research books, auditory learners could listen to books on tape or podcasts, intrapersonal learners could personally interview engineers, and interactive technology–geared learners could conduct Internet searches.

For the magnetism unit's culminating activity, logical-mathematical or visual-spatial learners could build a model or simple machine that uses magnetism while verbal-linguistic, musical-rhythmic, bodily-kinesthetic, or interpersonal learners could work with partners to produce a skit or song about magnetism. For a project incorporating emotional memory and verbal-linguistic intelligence, a student could explain verbally or with a graphic organizer the relationship between magnetism as a property of physics and magnetism as a way to describe physical and emotional attraction between people or animals.

Comets for Every Student (Grades K–4)

Students tend to enjoy the wonders of science, and astronomy is a particularly compelling field. Except in areas with light pollution, the night sky is a resource that all students can access and that most have pondered. This lesson makes the most of that natural interest.

Objectives: Students will learn about comets' composition, named parts, astronomical relevance, and theories of origin through multisensory lessons that engage multiple intelligences and learning styles. Students will activate several memory systems in their investigation.

Demonstration: A dramatic and effective way for teachers to begin a unit on comets is to make their own mock comet right in front of the class. This activity will create a strong episodic and positive emotional memory that students will remember for a long time, and it will provide a relational memory on which to link new information. The "ingredients" for a six-inch comet (provided by the National Science Foundation; visit http://education.jpl.nasa.gov/educators/comet.html) include two cups of water; two cups of dry ice (frozen carbon dioxide); two spoonfuls of sand or dirt; one tablespoon of ammonia; and one tablespoon of organic material (dark corn syrup works well). Other materials to have on hand include an ice chest; a large mixing bowl (plastic if possible); four medium-sized plastic garbage bags; work gloves; a hammer or rubber mallet; a large mixing spoon; and paper towels. Instructions for constructing the comet follow:

1. Cut open one garbage bag, and use it to line the mixing bowl.

2. Place the water in the mixing bowl, add sand or dirt, and stir well.

3. Add the ammonia and the organic material, stirring until well mixed.

4. Place the dry ice in three garbage bags that have been placed inside one another. Be sure to wear gloves while handling the dry ice to keep from being burned.

5. Crush the dry ice by pounding it with the hammer.

6. Add the dry ice to the ingredients in the mixing bowl while stirring vigorously, until the mixture is almost totally frozen.

7. Lift the comet out of the bowl using the plastic liner and shape it as you would a snowball.

8. Unwrap the comet as soon as it is frozen sufficiently to hold its shape.

9. Place the comet on display for the students to observe, discuss, and take notes on as it begins to melt and sublimate. (Sublimation is the process of a solid turning into gas without going through a liquid phase, which is what carbon dioxide does at room temperature and what comets do under the conditions of interplanetary space when they are heated by the sun.)

The dry ice comet is reasonably safe to touch without getting burned, but it is still best for students to use a spoon or a stick to examine it. As the comet begins to melt, the class may notice small jets of gas coming from it. These jets are gaseous carbon dioxide escaping through small holes in the still-frozen water. Teachers can build an episodic memory by explaining that this type of chemical reaction is also detected on real comets when jets expel sufficient quantities of gas to make small changes in the comets' orbit. Comparable occurrences include a jet engine propelling a jet or a burning fuse propelling a firecracker to twist and turn. Metaphors build relational memories, so teachers may want to ask students what else moves when gas escapes or engines burn fuel.

Pre-assessment: Using K-W-L, brainstorming, and open-ended class discussions, teachers' next step is to evaluate what students know and want to discover about comets. Students may not have investigated comets formally, but most have heard of or wondered about them. During these discussions, teachers can use their own enthusiasm to stimulate students' latent interest and tap into their prior wonderings. When teachers are enthusiastic about a topic, they can frame the subject matter in a way that will catch students' interest by relating the subject to something they have experienced in reality, films, readings, or their imaginations.

Model making: Students next create a model comet using crumpled newspaper for the head (coma) and aluminum foil strips for the tail. Having students repeat the word *coma* while compressing the newspaper into the comet's head blends verbal-linguistic with bodily-kinesthetic and naturalist experiences to reinforce relational and automatic memory. It is always valuable to find ways for students to experience success in learning styles in which they are not especially confident or competent. In this activity, students don't need to be artistic or have well-developed fine motor coordination to make their comet models look good.

Music, poetry, and movement: Next, the class can engage in some multisensory activities, such as listening to a song about comets ("Halley Came to Jackson" by Mary Chapin Carpenter, for example); reading a story about comets (*Maria's Comet* by Deborah Hopkinson, for example); or dancing as individual comets across the sky and then forming a class comet, with some students clumped in the coma and others branching off in the tails. These activities engage intrapersonal, interpersonal, bodily-kinesthetic, naturalist, and musical-rhythmic learners and build emotional, automatic, episodic, and relational memory.

To complete the activity, students can select a way to respond to what they learned, felt, saw, heard, and touched. They can write a haiku about what it feels like to be a comet; create a graphic organizer demonstrating the relationship of comets to the universe; diagram and name the parts of the comet and what they are made of; write a song or create a dance depicting one of the theories of the origin of comets or the elliptical orbits they follow; chart the dates and frequency of appearances of one or more of the known comets visible from the earth and predict the date of the next appearance; describe the state of technology or civilization that coincided with the last three appearances of Halley's comet; or create an original legend in the style of American Indians or Tall Tales that includes a comet's appearance.

Assessment: For logical-mathematical, bodily-kinesthetic, and visual-spatial learners, it can be fun to make different comets to determine which design aspects (for example, length of tail, number of strips of foil in the tail, size of head) cause comets to fly the farthest or the most accurately. Logical-mathematical and visual-spatial learners will enjoy looking at astronomy maps and predicting from where on earth returning comets will be most visible in the coming years. Students who have strong musical-rhythmic or bodily-kinesthetic intelligence might enjoy putting on a play about the discovery of a famous comet, whereas intrapersonal learners could read about comets in books or on the Internet and prepare charts to post on bulletin boards.

STUDENT-CENTERED ACTIVITIES

Student-centered activities are another important component of an enriched, stimulating learning environment. These open-ended discussions and explorations keep all students connected with the learning experience and build strong neuronal circuits and sustained memory storage.

Not all lessons are suited to a student-centered approach. When learners need the structure of clear, specific presentation of information—with no room for personal interpretation and opinion—then open-ended discussions are not appropriate. For example, facts that serve as the foundation for further learning need to be explained in a straightforward manner. There is no purpose in having students debate the need to use capital letters to begin sentences. This type of knowledge is learned initially through rote practice and is reinforced by exposure and practice.

Student-centered activities are valuable because they give all students the opportunity to personally interact with new knowledge, to mentally process or manipulate ideas. In the following sections, I discuss these research-based strategies and provide guidance on how to adapt them for inclusion classes.

Student-Centered Questions

In supportive, respectful inclusion classrooms, all students benefit from whole-class discussions of thought-provoking questions. Well-crafted open-ended questions leave room for multiple points of view, solutions, types of reasoning, examples of supporting evidence, and opinions. Ideally, these student-centered discussions generate thinking, provoke interest, and stimulate students to use such higher-order cognitive processes as analyzing, reasoning, making comparisons, and forming judgments. If a topic offers enough real-world or personal relevance, it will stimulate students' executive functions and keep them focused, alert, and engaged as they build more relational connections and stronger long-term memories. These discussions also give teachers the chance to gently but clearly correct any misinformation expressed by students. Although the goal is for students to share *opinions*, teachers need to correct factual errors or they will be harder to unlearn later.

Successful student-centered question-and-response discussions increase student engagement, lower affective filters, and invite student participation. Open-ended questions are inclusive and encourage students to actively listen and *think*. Because the questions do not have a single correct answer, multiple opinions or interpretations are valued, especially when students support them with reasons. Students at all learning levels can learn at their own pace, and they feel free to participate in class discussions without fear of being wrong.

A cautionary note: teachers should avoid the temptation to continually call on students who they believe will add required curriculum content to the discussion or provide clues to point classmates in a desired direction. Avoiding the lure to call on these students too frequently will pay off in the long run as more students develop their executive functions of judgment and critical analysis. Students will also build active listening skills when they keep in mind that their opinions are more interesting to their classmates when they are different from those already stated.

A stimulating, open-ended question asked at the right time can move students to experience intellectual excitement and discover a joy of learning that they may have lost. Research has found that dopamine levels in students' brains increase when they are engaged by whole-class discussions (Black et al., 2002). When student-centered questions and discussions are captivating, even reluctant learners will be inspired to give voice to their personal opinions.

Positive feedback for good reasoning encourages active thinking and participation among LD students. The acknowledgment of reasonable aspects of their responses can make students more open to corrections of the erroneous parts. For example, suppose that the question "If you were an explorer to the New World, why do you think you would have made the dangerous journey?" draws the response, "I would be curious about new places, and I'd want to eat American food like hamburgers and corn dogs." One supportive response could be, "Good thinking, curiosity is a strong motivator. Although the people living in the Americas in the 1400s did not eat hamburgers or corn dogs, you bring up a very important reason for New World exploration. Food was one of the top reasons that explorers set out, because the people in their home European countries wanted food spices that traders could get only from Asia."

Student-centered questions are a great way to begin a unit. When students offer opinions, they have a personal investment in gathering information to defend their opinions, so they will be more attentive to the lesson that follows. Global learners will use the discussion as a jumping-off point from which to enter subsequent lessons, while sequential or analytical learners will be alert for information that fleshes out the global ideas discussed. Here are some examples of student-centered, open-ended questions to kick off units of study:

- What can you do that all other living things can also do? In your opinion, is a seed alive when it is in the package, before it is planted? Why or why not? Is fire alive because it "breathes" oxygen, "digests" paper, "excretes" ash, and "reproduces" by spreading? Why or why not?
- What do you think is a fair voting age? In your opinion, should people be required to take tests showing that they are informed about the candidates to get licenses to vote, as they do for driver's licenses? Why or why not?
- Why do you think we do—or don't—need punctuation rules?

- Do you think it matters if words are spelled correctly?
- What do you think is the purpose of homework?

Student-Centered Lessons

Like the best student-centered *questions*, student-centered *lessons* should promote optimal brain stimulation and reasonable challenge for each learner through creative and interesting problems to solve or discoveries to make. Student-centered lessons connect all learners to new instructional material by incorporating students' individual interests, strengths, and learning styles. Students engaged in these lessons experience heightened brain activity as the information passes more quickly through their brains' affective filters and into the information-processing centers. Successful student-centered lessons

- Reach students through varied sensory inputs, increasing the likelihood that at least one sensory stimulus will resonate with each learner.
- Provide opportunities for students to connect personally with the material. A variety of entry subtopics offers more than one hook to connect multiple student intelligences to the main topic of study.
- Deliver information that students feel is relevant to their lives.
- Provide choice in how students can interact with and manipulate the information.
- Take place in a receptive, cooperative, and respectful classroom community in which students practice active listening and mutual support.
- Acknowledge student participation and include frequent, specific feedback.
- Offer flexibility in terms of the academic schedule. Now and then teachable moments will arise, or students will want to follow tangents. These tangents can be related to current or future units of study, or they can be so engaging that they inspire

students to learn more about the content independently. A tightly scheduled curriculum that limits students' pursuit of these exciting ideas can lead to frustration and lost learning opportunities.

- Provide opportunities for students to distinguish facts from opinion. For example, they can use a modified K-W-L chart in which the K (what students know) is separated into three sub-categories: facts, might-be facts, and opinions. Students evaluate information they receive by placing it in one of these categories. As the unit progresses, they can revisit the original K-W-L chart and see for themselves what really was fact, supported opinion, or unsupported opinion. This process of putting information into categories mimics the way the brain makes relational memories and builds the executive function of analytical judgment.

- Integrate assessment opportunities that are suitable to students' learning and testing strengths. Feedback may positively reinforce successful participation and good choices, or it may remind students of strategies that will help them get on track to achieve their individual goals.

DRAMATIZATIONS FOR MOTIVATION AND INCLUSION

Dramatization is a powerful strategy that enriches lessons with visual stimulation and the sensory activity of movement. Dramatization is not just for formal class plays; it's a powerful form of learning that is inclusive of multiple learning styles, especially those of visual-spatial and bodily-kinesthetic learners. Skits, improvisations, and reenactments provide opportunities for LD students to enter topics of study through creativity, imagination, and movement. Dramatization also encourages students to engage in activities that might be outside their learning-preference comfort zones. The following activity provides an example of how teachers can integrate this strategy in their own classrooms.

Social Studies Skit Activity (Grades 4–8)

This rigorous activity invites students to demonstrate knowledge according to their learning strengths while gaining a thorough understanding of the social studies chapter or unit's material. In addition, students improve their ability to work with others in cooperative groups.

Before they are actually placed in groups and assigned a section of the chapter to dramatize, students read and take notes on the entire chapter. This assignment ensures that they are familiar with all of the lesson's content, not just the segment they will be assigned later. Next, students receive their assigned pages for the dramatization but aren't yet told the names of their groupmates. Before the groups meet, all students must demonstrate a grasp of the information in their assigned pages, ensuring that they have individual accountability for the project. The teacher meets individually with the students to decide together how they will demonstrate what they learned from their independent reading. The students may want to show the teacher their notes, answer the questions that the teacher attached to their group assignment, or make a graphic organizer. This individual response requirement is learner-appropriate. For some students, it is not a realistic goal to understand everything they read in the text; a reasonable challenge for them may be to write an outline using the main topics designated by bold print in the chapter. One level higher would be to include one fact from each subsection. By demonstrating their familiarity with the material orally or in writing, all students will gain a degree of mastery of the background knowledge that will allow them to participate successfully in the group activity.

Another purpose for this miniconference is to bolster the confidence and competence of LD students who are especially challenged by reading comprehension. For some, coming to the conference with a list of three facts from the assigned pages may be a reasonable initial challenge. For the remainder of the miniconference, the teacher can provide prompts or direct instruction to prepare these students to join their groups. This one-on-one time increases student mastery and enables them to participate in and contribute more to the group activity, leading to increased self-confidence and a more positive reception by group partners.

Next, the class engages in preliminary activities to prepare for cooperative group work. In forming the groups, the teacher should make sure to integrate students with a variety of learning strengths. If possible, each group has no more than one student who needs extra structure and supervision; AD/HD in particular can make group cooperation problematic. The teacher provides an explanation of cooperative group behavior, followed by a rehearsed student demonstration. In the demonstration, the teacher acts as an uncooperative student while the modeling group of students dramatize how they might effectively respond to that student's disagreement, conflict, anger, or refusal to participate. Students can portray several possible responses, such as active listening, turn-taking, compromise, and consensus.

After this demonstration, the groups form and engage in team-building activities, such as creating names, mottoes, cheers, flags, or posters. These activities tap multiple intelligences and open up participation opportunities for LD students who may not be initially recognized by their partners as valuable to the group.

Next, the real group work starts. Although each group is assigned a specific topic to cover in its brief skit, the choice of how to dramatize the historical events is largely left up to the students. The following are examples of prompts given to 5th grade students for their skits about the colonization of New England.

Group 1: One of you is an interviewer, and three of you are representatives of the colonies of New Netherland, New York, and Pennsylvania. After choosing an interview format (e.g., television talk show, quiz show, live interview), you should ask and answer questions about why your colony was established and what it is like living in your colony on a daily basis. Your discussion should include how your colonies are similar to and different from one another.

Group 2: Half of you are members of the Lenape Delaware Indian Tribe and the other half are members of William Penn's group of Quakers from England. Show through a debate, television talk show, or other approved format what topics you might have discussed at your meetings, including why Penn's group wanted to start a colony. Where was it? What did Penn's group promise the Delaware Indians? Why were the Delaware Indians concerned about what might happen if Penn were to die?

Group 3: Imagine the class is a courtroom. Half of you are Quakers and the other half are representatives of the English government. First, those of you acting as Quakers explain to the courtroom what rights you want. Why did you form your colony? Who is your leader? What makes him a good or a bad leader? What are your beliefs about peace? Next, those of you representing the English government will argue your beliefs to the classroom court. For example, why did the English government want to punish the Quakers? How did the government punish them? Why were they called Quakers? And what are *your* beliefs about peace?

Group 4: You are a group of English settlers who came to New England. One or two of you plan to settle in New York, one of you in New Jersey, and one or two in Pennsylvania. One of you is a newspaper reporter who interviews the group to find out why each colonist came from England to the New World. Interview questions should include some of your own in addition to these: What do you hope will be better here than in England? What have you heard from people already settled in New Jersey, Pennsylvania, and New York about what their settlements are like? What are you concerned about in your colony?

The skit writing and practice process takes three to five periods of 30 to 40 minutes each, depending on the grade level and cooperative experiences of the students. To avoid distraction, the teacher should not permit props or costumes until the last rehearsal session, and the use of these should be kept to a minimum. Students will be recognized for their creativity in dramatizing their material with words and actions, not for their use of props or scenery. On the final rehearsal day, each group can spend 15 minutes going through the costume and prop box or making simple props from paper. The teacher may allow students who are particularly interested in this facet of dramatization to work on props or costumes at home or during recess.

After each group performs its skit, the audience of classmates asks group members to explain who they were and what they did. After the group answers the class's questions, each performer asks a previously prepared question of the audience. This exchange further increases students' mental manipulation of the information. Because students know that their responses to questions will be part of their grades, they are motivated to pay attention to the skits and ask questions about parts they don't understand before they are called on to answer questions about the skits' content. In addition, part of students' grades will be determined by the questions they create for their audience, so they should discuss their questions and answers with their partners beforehand to avoid duplicate questions. This is also an opportunity for students who need more support to gain from their groupmates' insight and expertise.

To assess the dramatizations, the teacher can provide students with rubrics both to assign group grades and to individually rate their own participation and cooperation. The rubrics can be adapted to students' realistic challenge levels and include appropriate accommodations. The teacher can also assess students according to their success in reaching individual learning objectives.

CROSS-CURRICULAR LEARNING

Making real-world connections to curricular material is one of the most powerful strategies teachers can use to create an enriched classroom that motivates and engages students. In a perfect world—or even in a perfect classroom—we would always know and believe in the value of what we are doing with our time. As educators, we must strive to help students believe that their time is valuable and that they are not wasting it when they commit their attention to our classes.

Students should spend their time and energy on things they care about. Accordingly, an important part of our job as educators is to show students why the information we offer is something they should care about. That task is easy enough when the subject is shooting model rockets, but explaining the direct and explicit value of our lessons is more challenging when we're teaching Latin verb conjugations or prime-number factoring.

To show my students that my goal is to make their classroom experiences worthy of their time, I encourage them to (gently and politely) hold me accountable. I tell them that although I can't always promise my answer will be satisfactory, they have the right to come to me before or after class and ask, "Why is this information important for me to learn?" Although I may have convinced them earlier in the year that the study of history has current-day relevance and personal value, by the time we have completed our studies of the French and Indian War and the American Revolutionary War and are about to embark on the American Civil War, they have a right to ask how studying yet another war will add to their worldview or value as future voters, senators, or even generals. When planning lessons, teachers may want to place a reminder on their desks asking, "Why do I need to know this?" The message prompts teachers to build a curriculum that provides students across the ability spectrum with reasonable answers to that valid question.

Cross-curricular units are thematic multidisciplinary explorations that link curriculum to students' interests, lives, community, and world. Such units help the "must-learns" go down with a spoonful of sugar as they weave required material into a context with enough threads to tie in all students' learning strengths, skills, and developmental levels. They not only increase students' interest in the material but also are vital for students' ultimate success in higher levels of education and employment. The structure of cross-curricular units corresponds to the cross-referencing neuronal connections between brain areas storing related memories. Well-structured thematic approaches prompt students to see the connections between subject areas and thereby help students pattern new information with existing memories already coded and stored, resulting in stronger long-term relational memories.

Thematic units involving several subjects are particularly appropriate for the diverse range of students in inclusion classes. At least one of the multiple subjects involved is bound to incorporate at least one of a given student's strengths, and the variety of activities and approaches enable all students to fully explore the theme of the unit. For students weak in one subject area and strong in another, investigating a topic through both subjects facilitates transfer of interest or aptitude across the curriculum. For example, if a student is shy and withdrawn in every subject but math, incorporating math into a lesson in another subject area will increase her interest and participation. A computer expert who has difficulty with writing may shine in a language arts unit integrating Internet research. Making posters of Egyptian hieroglyphics would help connect non-history-loving artistic learners to the study of that historical period or geographic region. And playing rhythm instruments to kick off a science lesson on sound can reduce English language learners' stress at the prospect of complex new vocabulary (thus lowering their affective filters and opening them up to learning), as well as enable bodily-kinesthetic and musical-rhythmic learners to connect with the topic. The best cross-curricular units build students' confidence—first in their areas of strength, and later in the other intelligences they use in their goal-directed pursuits.

Thematic units also help consolidate topics in a crowded curriculum and can incorporate mandated content more efficiently and in richer contexts (Shanahan, 1997). Such lessons enable students to find value in the less-engaging information that they must learn by semantic memory, often for standardized tests. For example, students who enjoyed a unit on the American Colonial period may be more engaged in a unit on the War of 1812 if the teacher links the two subjects through compare-and-contrast activities, a timeline investigation of the military technological advances in weapons or ships, or an inquiry about how terrain and geology influence battle outcomes.

It is more difficult for all students to reach a deep level of comprehension of a lesson when they do not see how the information is applicable to their lives. Real-world connections support students' learning differences and motivate them to use and develop their learning styles when they approach difficult material. Integrated lessons make it easier for teachers to demonstrate the value of the information—the big picture that is so important for global learners. For example, interpreting scientific notation for large numbers requires specific math skills. Students will value those skills more when they see how the application of that math will help them

---

**Cross-Curricular Unit Involving Parents
and Community Members as Speakers**

Topic: Communication and Media

Potential speakers:

- Newspaper reporters and editors
- Radio and television personalities
- Representatives from the public relations/advertising field
- Post office workers/administrators
- Experts on animal communication, interstellar communication, language translation, computer programming, ancient communication such as hieroglyphics, sign language, Morse code, and Semaphore flag signals
- Reading for the Blind and Visually Impaired representative
- Ombudsmen, such as volunteers who help people communicate with legal, financial, or medical professionals
- Authors, poets, and songwriters
- 911/emergency communications operators
- Code analysts/cryptographers
- Military communication specialists

achieve interesting goals, such as determining the distances between planets and galaxies. The more subject areas and learning styles that teachers can connect to the fund of knowledge to be mastered, the more likely it is that all students will find at least one authentic use of the material they are required to study.

In addition to their academic benefits, cross-curricular units strengthen ties between school and community, teachers and colleagues, and teachers and parents. Bringing community needs and issues into cross-curricular lessons lends authenticity to the reasons behind community service, which is often a requirement of the middle or high school curriculum. It sends a powerful message to students to see the teachers they respect sharing valuable classroom time with outside experts or representatives of organizations that benefit the community they live in.

In particular, including parents as information resources in cross-curricular units has multiple benefits for inclusion classes. Parent participation can increase the classroom status and self-esteem of students who need it most—LD students, new members of the class, physically challenged students, or any students needing more confidence to build connections with classmates. Students also connect more powerfully to a unit of study when they see how adults apply the academic content to interesting jobs. (See "Cross-Curricular Unit Involving Parents and Community Members as Speakers" for an example of a unit involving parent participation.)

In addition, parents who get involved tend to promote stronger community connections to and confidence about the school. These connections model positive feelings about school to students, who are motivated by their parents' evident respect for their school. Parents are also more likely to participate in other school activities after being invited into the classroom, and they feel more confident that their children are being taught by caring teachers who see the big picture of education.

Whether or not cross-curricular units involve outside speakers or field trips with parents, it is beneficial for parents to know what has been planned for their children. Communicating with parents about these units can prompt parent-child discussions that validate the importance of the unit of study. Then when the students talk with their parents about what they are learning, they build a greater mastery of the subject. (See "Cross-Curricular Unit Described in Teacher-Parent Communication" for an example of a teacher communication to parents.)

A final and important benefit of cross-curricular activities is that they allow teachers to grow and learn along with students. Whatever we do to keep our teaching fresh is picked up by our students, who are buoyed by our enthusiasm. Just as students enjoy the stimulation

Cross-Curricular Unit Described in Teacher-Parent Communication

Victor Dominocielo-Ho teaches middle school science at Santa Barbara Middle School and keeps parents informed about his cross-curricular units of study. The thematic unit called "Genetics and Evolution" includes science, English, and history and incorporates class discussion, family discussion, use of primary sources, dramatization, and examination of current events. The following is an excerpt from his communication to parents about this unit.

> We finished reading Chapter 4, in which we learned about human inheritance, genetic disorders (cystic fibrosis, sickle cell anemia, hemophilia, Down syndrome, etc.), and advances in genetics, such as cloning, DNA fingerprinting, and genetic engineering. Chapter 5, which we'll be studying over the next few weeks, details the scientific study of evolution. As you have probably heard, in history class Marlene will be researching and presenting the Scopes Monkey Trial, and in English class the students are reading *Inherit the Wind*. In science class we learn about the "nuts and bolts" mechanisms of evolution and some of the history and development of evolutionary theory. In order to produce knowledgeable students, we discuss elements of the current controversy surrounding evolution. If you look back to your first newsletter, we laid the foundation for this subject at the very beginning of the year with class discussions on the differences between science and religion.

and novelty of interpersonal relationships, challenge, and real-world connections, so do teachers. The following cross-curricular unit exemplifies these crucial and captivating qualities.

IDITAROD CROSS-CURRICULAR UNIT (GRADES 4–8)

Each March, the Iditarod Trail Sled Dog Race captures the imagination of people worldwide. I have developed a cross-curricular unit based on this exciting event that connects to such a variety of interests that I have yet to meet a student who remains disengaged. From the time students have their hands stamped with the paw print of a Husky and receive the names of the three mushers they will represent in the race, the excitement is palpable.

Planning and Early Activities

At the beginning of the unit, students spend a few minutes writing a list of what they know and what they think they know about Alaska and the Iditarod race. To promote verbal communication for students who are reluctant to share their ideas in whole-class discussions, teachers can provide a few minutes for partner pair-share, a routine that enhances all students' comprehension and communication skills. Pair-share provides a smaller, safer environment for the students who are challenged by the activity while enabling those who work at a higher cognitive level to increase their understanding of the topic. After the pair-share activity, students can offer their partners' ideas (with permission) or their own to create a whole-class K-W-L list. Other possible pre-Iditarod activities include

- Inviting guest speakers to the class who will provide information and realia about Alaska or the Iditarod. Students can add what they learn to their K-W-L charts.
- Studying the geological and historical elements of Alaska's Bering Strait and the importance of the land bridge that once existed between Asia and North America.

- Working in cooperative groups to construct posters or models that place a scale map of Alaska on top of a map of the U.S. mainland. Students will discover that at more than 656,400 square miles, Alaska is the largest U.S. state, stretching approximately 2,000 miles from east to west. The map overlap can center on students' own town to give a more personally relevant comparison. This activity taps students' math, art, geography, and research skills.

- Reading and engaging in a whole-class activity about *Black Star, Bright Dawn*, a novel about a teenage girl who represents her small village in an Iditarod race.

- Investigating an area of personal interest related to Alaska and presenting findings in the form of a report, a PowerPoint presentation, a model, a video production, a debate, or a simulated news story. Possible topics include the controversies over oil drilling; physical geographical features, such as volcanoes, glaciers, icebergs, or earthquakes; the fishing industry; native crafts; sled dogs; wildlife found along the Iditarod trail; famous women in Iditarod history; and the effect of the Iditarod on Alaska's economy.

During the Race

As the race approaches, the class receives updates from the official Iditarod Web site (www.iditarod.com) about snow conditions, mushers in the running, new rules, and predictions about the coming race. After the mushers are registered, the teacher drops papers with the names of the 60 top-ranked competitors into a model of a dog sled, and students each pick three mushers. (They get three because there is a high dropout rate.) Students then conduct Internet research and prepare a short presentation on one of their mushers in a format of their choice—for example, portraying their musher in a class interview or writing a formal business proposal to a company explaining why the company should sponsor them.

For subsequent activities, students can create posters mapping the race route and describing what their musher would expect to find at checkpoints along the way; write journals from sled dogs' point of view about what their lives have been like leading up to this year's race (including how they were bred, selected, and trained); develop a pen pal relationship with an Alaskan student who lives in one of the towns along the route; or use a graphic organizer to compare the life history of one of their mushers with that of a famous musher from a previous race.

Academic content takes on new meaning when connected with this thematic unit. As students get to know their mushers, choose how they will conduct their individual investigations, and select presentation modes, they become personally invested in the unit. With motivation and engagement high, they are primed to study subjects that may have been previously frustrating (due to excessive challenge) or boring (due to insufficient challenge). Because the unit provides choice in a variety of contexts, individualizing goals and approaches is a natural process that doesn't make any students feel different from their classmates. In addition, the diversity of presentations and projects is more enjoyable to the class than a series of single-mode presentations. Possible projects and activities include the following.

Grammar exercises. During the Iditarod race, many regular class activities take on added real-world and personal excitement—even grammar exercises. Here are a few examples of warm-up sentences for students to review and correct at the beginning of each class.

- On the Iditarod trail sled dog race track I founded snow storms moose and wolves that slowed me down and mean danger
- The Iditarod begun in anchorage Alaska on March 5 2006 and it's headquarters was located in anchorage Alaska
- what do the musher use to sea in the swirling snow ice dark and winds

Math problems. Regardless of the grade level or topic of math study at the time, teachers can easily adapt word problems to relate to the big race. Examples include the following:

- You know how long the race is. Looking at today's results of how far your musher has traveled, calculate the percentage of the race that he or she has completed and his or her average rate of travel.
- At this calculated rate of travel, when might your musher finish the race?
- How much faster would your musher need to travel to catch up to the first-place musher in the next 24 hours?
- If your musher travels at the current average speed with six dogs, what might his or her speed be if one of the dogs had to be pulled from the race because of injury?

Cities on the trail. In this activity, students select points along the race route to investigate and report on through models, charts, travel posters, and scientific analyses. When their mushers arrive at their designated checkpoints, the students share their presentations. For each city on the trail, students have a multitude of topics to explore, including indigenous native populations, local businesses, geography, and cultural characteristics. Students who select the same checkpoint may work in pairs or small groups to pursue the topic that pertains to their area of interest. Students may also decide which role to take on for their presentations: historian, geographer, geologist, town mayor, local business owner, zoologist, or botanist. The choice this activity offers in terms of topic of exploration and presentation approach enables teachers in inclusion classes to build strengths and differentiate realistic challenge. With teacher guidance, students can investigate as many or as few aspects of their cities and make their presentations as detailed or as simple as suits their abilities.

Students interested in zoology could investigate an animal native to their town's geographical area and report on that animal's habitat, predators, prey, migration habits, climate adaptation, food, camouflage, and life cycle. They could deliver this information in a report, on a chart, through an oral presentation, or in a narrative about the animal's life written from the animal's perspective. Budding geologists and geographers may be interested in investigating the physical features of their town's region. If a student's chosen town is near glaciers or icebergs, he or she could research and report on these arctic phenomena. If the Great Alaska Earthquake of 1964 occurred near a student's town, that student could investigate earthquakes in general, and that one specifically. If there is a volcano near a student's chosen town, the student could investigate its eruptions, as well as volcanoes in general. Information on the Pacific Ring of Fire (www.crystalinks.com/rof.html) will show students how many active volcanoes there are along the Aleutian Trench in Alaska. Students interested in botany may want to investigate the plants native to their town's region and, in general, how plants adapt to the frozen ground of the tundra.

To keep group members learning about one another's investigations rather than simply conducting separate research in parallel, teachers can set aside time each day for students to give mini-reports to their group about what they discovered and to exchange feedback. Each group documents new facts on its K-W-L chart, which the teacher may use for assessment purposes. This process keeps students on track and accountable to be productive each day, and the *W* (what students *want* to know) questions the group asks will prompt students to conduct further investigation in these areas of interest, just as a real scientist would.

Logistical planning. Students can engage in hands-on activities to address various logistical issues of the race, including designing and creating (and discussing the reason for) sled dog booties; investigating solar energy and creating a solar oven that mushers could use to heat or defrost their food; planning meals for mushers and sled dogs based on calories needed per hour, day, and week, taking into consideration the calories provided by different foods and the weight of the food and food preparation items.

Whiteout storm rescue. For this activity, students plan and demonstrate a rescue for a musher lost in a whiteout storm using rope and "snow screens" that simulate what a person sees—or doesn't see—during a whiteout. For a simple snow screen, students could use a plastic bucket placed over the head or a white blindfold. This activity is great for bodily-kinesthetic learners, especially if they can move about in a large, unobstructed outdoor area, such as the playing field. Students not usually comfortable as discussion leaders in class can be encouraged to work with a partner to create this simulation for their classmates to enjoy and learn from. The student demonstrators can also give classmates the opportunity to experience a whiteout rescue by dividing the class into teams and having them plan rescues using only a rope tied to a wooden stake anchored in the ground and wearing blindfolds.

Alaska Day. When the last musher has completed the race, the unit concludes with a celebration of Alaska Day. Groups present their research about their towns on the race route through oral reports; newspapers; dramatizations; charts; models; debates; mock trials (for example, to present the facts about oil spills, oil needs, and the Exxon Valdez Alaskan oil spill disaster); or simulated local news broadcasts from students' towns. The culminating Colony Day activity described in the appendix (pp. 187–190) can provide some ideas for adding to the learning and fun of Alaska Day with Alaskan foods, games, music, and costumes.

CULMINATING ACTIVITIES FOR ACTIVE INCLUSIVE LEARNING

Too often, a unit of study ends with a test, after which the next unit begins. But schools celebrate graduations and the end of sports seasons, so why not the successful attainment of wisdom? Culminating activities give students time to reflect on what they have learned and celebrate the goals they achieved, ensuring that the unit ends on a positive note.

A special designated day or celebration isn't feasible for every unit, of course. For most units, students can simply choose from several activities to honor the knowledge that they have acquired. Some students will choose to record their reflections in a journal, whereas others will prefer to create graphic organizers. Other options include creating scrapbooks, computer graphics, games, songs, or models. To enrich students' multiple intelligences and enhance their abilities to respond to information through various learning styles, teachers should encourage students to engage in a different culminating activity for each unit. Initially, students will likely choose activities that match their learning strengths, but with encouragement and modeling they will want to try alternative activities that classmates have used and that seem appealing. The class can even post a list of student experts on different types of projects so that students can ask one another for help during designated project time. As the year goes on, students of all ability levels will continue to set and reach achievable, satisfying goals in which they are invested. Gifted students will build the confidence to take risks in areas in which they may not be the best in the class, and students who have long felt incapable of learning will grow to see themselves as active participants in a community of learners.

In this era of accountability, it sometimes seems that the most popular culminating activity for a unit of study is a formal test simulating the way students' knowledge will be assessed on future standardized tests. Fortunately, teachers' wisdom and creativity can help ensure that culminating activities both celebrate knowledge acquired and shared and provide opportunities for reinforcing memories and connecting new knowledge with frontal lobe processing centers. The following culminating activities are adaptable to multiple learning styles, subjects, and grade levels.

Americana Experience (Grades 4–8)

In 1999, I was a student teacher in the classroom of Beth Yeager, a 5th grade teacher at McKinley Elementary School in Santa Barbara, California. One of the engaging activities I observed in Yeager's class was her Americana Experience, designed to wrap up students' study of U.S. history from the Revolutionary War through Westward Expansion and the Civil War. In this culminating activity, students work individually or in small groups to set up a booth or learning station that portrays—through models, costumes, theatrics, food, music, art, simulations, games, or books—a person, a battle, an invention, a miniature room, or a similar representation of some aspect of early America. Parents and students from other classes are invited to tour this Museum of Americana. (Other possible themes include a State Fair or a World's Fair, for which students' booths represent the historical, geographical, or cultural heritage of their state or country.)

In the Museum of Americana, I saw students who never spoke in class come alive as they discussed the inventor of the potato chip and gave samples. A boy who had not previously connected with history devoured illustrated books about early locomotives; when visitors came to his booth, he spoke with animation and an almost encyclopedic knowledge about how the building of the transcontinental railroad changed daily life in the United States.

A girl with a learning disability that severely limited her reading level sewed wonderful period dresses for her and her partner to wear as teachers reading from a primer in their one-room prairie schoolhouse. When visitors came to their classroom, this student was able to take her turn as teacher because the primer was at a lower grade level. For the first time, she was comfortable reading aloud. After the Americana experience, she told me that she had begun reading aloud to her stuffed animals at home from library books. In addition, she grew in class status for her sewing and design skills and became close friends with her academically advanced project partner. That friendship led to a natural peer tutoring relationship.

Ethics Unit Bake Sale

This culminating activity can follow a cross-curricular unit about ethics and ethical dilemmas. It works well during the holiday season as a replacement for the more traditional Chanukah, Christmas, and Kwanzaa activities. First, students select a cause that they want to support. My 5th grade class decided to donate the proceeds of their bake sale to the local humane society and to a former graduate of the school who was serving overseas in the military. They used their mathematical knowledge to increase recipe quantities, determine prices, calculate discounts for purchasing three items, and count their earnings. When they wanted to see if they could get markets to donate food items needed for their baking, they learned how to type business letters in the computer lab. They used their artistic skills to make advertising posters, and their dramatic flair to go about the schoolyard encouraging potential customers with jingles and slogans.

The main goal of this activity, however, was to practice the skills in cooperation and conflict resolution that they had worked on during the ethics unit. Students were also able to practice the Golden Rules they had each written in their own words after discovering that the religions they investigated seemed to have a version of that tenet in common. The tangible product was seeing their cooperation work toward raising money in a way they chose for causes they chose. The choices they made resulted in learning that was diversified, inclusive, intrinsically motivated, and fun.

LEARNING CENTERS TO COMPLEMENT MULTISENSORY LEARNING-STYLE DIVERSITY

Although teachers in inclusion classes don't have much time to meet individually with students, holding one-on-one miniconferences at the beginning of the school year builds trust between students and teachers and enables teachers to discover students' learning-style preferences, interests, and talents. Teachers should also meet with students individually throughout the year to evaluate progress, assess mastery, provide feedback, and develop and modify appropriately challenging goals as needed.

One successful way to free up time for these miniconferences and to meet the multisensory needs and diverse learning preferences of students in inclusion classes is to set up learning centers. Placed throughout the classroom, these centers provide self-contained learning opportunities for independent or peer work that address the needs of a diverse range of learners. Ideally, they offer appropriate and individualized choice, accommodation, interaction, and challenge to prompt students to reach their optimal learning potential. Planning learning centers is often a time-consuming process, but once they are set up with supplies and activities, they become places of engaging, interactive learning that can be used year after year.

Teachers should try not to introduce more than one or two learning centers during a class period. They can add new centers later, after students have had some time to learn the proper behavior and process for each station. When introducing new learning centers, teachers can model and lead discussions on how students should deal with conflicts independently before resorting to teacher mediation. After this introduction, students may engage in supervised center work, with the help of instructional aides or parent helpers when possible.

When outside help is not available, students who have mastered a center can guide others. Because learning center activities are differentiated for a range of learning strengths, it is likely that all students in an inclusion class will have one center where they excel and can spend a period assisting others. Students will need instruction and practice in guiding classmates through an activity rather than doing it for them. Some useful guidelines for peer experts include, "Don't use your hands" and "Give hints, not answers, so that your classmate can have the fun achieving his or her goal that you had achieving yours."

Consistency in the organization and placement of the centers also helps with management. Elementary classrooms can arrange learning centers by subject, whereas single-subject classrooms can stage centers by topics generally explored in each unit of study. For example, common science learning center topics might include scientists who are active in the field; problem investigation; interaction with manipulatives demonstrating scientific phenomena; discovery centers for new investigations; and final product development centers for creating posters, reports, and models. When teachers keep the purpose of each center consistent throughout the year, students will pick up on the flow and know where to go during the discovery, investigation, and culmination phases of each unit of study.

Learning centers also develop students' abilities to work independently, prioritize, focus, cooperate, and stay organized. Clear instructions and extensive initial supervision within a strong, supportive classroom community will set the tone for successful independent center work throughout the year—leaving teachers with more time for those critical one-on-one connections with students.

To be accessible to LD students, learning centers need to provide clear instructions and present the required tasks in stages. Some LD students might be appropriately challenged by stage 1 in all centers, but most will probably be able to achieve stage 2 in a few centers that tap their individual capabilities. Teachers may want to make suggestions in these students' learning logs, next to the name of each center, to guide students to their ideal level of challenge. Usually the centers' activities build on one another, so students who successfully complete stage 1 may progress to stage 2, even if is not listed as a goal on their learning log. Because several students with diverse abilities can work at a center independently but simultaneously, students who have not yet reached the higher stages will have the opportunity to observe what they could achieve with more experience and practice.

Teachers can hold students accountable for their learning by having them create final projects or complete cards after center work indicating which centers they worked on that day and what they learned. Each center can have a box containing individual cards for all the students so they can keep track of their progress. Alternatively, cards can be kept in a pocket in students' individual learning logs. At the start of each unit, students can label pages in their logs with the names (or diagrams) of each specific center. Each center's designated page will need to specify the level of mastery assigned to the student and document the student's progress before the student turns in the card or adds the progress to his or her learning log for assessment and feedback (Bender, 2002; Ramey, 1996).

ENRICHING ALL STUDENTS' EXPERIENCES

All students can benefit from enriching, stimulating learning environments. Developing thematic units, multisensory lessons, and activities that resonate with all learning styles offers greater opportunities for LD students to engage in the lessons and extends opportunities for all students to challenge themselves—and succeed.

CHAPTER 5

REVIEW AND TEST PREPARATION STRATEGIES FOR DIVERSE LEARNERS

Practice doesn't make perfect—it makes permanent.
—MADELINE HUNTER

So far in this book, I have discussed how teachers can create enriching and multisensory lessons, power student investigations through motivation and choice, and help students set and reach appropriately challenging goals. But to solidify learning and develop long-term memories, students must engage in a final process of strategic review, which involves the manipulation of academic content through the executive functions and the repeated activation of the brain's new neural circuits. Teachers in inclusion classes can implement numerous strategic review and reinforcement strategies aligned to multiple learning styles that will allow the information to become part of students' permanent memory banks, available to build on and connect with all future learning.

USE IT OR LOSE IT

As we know, the brain is plastic, changing structurally with new learning. Although most of the neurons where information is stored are present at birth, dendrites that connect and enhance communication among neurons grow throughout a lifetime, increasing in size and number in response to learned skills, experience, and information.

Once these dendrites are formed, the brain's plasticity enables it to reshape and reorganize the networks of dendrite-neuron connections in response to increased or decreased use of the neuronal pathways (Giedd et al., 1999). The regularly used pathways and connections are maintained and hard-wired into the brain, whereas others are eliminated, or *pruned*. Pruning generally happens when a practiced routine or thought process has become so well established over time that the steps building up to the action or memory can be eliminated. When a process become automatic, the dendrites and synapses that were originally used during the early stages of acquiring the skill or knowledge—such as learning to speak a foreign language or to play piano—are no longer stimulated or needed, and are thus pruned to streamline the brain's superhighway of circuitry.

Because unnecessary brain network connections don't need to be supplied with nutrients and oxygen, their elimination leaves these elements available to support other networks—an efficient process. The downside of this "use it or lose it" phenomenon lies in the decay of neurons that store memories that are still required, but that are not used or stimulated often enough to be successfully maintained. Accordingly, the ideal way for students to review new information is to access it repeatedly in the context of subsequent learning activities and skills. For example, vocabulary lists could correspond to the vocabulary found in books that students are about to start reading, or the teacher could review addition facts at the beginning of a unit on multiplication (a process that students initially learn as a series of additions).

METACOGNITION FOR REINFORCEMENT AND REVIEW

More and more top-rated colleges and universities have begun to recognize that the bright and motivated students they admit often experience difficulty with college classes' reduced assignment structure and relatively few formal assessments (Vermetten, Vermunt, & Lodewijks, 1999). Study skills specialists at the university level acknowledge that many of the students who come to them for help never needed to study much in high school and have never intentionally identified their study strategies (McGuire, 1998). Once these students are taught to recognize their learning strategies and practice metacognition, they are usually able to regain their academic success.

Metacognition helps students of all ages and abilities to develop an understanding of their own strengths and weaknesses and of the strategies that are most useful to them in specific situations. To help students practice metacognition, teachers can explain to students why they are teaching them a new strategy or having them use a previously practiced one.

For example, when students are learning how to self-edit for comma placement, they might be taught the strategy of reading the sentence aloud and listening for natural pauses. After explaining the strategy and its benefits, teachers can use an overhead projector to display sentences with omitted commas while reading the sentences aloud, pausing at the places where commas belong.

Next, students can complete worksheets containing sentences that are each missing a single comma at a natural pause in the sentence. Gradually, the sentences become more complex, and teachers formally introduce the concept of dependent and independent clauses. Even after learning these formal grammar rules, students can see that the natural pause strategy still often applies. The next worksheet distributed contains sentences with more than one missing comma, with the number of missing commas noted at the start of each sentence. Teachers work along with students during this guided practice, showing them the correct answers at the completion of each sentence. This guidance prevents the cementation of incorrect information and provides immediate positive feedback for correct comma placement (Bender, 2002).

When it is clear that the students understand the strategy, they can work on sentences in small groups with a list of grade-appropriate comma rules. They can refer to the list to explain to one another where they believe commas should be placed in the sentences. During a culminating whole-class brainstorming activity, group representatives can offer their groups' solutions and the thought process behind them, as their responses are written on the board.

To wrap up the lesson, teachers can add "Read quietly aloud for self-editing" to the class strategy list and write, "Natural pauses may be the places where commas are needed" in the "Uses of This Strategy" column. Some students may immediately think of other times they have found reading aloud helpful to them; these can also be discussed and added to the list. In subsequent self-editing lessons, teachers can demonstrate how reading aloud can also help students identify run-on sentences or words that are repeated too often. After practicing the strategy in these situations, they too can be added to the strategy's column of uses.

In an inclusion class, this overt discussion of strategies is critical for some students and valuable for the rest. Although some strategies will seem simplistic to advanced students, the metacognitive process of taking note of the use of strategies and when they work will expand every student's learning potential. Trying different strategies and discovering new uses for them can even become a fun type of detective activity.

When students use metacognition to actively and consciously review their learning processes, their confidence in their ability to learn grows. They begin to attribute outcomes to the presence or absence of their own efforts and to the selection and use of learning strategies. Students with LD, many of whom have never thought of themselves as capable of learning, realize that some of their errors are due not to ignorance, but to not knowing the effective strategy to use. Once students identify useful strategies and use them repeatedly, they experience a powerful boost in confidence. Similarly, they will develop more perseverance as they discover that when their initial effort to solve a problem fails, they can succeed by approaching it with a different strategy. Students are actually learning to be their own tutors and guides.

To reinforce the process of metacognition, teachers can ask students to write down the strategy they used after successfully completing an activity, especially if it was in an area in which they had not previously succeeded. For example, when I find that a student has demonstrated significant improvement in his math homework, I'll ask him what he thinks he did right. He might say that he turned the page 90 degrees to make the horizontal lines into columns that kept his numbers organized for more accurate multiplication. Writing down his successful strategy will both boost his confidence and cement the strategy into his repertoire.

STRATEGIC REVIEW

When new learning is isolated from past knowledge or is particularly complex, students will need frequent reviews early on to reinforce the memory circuits formed by the newly sprouted dendrites. Before launching a review session, teachers should assess their students' knowledge. What do the students know? What do they need to know to accomplish mastery? Which methods effectively reach individual students? What are students' individualized goals, and how will their progress toward those goals be evaluated? Teachers can glean some of this information from students' learning logs or notebooks. After this pre-assessment, teachers will be ready to apply the following practices to support and stretch the learning strengths of all students.

Multisensory Review

Review sessions should provide opportunities for students to connect with the information through different learning styles than those they used when they first learned the material. Multisensory review sessions specifically and intentionally support the diverse array of learning styles and intelligences found in inclusion classes. For LD students who did not code the information into usable patterns when it was initially taught, review sessions that embrace their learning strengths will be their opportunity to successfully process the knowledge. These students' goal is to discover which strategies engage their brains through their learning strengths as they connect to and reinforce the neural pathways of the newly stored information.

For example, review sessions for auditory learners may involve listening to parts of recorded text or lecture material or speaking the information aloud to themselves, classmates, family members, or even pets, whereas verbal and interpersonal learners might benefit from working in study groups in which they discuss and quiz one another on the information. Students who respond better to diagrams and pictures can use the pictures and tables in their texts and notes as prompts to verbalize the information conveyed, or they can write explanations of the diagrams on paper or on a blackboard (if they respond best to large motor activity).

Bodily-kinesthetic learners and students with focus issues can highlight or draw sketches with connecting arrows in their notes or in the margins of texts they own. If the books are school property, there may be older, damaged copies that they could have for writing in. Alternatively, they could use sticky notes to emphasize important review points in textbooks and class notes.

Gifted or accelerated students can benefit from the stimulating challenges provided by review sessions that are geared to their less-developed learning strengths. Because these students already have the basic knowledge of the lesson patterned in their memories, their brains will be open to processing the information in less-familiar ways. Opportunities to practice these less-developed intelligences are as valuable to these students as cross-training is for athletes. For example, students whose brains successfully coded new information from a lesson on calculating fractions through auditory or analytical functions will be open to exploring fractions through less-familiar learning styles—say, in a review session geared to global or visual learners. The analytical thinkers will feel comfortable engaging in these review activities—which might involve coloring fractions of pictures of animals ("color approximately one-fourth of the paws on this dog")—because of the patterns that now exist in their brains. These students will have the confidence to explore and develop their less-used creative or global learning processes.

Note Taking

Sharing notes is a valuable way for all students to hone their note-taking skills and gain metacognitive awareness of which content is crucial and which is not. Teachers can ask students who have clearly written notebook entries to share them verbally or post them on a bulletin board for the benefit of students who don't have adequate notes. Hearing or reading different styles of notes will connect with different learning styles. When appropriate, and if the skilled note-taking students agree, teachers can provide photocopies of good student notes to LD students after they have made their own best attempts. This practice will both guide students on how to improve their own notes and ensure that they have complete notes to study from.

That said, teachers need to make sure that they use note sharing as a temporary scaffold rather than as a permanent crutch that could lead LD students to make less than their best effort. It is also important to consider how students will feel if they see their best efforts as significantly inferior to those of a classmate. But as long as LD students are improving their note-taking skills over time, and the classroom structure provides other opportunities for them to produce exemplary work, giving them good sample notes to study from can be a reasonable support.

Teachers can also confirm the accuracy and completeness of students' notes by having students compare their notes with those in a file of best-work notes from previous years. This process allows students to fill in missing information and challenges them to recognize what information they excluded. Writing the added notes in a different color will assist students in this analysis. After correcting their notes, students can verbalize or write what they learned about the newly added information.

Teachers should go beyond showing students samples of good notes, however, and ensure that students are actually improving their note-taking skills. After all, students can only practice, review, and master information that they have organized and saved in a format that is accessible to their learning styles and skills. If students are to use their notes to study authentically important as well as test-critical information (which, unfortunately, are not always the same), their notes must be complete, accurate, and understandable to them.

A strategy that motivates students to work at their note-taking skills is administering open-notes tests. Students realize the value of complete and organized notes when the notes enable them to efficiently find information that will help them answer test questions. Of course, some students may go overboard and copy almost an entire chapter's worth of text into their notes. To preempt such a situation, teachers can place a limit on how many pages of notes or note cards students can use for tests. This limit will develop students' abilities to select important information from their texts and omit extraneous data. It's also another opportunity for students to exercise the executive functions of prioritizing and judging.

One way for students to assess and improve their notes is to consult a checklist that helps them categorize components they omitted from their original notes. The checklist could ask,

- Did I recognize visual cues in the book, such as bold, large, colored, or italicized words, sidebars, and section headings?
- Did I write down information that the teacher emphasized after giving such prompts as, "Write this down"; "I'll stop for a minute here so you can include this in your notes"; "This is an important piece of dendrite food"; "In conclusion"; or "This diagram shows how it all comes together"?
- Should my notes have included certain names and dates that I missed? Why didn't I include this information in my notes, and how would including this type of information in the future improve my note-taking success?
- Did I leave out examples or real-world connections that were discussed in class or written about in the text?
- Did I separate my notes into appropriate categories, include page numbers and important definitions, and distinguish fact

from opinion? When I gave my opinion, did I back it up with specific supporting information?

The goal of this self-analysis is to help students recognize how developing an awareness of their notes' omissions contributes to their note-taking success. Good note taking builds brain-processing skills and increases students' abilities to transform raw information into owned knowledge.

Team Review Activities and Games

Conducting team reviews through a game format enables teachers to group advanced students with classmates who need support to participate in whole-class reviews. Students are more comfortable participating in convivial review competitions when they can collaborate on team answers rather than having to give individual answers. Teachers can also add components to the review that provide inclusion opportunities for multiple intelligences, and the fun format of a game show promotes dopamine release, thus adding to students' focus.

Team presentations. For this activity, teams collaboratively lead a review connecting the content to the topic. If the topic is the Summer Olympics and the test is on parts of the body, for example, a team might make a graphic organizer of a human figure showing different body parts playing different sports all at once. While the right foot is skiing, the left foot is snowboarding, and the arms are lifting an ice-skating partner overhead. Because the activity requires sports knowledge and art skills, more students have an opportunity to participate through their areas of interest while actively reviewing the material. Presenting their organizers on the overhead projector reinforces the test material through visual and auditory channels and gives teams the added fun of using the teacher's special tools.

Hot potato. This activity begins with the teacher announcing the topic of review to teams of four to six students, who then pass a clipboard around their circle with a sheet of paper and pen attached. Each student writes on the sheet something he or she recalls about the subject. A student who can't think of something to add may ask the group for help but must actually write the words down (in any spelling or handwriting). In this way, students still benefit from the review and feel like full participants. Representatives from each team take turns reading aloud their data, skipping the items already noted by other teams, until all items are reported. The team with the most correct data points not written by any other team wins. Because items included on multiple lists are not awarded points, students are motivated to listen to opponents' answers, thus enhancing the review. Any class member may challenge the accuracy of a fact, and the teacher is the final judge.

Quiz games. Students on each of two or four teams use their notes or texts to create one or more quiz questions for the next day's game. After students write their questions and answers, the groups review them to ensure that the questions are fair and the answers accurate. Each group hands in its final list for teacher approval, and the teacher codes each question for difficulty. During the game, the teacher selects an appropriately challenging question for each student. For added support, students can consult with one "lifeline" team member before giving a final answer.

Technology for Review

Technological advances can help even the playing field in inclusion classes by presenting information through alternative sensory pathways, connecting with students' varied learning styles, and increasing opportunities to visualize and manipulate abstract concepts in concrete ways. Specific academic computer programs and Web sites can be assets for practice and review because they stimulate auditory, visual, and kinesthetic sensory inputs and can make review and practice more enjoyable and efficient. Some students don't have Internet access at home, but most do have this access in school computer labs or libraries. In addition, many current textbooks in mathematics, history, and other subjects have CD-ROM versions or extensions of the texts or Web pages with interactive activities for students and teachers. Well-designed programs can also provide feedback while customizing each student's review material according to areas in which they have assessed deficiencies.

Computer feedback systems. One example of classroom technology that can engage all students in active learning is a computer system that provides personal feedback about student comprehension of the lessons as they are being taught. This immediate feedback assesses how well students are listening, what they already know, what new material they comprehend, and what remains confusing to them after the lesson is completed. Many teachers already glean this information by watching and listening to students or by questioning them and encouraging them to ask questions during class. Yet we know that some students appear to be engaged while daydreaming, while others who claim to have no questions don't truly understand the material.

In computer feedback classrooms, students have notebook-size data entry units at their desks that directly feed their input into their teachers' computers. When teachers ask a question about the material that has just been covered, students type in their individual answers—usually yes-or-no, numerical, or multiple-choice. Students can also indicate when they are confused and need more explanation or when they are bored because they already know the material. A grid shows teachers each student's response and a tabulation of what percentage of the class "gets it." This information tells teachers whether they can proceed or need to teach the material again in another way.

E-mail response technology. This technology is another way for teachers of any subject area to assess students' knowledge, although it's contingent on students having access to computers where they do their homework and on teachers having some time in the evening to check their e-mail. It also works best when assignments are given more than 24 hours in advance of their due date. In classes using this technology, teachers pose comprehension questions about reading assignments, and students e-mail their responses to the teachers' computers before the next class. Students can also submit questions and indicate any parts of the reading that confused them. By reading students' responses before class, teachers know which parts of the reading need clarification and review.

This homework keeps students individually responsible to keep up with the work—no "lost paper" excuses. In addition, the e-mail response system is particularly helpful to students with LD and to those who find it difficult to admit in class that they are not following the lesson or the text. When students have e-mailed their concerns to the teacher before class begins, they enter class trusting that if they pay attention, the questions they e-mailed will be answered without their needing to raise their hands. Systems like this also help students feel a connection to the teacher outside the classroom; technology becomes a uniter, not a barrier.

Calculators. Calculators are another useful classroom technology for inclusion classes, offering students with LD the opportunity to advance their mathematical knowledge without being stuck because of limited ability to retain basic arithmetic. One concern with calculator use is that students can become dependent on calculators to do basic math before they have mastered the arithmetic skills and abstract concepts of addition, subtraction, multiplication, and division of positive and negative numbers. Luckily, alternative calculators can help students grasp these concepts and develop mathematical understanding. For example, the Casio ClassPad is valuable for a variety of learning styles because it can be used with keys or with a touch pad and stylus. Students can manipulate numbers and variables in equations using keys or the stylus, and they can drag or copy and paste equations or expressions to reuse for practice with other numbers. Visual learners can view an equation as a graph, enabling them to see the relationships among the numbers and the relationship between algebra and geometry.

Computer review systems. Positive reinforcement and feedback can be a powerful factor in student learning. Teachers don't always have the time to provide that external reinforcement to every student, so this is another area where technology can come in handy. A well-structured computer learning assist system gives positive, authentic feedback to students and reinforces neuron circuits in their brains. In selecting a computer review system, schools should be sure that it provides suitable progress feedback to teachers and students at any time and that each new lesson starts with a review of the material previously learned.

A well-engineered computer adjunct can enhance students' memory connections, pathways for access, and retention of the material they learn in class and read in their texts. The feedback should directly connect to the learning that just took place and to information that was learned in earlier lessons and tested in periodic assessments. The programs also need to provide prompt, appropriate review to fill in knowledge gaps. Some computer systems evaluate only students' recall of the topics taught since the last assessment and fail to adequately address long-term memory retrieval. If a student has forgotten things learned earlier in the course, the assessment should recognize and report these gaps when it measures true mastery. The best systems use all of this information when evaluating an individual student's readiness to proceed and make those assessments easily accessible and comprehensible for teachers and administrators to review. One such system is ALEKS (Assessment and Learning in Knowledge Spaces).

When learning is exciting and engaging, the results will more than offset the planning and prep work involved in the initial configuration of techno-classrooms. Smiles will replace groans, eye rolls, and disruptive behavior. Students will be more cooperative and responsive, teaching will be more effective—and, yes, even standardized test scores will increase.

TEST PREPARATION AND TEST-TAKING STRATEGIES

Even though standardized or traditional formal testing may not be the best way of assessing what all the students in inclusion classes know, these tests do have a place in the curriculum and help prepare students to do their best in subsequent formal testing situations. In addition, teachers can use them to measure students' ongoing progress, assess the success of various interventions, and highlight areas in which students might benefit from extra help or an alternative method of teaching the material. Several commonsense approaches to test preparation and test taking can reduce anxiety and improve test performance.

Frontal Lobe Executive Functions: The Ultimate Study Skills

When we really consider the brain processes that go into deciding what, how, and when to study, it turns out that the frontal lobe executive functions of organizing, judging, analyzing, and prioritizing are the essence of efficient studying. When students receive instruction geared to their learning strengths and then practice the strategies most compatible with their intelligences, they will be better able to develop the executive functions needed to process and store important information for retrieval during future situations, such as tests. Students can reinforce the following executive functions by regularly practicing—and building metacognitive awareness of—several useful strategies.

- **Organization**. Students can hone their organizational skills through such activities as identifying main ideas or global themes from texts; creating graphic organizers that prioritize secondary information; and taking, revising, and comparing their notes with samples provided by classmates or teachers.
- **Judgment**. This executive function encompasses self-checking strategies, such as self-editing; estimating or checking math accuracy; planning use of time; looking for clues to answer questions in subsequent questions; and monitoring focus.
- **Analysis**. Students with good analytical skills can gain an awareness of the types of mistakes they commonly make. Reviewing these while they study can help them avoid such mistake patterns

as copying problems incorrectly; failing to analyze whether their answers make sense; forgetting to read the entire question and answer all parts of it; and missing important words in the instructions (for example, the *not* in "Which answer is not correct?").

- **Prioritization**. Students can hone this executive function by learning to separate low-relevance details from the main ideas. Learning how to prioritize will enable students to make the most efficient use of study and testing time.

Prediction

Prediction is a strategy that can help students get an idea of what to study for the test. Before students begin preparing for a test, and after they are equipped with complete notes, teachers should have them predict what information from their notes they believe will most likely be on the test. Students can check the accuracy of their judgment by writing down their predictions before the test and then later comparing their predictions with the actual test questions.

Prediction builds motivation by increasing personal connection with the outcome. Students want to see whether their predictions were correct, so they have authentic interest in going back and looking at their predictions after the test. What did they predict correctly? What did they miss? Is there a general category that they should consider when they make predictions next time, such as the timeline or the examples and facts in their notes that supported the theories? To encourage prediction as a test preparation strategy, teachers can collect students' predictions before a test and give bonus points for making reasonable predictions and jotting down answers to those predicted questions. Students needing more accommodation might need to use these predictions and notes when taking tests early in the year as they build skills and confidence.

Students can do their predicting alone or in a partner pair-share, as long as they are actively thinking about their own notes. Teachers can model the prediction process by placing a set of complete notes on an overhead projector and asking volunteers to suggest which information is likely to be included in test questions. Then they can show the class sample test questions based on the crucial material found in the notes and lead a class discussion comparing the sample questions with the class predictions. Assuming there's some gap, students can examine why they missed certain information included in the test questions and whether there was some commonality in their incorrect predictions.

Just like solving word problems in math, evaluating test predictions requires logic and judgment to know which information is not essential. Writing down their impressions takes students to a higher level of cognition, and discussing their impressions with partners or teachers reinforces new goals and strategies to use next time. By gaining this metacognitive awareness, students build the strategies best suited to their learning styles and most crucial for coping with their learning differences.

Final Review

After teachers have told students what material the test will cover and what types of questions to expect, they can have students individually verbalize or write a few sentences about what they took away from the explanations. There can be a surprising discrepancy between what teachers think they have made clear about test expectations and what students actually absorbed. Because tests can be a source of anxiety, students' affective filters may have blocked some information about the test. This check-in tells teachers what they need to focus on in final review sessions and test preparation discussions, enabling them to correct misconceptions and make individual test preparation more efficient. While teachers give individual feedback to some students, other students can use the time to check their own personalized study guides, reviewing the lists of test errors they have been prone to make and their successful test-taking strategies. They can then prepare personal guides that list their test question predictions and material that they have been told will be covered and write a corresponding list of learning style–specific strategies to use to avoid common mistakes and maximize their strengths for this particular test.

Essay Test Preparation

Preparing for essay tests in simulations that approach the real testing climate will build confidence and reduce the anxiety of the unfamiliar. Teachers should remind students which strategies worked previously for their styles and give them opportunities to practice and receive feedback on essays similar to the ones they can expect to write on tests. For many students, especially strategic-analytic thinkers, essay test practice will start with making a list of all the ideas they have, followed by organizing the ideas into categories and then into outline form before they start writing. Global thinkers may start with a graphic organizer, coming up with their big ideas first and then following with branches for ideas that they brainstorm to support that idea.

In some cases, teachers may want to allow students to devote their essay practice time to writing detailed outlines that demonstrate what they know about the essay topic instead of getting bogged down putting these facts and evidence into essay form. This strategy is useful for students who have satisfactory writing skills but are challenged by remembering the important facts or organizing the facts into a sequential outline. Students who are most challenged by writing opening sentences might first want to list the information they think should be included in the paragraph and work backward to formulate a sentence that leads into that information.

Peer editing can reinforce all students' knowledge of the factual material. Even students who are limited in their ability to check essays' grammar, spelling, vocabulary, and punctuation can still provide their partners with a great service if they evaluate what is perhaps the most important characteristic of a satisfactory essay answer: is the statement made in the first or second sentence supported by relevant details and examples?

Explicit Strategy Instruction

For many students, studying is a frustrating challenge until they learn specific strategies suited to their intelligences. Some LD students may demonstrate their knowledge best in class discussions and other verbal, informal assessments, so the full extent of their knowledge may not be reflected in their standardized test scores. These discrepancies may become apparent in these students' higher grades for class work and lower scores on standardized tests. Often, the problem is the test and not the student, because the typical standardized test tends to measure rote memory rather than conceptual understanding.

Students with learning difficulties may need explicit and extensive instruction in study strategies, including prioritizing, judging the main ideas of paragraphs, knowing which details are important and which can be set aside, planning ahead for most efficient use of time, checking the logic of answers, using estimates to compare with their math answers, and self-editing writing samples. Just as students can be taught a variety of strategies enabling them to organize their thinking about new academic content, they can learn and practice specific test-taking strategies that give them the tools to truly show what they know on standardized tests (Wunderlich, Bell, & Ford, 2005). For example, when students need to memorize content, they could use the information to create rhymes, songs, or raps; illustrate the information through drawings; dramatize the material; rehearse the content with a partner; create flash cards; or pretend they are teaching the material to the class mascot, a favorite superhero, or a rock star, using a chalkboard or whiteboard. When students feel good about study strategies that they have developed, they should be encouraged to teach them to the class in subsequent review sessions.

Test Modifications

Test modifications are an important adaptation for some students. Teachers should discuss any modifications with students in advance, ensuring that students know they are not taking an easier test, but rather one that is designed to prevent confusion and test what they really know.

Teachers can provide study guides with sample questions for LD students who misread or have difficulty understanding test questions, misunderstand nuances in the test language, struggle to determine what's most important, or don't easily differentiate between similar multiple-choice answers. It may also be a necessary accommodation to provide alternative tests of the same information but without the questions that can be confusing to these students. For example, changing multiple-choice questions to true-or-false questions or providing questions that offer a choice between two rather than four answers can assess students' knowledge while making it easier for them to show what they know.

Students with visual-spatial or fine motor difficulties may have difficulty filling in Scantron forms rapidly and accurately or copying answers onto a separate answer sheet. It may be reasonable for these students to write their answers directly onto the test booklet. The teacher can then later copy their answers onto the Scantron form. Some students also benefit from using an index card to follow the text so that they don't skip lines when they come to the end of a sentence.

Test Day Preparations

Routines that the whole class participates in before taking the test can help release anxiety, easing students out of the basic survival mode that releases fight-or-flight hormones and neurotransmitters that overwhelm their reticular activating systems and affective filters. For example, teachers can tell a joke or wear a funny hat to elicit laughter: the deep breathing and muscle stimulation of laughter release endorphins and acetylcholine and increase oxygen flow. These positive biological factors enhance focus and test performance.

Before the test starts, teachers should make sure that students have gone to the bathroom, have all necessary supplies and notes, and have water if necessary. Students who need to leave their seats during the test can disrupt the concentration of classmates. Teachers can then read aloud the test instructions as students follow along in written form; the students should repeat the instructions back as the teachers record them on the board or overhead projector. Teachers also need to confirm that students know what to do when they finish the test and that they understand the meaning of the times written on the board (for example, time elapsed or time remaining).

Teachers should also remind students before starting the test to calculate how much time to allocate to test questions and to write themselves a note about what time it will be when they should move on to the more time-consuming questions. Ideally, students have already engaged in practice sessions and made their own pacing plans. Students who are most challenged by the word problems in math, for example, should know to plan extra time to interpret these problems in the ways they have practiced. Similarly, students should be aware of the point-value system for tests so that before starting, they can determine the questions that carry the most point value and plan to devote the most time to those. Teachers should encourage students to write down these specific plans.

Often during test preparation and study sessions, students have learned key formulas, mnemonic devices, or acronyms that they use to internalize the material. Teachers can remind students who benefit from these memory prompts to write them all down in the margins or at the top of their tests before they even start reading the questions. Writing down their memory hints in a relaxed and positive state, before they start answering the test questions, will help students stave off anxiety from reading questions they don't think they know how to answer.

After the Test

After the test is the time for students to add metacognitive strategies that they found helpful to the class list and to evaluate the predictions they made about the test. Unless students have this time to review their test results, they may never do so. To ensure students' accountability for going through this process, teachers should ask students to respond to teacher comments in writing, remark on the patterns of their errors, and then return the tests to the teachers. As with any process that might cause students to feel criticized or defensive, teachers can ask students to first respond to the positive comments and write down what they did to succeed in those areas.

It may be helpful to give students suggestions on what to evaluate in their error review. Did they leave questions unfinished at the end? If so, do they think they knew the answers to some of these, and could have skipped more difficult questions along the way to get to the last questions (and gone back as time allowed)? In other words, did they get the most points for the effort and time spent? Were any of their errors due to not following instructions? Could they have underlined key words in the instructions and reread them before answering the questions? Did they make mistakes because they didn't review sections of the test material, because they didn't focus on the information they were given about what the test would cover, or because they didn't ask for help in understanding items they knew would be on the test but that they were confused about? Teachers should do their best to return tests promptly so that students can learn what they were confused about before going too far into the next unit.

LOOKING AHEAD

Strategic review and study practices are vital for maintaining and nourishing the garden of new knowledge so successfully planted. Link them with test preparation and test-taking strategies, and students will be able to access this information for winning results on those looming standardized tests—and, more important, for the rest of their lives.

AFTERWORD:
WHAT THE FUTURE HOLDS

When applied to the classroom, brain research can both drive the learning process and enliven the minds of students. As the research continues to build, our challenge as educators will be to develop and use new strategies that bring the fruits of the research to the students in our classrooms. This challenge will be a fascinating and exciting one to work toward, and the more we learn about the structure and function of the brain, the more prepared we will be to meet it.

TEACHER-RESEARCHER PARTNERSHIP

The last decade has witnessed extraordinary progress in building links between neuroscience and classroom instruction. Now educators can find well-designed scientific studies to help them determine the most effective ways to teach students as individuals in inclusion classes. Recent advances in technology have enabled us to view the working brain as it processes sensory data into stored knowledge. We have seen how functional brain imaging, scanned while individuals perform discrete cognitive tasks, reveals increased metabolic activity in predictable, specialized neural systems as the brain meets those demands. We have come to understand that the brain uses patterning to connect new sensory input to related memories and discover new meaning (Olsen, 1995). We have found that the frontal lobes perform the highest cognitive functions when they manipulate these relational memories in new ways to analyze, compare, contrast, predict, judge, plan, and discover new meaning.

I concur with John Mazziotta, chair of the UCLA Department of Neurology, that brain research has already suggested and will continue to suggest teaching strategies and curriculum based on what the brain is *wanting to do* and can do best. Mazziotta's work with the International Consortium for Brain Mapping is dedicated to the concept that the human brain map will continue to reveal mechanisms involved in memory and learning and help define additional strategies for better learning. Mazziotta sees PET scanning as an important tool to identify presymptomatic students at risk, thereby allowing early intervention. For example, isolating the precise genes that cause a predisposition to such conditions as AD/HD or dyslexia in families could allow earlier prediction for at-risk children and ensure that they are provided with enriched environments to stimulate and strengthen areas of weakness before they enter school.

As the research continues to build and educators become knowledgeable about the neurology of learning, brain researchers will look to informed educators as partners. Teachers will tell researchers which strategies they find successful so that researchers can investigate what is happening in students' brains when those strategies are used. In turn, researchers will make their data accessible to teachers, who can then develop new strategies that make use of that information.

We are teaching in an era of evidence-based education. We rely on objective scientific research rather than philosophy or opinion. We cannot risk teaching students with unproven tools. We must insist that the programs, strategies, and curricula required by our school districts reflect current knowledge about effective learning.

The father of multiple intelligence theory, Howard Gardner, was confident that research would support his cognitive theories but not convinced that the information would inform teachers' practice and be used to reach challenged learners (1999). Now that neuroimaging and brain mapping have confirmed the brain regions that show variable activation associated with different learning styles, more strategies are available to evaluate functional changes in students' brains after specific strategies have been used. As more data are gathered, even more specific recommendations for students with defined learning strengths and challenges will come to light.

It is classroom teachers' challenge to incorporate the strategies we do have into students' daily lessons. This challenge has been intensified by the highly structured curriculum that some schools have adopted to prepare students for standardized tests. We now have the documentation to validate our best brain-compatible strategies—if only the powers that be will listen.

MAKING A DIFFERENCE

Consider the most effective strategies for creating a fun and individualized learning environment, and you'll realize they are what you find in every classroom where students

- Work at their own pace toward appropriately challenging goals.
- Are aware of real-world applications.
- Feel personally connected to their studies.
- Are exposed to multisensory teaching and review.
- Work together in a classroom community that honors all individuals' talents.
- Receive ongoing, individual feedback and know they are acknowledged for their improvement and progress—not just their final products.

At the end of the day, how do you know if you succeeded in enriching each one of your students? Look at their names or their photographs and consider whether you opened them up to new knowledge and experiences. Did you engage them through their learning strengths? Did your class's activities help them make personal connections and reach their highest potential? Did the day show them both the value and the joy of learning?

Each time you helped even a single student feel special, you made a difference. If you spent time and thought in helping students show you who they are, and if you appreciated them as individuals, you made a difference. If you responded to students authentically and they recognized your sincere interest, you made a difference.

If you have established a supportive class community with opportunities for students to respect and encourage one another without fear of embarrassment if they try something new or make a mistake, you have moved your class toward safety and trust. You will know how successful you are. You will notice your students trying to do their very best because they learned self-respect from the respect you gave them—not just respect for knowledge and for their classmates, but respect for themselves. You made a difference.

APPENDIX: SAMPLE LESSON PLANS FOR INCLUSION CLASS ACTIVITIES

In this section, I offer several detailed lesson plans for different grade levels and subjects. These lesson plans are meant as guides to show the neuro-*logic* behind the strategies that make them useful for inclusion classes. For all of these lessons, teachers can guide individual students in determining reachable, reasonably challenging goals and provide appropriate structure for their needs. Including a variety of presentation formats and accommodating all students according to their learning or developmental levels will ensure that students do not perceive individual accommodations as evidence of limitations.

EXAMPLE 1: EXPLORER REPORT

This cross-curricular lesson's theme is "Challenge and Exploration." In this lesson, which can be adapted for 5th–8th grade classes, students each investigate a historical figure who played a role in the exploration of the New World. The unit provides multiple points of entry for diverse intelligences and interests; students can choose their explorer and can decide how they want to conduct their investigation and present their findings. Certain segments of the investigation prompt students to practice their less-familiar learning styles, but students' collaborative work with classmates who have complementary learning styles, interests, and talents provide scaffolding for this expansion into unfamiliar territory. The lesson's overarching goals are to

- Integrate the study of historical exploration of the New World with the exploration of students' interests.
- Start the school year by establishing a supportive classroom community, building bonds of friendship, and generating respect and appreciation for individuality.
- Help students feel safe discussing their anxieties about starting a new school year with new classmates and teachers.

The objectives of this unit are for students to

- Compare and contrast cultural and societal similarities and differences.
- Recognize types of societal conflict and resolution both in history and in classroom dynamics.
- Use discovery science and research to investigate how technological development is often need-driven.
- Correlate geography and environment with settlement development (availability of food, shelter, protection, and clothing).
- Conduct research of greater depth than has been done in previous grades or units. Students will have some choice in selecting subtopics to investigate within a larger unit.

Before the unit actually begins, the class breaks into pairs to conduct peer interviews, providing an opportunity to build friendships and mutual respect. Instead of focusing on their academic differences, partners explore each other's heritage and draw parallels between why their parents, grandparents, or great-grandparents came to the United States and why the explorers came to the New World. Students also share feelings about the challenges they anticipate in the coming school year. After the interviews, students review their notes and introduce their partners to the class.

Making the Lesson Real and Relevant

The unit kicks off with the class sharing a personally relevant experience connected to the unit's theme of exploration—for example, an exploration day in the park. Students search for natural resources to build shelters, pretending that they are newly arrived explorers who need to set up temporary living areas inland from their ships. The students don't have to actually build the shelters as long as they are involved in the act of discovering and recording (sketching, videotaping, photographing, writing about) the resources available and deciding how they will protect themselves from the hazards they might encounter (animals, weather, native people). Students are encouraged to work in groups of two to four, including at least one classmate they don't know well. Teachers can tell students that including someone new in their group is a type of interpersonal exploration.

If feasible, teachers should include a hands-on project during the field trip, such as weaving a basket with grass or starting a fire with flint. The bodily-kinesthetic experience provides a concrete, personal connection to the more conceptual learning that will follow back in the classroom. As soon as possible after this out-of-the-classroom shared experience, students should write, illustrate, or use magazine or Internet pictures to create a personal journal entry about their day of exploring, including as many sensory descriptions as possible. What did they see, hear, smell, touch, and feel emotionally? Connecting to the experience through multisensory modalities increases emotional, relational, and physiological links to the learning experience, ensuring that the information is stored in multiple sensory storage areas of the brain. In addition, writing the journal entry from the perspective of someone from the historical time period will give the subsequent explorer investigation more personal relevance.

Suggestions for Organizing the Explorer Investigation

The following suggestions will help students organize and pace their investigations. Teachers may simplify or add more structure to them to accommodate students with LD.

- During the next few days, look at the list of explorers. Read in your social studies textbook or the encyclopedia about some of the explorers on the list who interest you or who are unfamiliar to you. Make a list of at least four names from the list. Students' names will be randomly picked from the name jar to choose their explorers in turn. You may not get your first or second choice, so be prepared with several choices.
- Look at the schedule of due dates and mark important dates in your assignment notebook or personal calendar or organizer. If you want to, you can even make notes on your calendar a few days *before* deadlines as helpful reminders.
- Gather information about your explorer from a variety of sources—for example, the school library, the public library, the Internet, magazines, primary sources, experts in our community, and CD-ROMs. After gathering your resources, read about your explorer. (*Note to teachers*: Allow for diverse independent reading levels by researching the school library's resources—how many books there are for each explorer, and at what grade levels they're written. Some students will need to select their explorer on the basis of the availability of books at their reading level.)
- Write down all the questions you have about your explorer. What more do you want to know about this person—his life, background, reason for exploring? This is your chance to investigate things about your explorer that you really are curious about and are interested in knowing!

Guidelines for Written Explorer Report

These guidelines take students step-by-step through the report-writing process. Teachers can adjust the requirements for the amount and detail of note taking, number of report questions, paragraph and page length, and number of sources according to each student's level of appropriate challenge. After distributing the same assignment instructions to all students, teachers can hold brief conferences with individuals to personalize the assignment goals for each student.

Introduction. Students should start by writing notes for their introductions. Their reports can start with an introductory paragraph including a lead sentence about who their explorer is and telling readers what they can expect to learn from reading the report. Students should also include a few of the most important facts about the life and adventures of their explorer. These do not have to be detailed because the reports will go into greater depth later on.

Next, students should go through the questions they wrote down after reading about their explorer, selecting those they really *want* to learn more about. They will need the questions to be broad enough to be able to write more than one paragraph in response; it's best to start with three or four questions because they might not find enough information to answer some of the questions. Students can demonstrate their knowledge of their explorer, the historical period, and their own critical thinking by researching questions like these:

- What was happening in parts of the world other than Europe and the Americas during this period in history?
- Why was exploration important during this historical period and to your explorer's native country?
- What challenges did your explorer face, and how did he overcome them? Include internal and external struggles as we have discussed in the historical novel we read in English.
- Show your knowledge of the natural and manufactured resources and technology of this time in history by describing what your explorer took on his journey and what he discovered at the destination.

- Demonstrate the importance of your explorer's journeys and why these explorations were valuable, or what negative effects they had on people.
- What tools of navigation, ship building, communication, protection, or battle did your explorer use? How did these tools come about, and how did your explorer benefit from their use?
- Which people were crucial or influential in your explorer's decision to travel, and how did they influence him?
- Compare and contrast the challenges you investigated during our field trip with those of your explorer.
- Would you have chosen to accompany your explorer on his adventures? Why or why not? What would you have suggested he do differently if you had been there?

Note taking and organization. The next step in writing the report is to take notes. On three-by-five-inch index cards, students can jot down information using the sources they find. Teachers should encourage students to summarize what they read and write down the information as phrases, avoiding copying word for word what the author wrote about the topic. Students should write down the source on each card, including the page numbers so that they can refer to it later. When students have finished writing the information on note cards, they should organize their notes in categories and in a logical sequence, grouping the cards together in piles that each correspond to one of the report's questions.

Outline. Now students are ready to write an outline, first figuring out the order in which their information should be written and listing the main ideas in that order. They should leave space between the main ideas so they can add details later. Teachers can tell students that their outline will be like an explorer's map for them to follow when they write the report.

First draft. Students should use their notes and outlines to write their first draft but put the information into their own words. Teachers should emphasize again that students must not copy the words from their books and ask if they need clarification on what constitutes plagiarism. Teachers should also remind students to follow the writer's workshop process that the class has practiced, consisting of four stages: writing, self- and peer editing, teacher conference, and revision. Students should include a bibliography documenting at least two references.

Schedule Checkpoints

Teachers can distribute the following checkpoint list to students to help them keep track of their project schedules:

- Check out explorer books from the school library, or bring in books from the public library or from home, on [DATE].
- Your notes about your explorer and at least three questions you want to investigate are due by [DATE].
- Your notes about your remaining questions are due by [DATE].
- Your report outlines and ideas for your secondary investigation are due by [DATE].
- The first draft of your report is due by [DATE].
- Your corrected, final report is due by [DATE].
- Beginning on [DATE], all students will present their explorer reports to the class. You will act as your explorer and have a choice of several presentation styles.

The Secondary Assignment

All students must complete a secondary assignment in addition to the main presentation and report. For this investigation, students must include evidence of their critical thinking and knowledge of the historical period. Again, teachers can provide individual accommodations to students, requiring them to provide more or less documentation of their critical thinking as appropriate. Some students may be sufficiently challenged by explaining in a one-on-one miniconference the thinking that went into their investigation, whereas others can be prompted to make their investigation more challenging.

Because students' grades will primarily be based on the written explorer report, teachers should encourage students to try something new for the secondary project. Students can choose a product to create—a model, a PowerPoint presentation, a chart or a poster, a board game, a video, or a dramatization, for example—and must use at least one classmate from the class expert list as a consultant, including his or her name on their list of resources. The support of a classroom expert and the fact that students are already acquainted with their explorer from the primary project help students approach this assignment with less stress. This project builds class community and strengthens students' interpersonal skills and less-developed learning styles. Here are some suggestions for secondary investigations:

- How have the tools that your explorer used—for navigation, ship building, communication, protection, or battle—changed during the last 500 years? What technological advances do you think are possible in the next 100 years?

- Write a journal that your explorer could have written detailing his experiences during a few days of his travels—things he saw, heard, tasted, feared, enjoyed, and dreamed.

- How would you apply what you learned about your explorer to a mission that you are going to lead to explore life on another planet—one that is habitable but previously unexplored?

- Create a map of your explorer's travels, marking the places he traveled to for his discoveries. Include a map key to explain your distances, directions, color-coding, and symbols. Label all important places on your map. Use your math knowledge of ratio and proportion to create your map to scale and write what the scale ratio is, including your calculations.

Multifaceted Learning

The "Challenge and Exploration" cross-curricular unit goes beyond history class to incorporate literature (including three historical fiction books—one for independent reading, a second to be read together and discussed, and a final, more challenging one to be read aloud by the teacher); math (for example, using knowledge of ratio and proportion to make maps); dramatizations (including student-written and -performed skits based on textbook sections about the exploration of the New World); and science (for example, observing computer simulations of how wind and tides affect boats, engaging in hands-on experiments with waves, and learning about nutritional deficiencies among seamen). Equally important are the social goals set out in the objectives of this unit: to build cohesiveness, respect, and appreciation for the different skills, talents, and interests that classmates in inclusion classes will share throughout the year.

EXAMPLE 2: LIFE IN COLONIAL AMERICA

In this lesson, students select an early American colonial settlement and investigate the daily life of its residents and neighbors, including such aspects as religious practices, agriculture, trade, education, government, celebrations, and relationships with American Indians and England. Students will look at how geography influenced the lifestyle and activities of their colonists and compare the factors that affected daily life in the colonies with the factors that affect their own daily lives. This unit can be adapted for students in upper-elementary grades through high school as a cross-curricular unit or as a single-subject investigation in history or geography. Teachers can also use the basic activities for a unit on a different historical period or geographic region. The goals of this unit are to

- Advance students' research and report-writing skills.
- Offer a choice of investigation techniques using multiple media and technology applications and incorporating text sources appropriate to individual reading levels.
- Give students practice using various types of graphic organizers and help them discover which ones are best suited to their learning styles and goals.

- Involve students in setting appropriately challenging goals.
- Provide opportunities for students to work according to their strengths as well as hone their less-developed intelligences.
- Provide ongoing assessment and feedback to students.
- Promote peer and small-group cooperative interactions.
- Give opportunities for students to start from a global perspective (the big picture) and move toward sequential, analytic processing.
- Encourage whole-class participation in discussions of topics that extend beyond the confines of verbal and mathematical academics, including distinguishing between fact and opinion; comparing and contrasting students' society with another society; investigating through a variety of approaches (including linguistic, bodily-kinesthetic, and mathematical-analytical) the relationship between geography and culture; and cooperatively planning for the highly anticipated culminating celebration of Colony Day.

General Instructions for "Life in Colonial America" Investigation

As in the exploration unit, teachers can modify the following instructions to suit the needs and abilities of their students—for example, by adding more rigorous cognitive activities (such as critical analysis) for some students and simplifying requirements for others. Again, teachers can give the same initial instructions to the whole class and then hold individual conferences to guide students to the choices best suited to their strengths and goals.

Students should use one or more of the graphic organizers that the class has used—or create one of their own—to record their discoveries and ideas about the topics they choose. The "who, what, where, when, why, and how?" questions apply to most topics. Students can add to their organizers as they gather more data from their research, which they may conduct through a variety of media, including videos, CD-ROMs, textbooks, interviews with local experts, library books, and the Internet.

Students may present their final written work in outline form with references, if they chose an alternative final project to a formal written report. The outline must be detailed enough to include the most important items that would be in the report. Making this option available to all students reduces any stigma that may be associated with this accommodation. Teachers can individualize the outline assignment by adjusting the amount of detail required according to ability or developmental level. Students have numerous options for final projects that connect their learning styles and interests to the unit of study, such as building models, giving oral reports, or creating colony posters.

Writing the Report

The following guidelines lead students through the process of writing their formal reports:

- Use the rubric provided and review the papers written by students in previous years investigating the changing nations of Africa and the tribes that lived in those nations. Although your topic is different, comparing those reports with your rubric will give you a good idea of what is expected for an *A* paper, a *B* paper, or a *C* paper.
- Begin with a global statement about how a society or nation can be built from different parts (colonies). Recall the class discussions about what constitutes a nation. Is it geography, arbitrary boundary lines determined by governments, common beliefs or goals, mutual needs, or other factors? Can a nation be successful if there are great differences among the colonies that are to be joined by a common government?
- Give your opinion about the main question you chose to investigate. There is no single correct answer; your opinion is as valuable as the arguments you use to defend it. Use a graphic organizer, such as a Venn diagram, to show similarities and differences between your colony and the new nation created when the colonies joined together under a central government.

- Consider how different climates and natural resources affect the ways in which people live and develop societies. Sometimes our choices in how to live are limited by where and when we live. People who live in the Arctic have developed clothes to suit the cold and social customs to celebrate important seasonal changes, such as the first snowfall or the spring thaw. People who live on a coast have different resources—such as fish for food and water to travel on—than those of people who live on rich soil, who can develop agriculture and grow extra food for trade. Which aspects of life in your colony were determined by outside forces, such as geography, climate, natural resources, neighboring populations, politics, and religion?

- While you write, remember to use facts you researched, keeping them separate from your opinions, as we practiced in class. You can use the same type of fact-versus-opinion graphic organizer you used during those lessons as you prepare this part of your report.

- Describe at least one custom (relating to anything from agriculture to recreation) unique to your colony and explain how the time period, geographic location, neighbors, religion, and other factors caused this custom to develop.

- End each paragraph with a sentence that summarizes or interprets what you wrote about rather than repeating the information in that paragraph. See the practice pages where you wrote sample summary sentences in class.

- Use a transition statement to begin some of your body paragraphs. Consult your list of transition words and the sample sentences you wrote in class that used transition words.

- Closing paragraphs should include one or more of the following: (1) a concluding global (general) statement explaining your opinion of how place (geography) influenced the way early settlers lived and why you believe geography has that importance; (2) whether you think our current society could learn something from the people in your colony; or (3) some cultural or everyday customs or beliefs in your colony that have parallels in your life in our society today.

Culminating Activity: Colony Day

The culminating activity of this unit on the lives and challenges of colonists in the New World is Colony Day, a celebration and "cerebration" (a play on words to indicate the **cerebr**al cortex acti-**vation** that takes place during thinking) that brings history to life. Colony Day enables students to access knowledge and demonstrate mastery though activities that challenge them at their most appropriate levels for growth and achievement. Incorporating these activities into a day of celebrations lowers affective filters and performance anxiety and reinforces the dopamine-mediated reward connection between fun and learning.

Colony Day presentations. Students hone cooperative and collaborative skills by writing and presenting skits that re-create events in history. Working alone or with partners, students portray people from the colony that they have investigated. Because students have already successfully completed their major research projects, receiving feedback along the way that helped them reach individualized goals, the pressure is off when presentation time arrives. They have made any necessary adjustments or corrections to ensure accuracy and comfortable familiarity with their topic. Students tend to see the Colony Day presentations as a celebration of their efforts and a time to share their special knowledge with classmates. Students who are not comfortable giving live presentations in front of the class could stage puppet shows or produce and show videos instead.

For their final presentations, students choose anyone from their colony to portray—an American Indian, a child of a wealthy family, or a slave, for example. Then they tell the class about their activities over the course of a single day or a few days—what they ate, how they played, what they did for work, whom they worked for, whom they did things with, or who worked for them. They can talk about their feelings toward the other groups of people in their colony, or perhaps toward the governor or the English king. Students have demonstrated in their reports and projects that they have mastered this content. Now they have the opportunity to share their expertise with their classmates and let them know what it would be like to actually have lived in their colony. Students can choose to customize their presentations in several ways. Here are some suggestions:

- **Props**. Props are especially helpful for students who have memory difficulties because they can use their props as prompts to remind them what they will talk about and in what sequence. For example, students can set up the props in the order in which they will discuss each part of their subject's life.
- **Costumes**. The use of costumes will help some shy students feel more confident and will demonstrate how acting out the role of another person can free them of their self-imposed confines. Masks in particular can help reserved students feel less exposed.
- **Video productions**. If live presentations are too anxiety-provoking, or if students are interested in the technology of videography, then pairs or groups of students who investigated colonies with similar lifestyles can create video presentations that combine technology, script writing, and acting.
- **Puppet shows**. Various students may enjoy crafting puppets for presentations. Some academically gifted students who would feel uncomfortable directly speaking lines that might sound too "brainy" to classmates may feel more comfortable if the words come from puppets. In addition, students who are challenged by memorizing lines can read from scripts that they or their groups have written, since the scripts remain hidden during the presentation.

Colony Day celebration. This activity is indeed a celebration that teaches by active engagement through all of the senses. Students become the colonial people they have "lived with" through their investigations and reports. Here are some sample instructions to students:

On Colony Day, you can work independently or with a group of two or three classmates who have a colony in the same region as yours. You will have a choice of preparing and bringing to class a food dish that would have been eaten in your colony, teaching the class a game played in your colony, or actually spending the afternoon as a person from your colony—dressed as he or she would have dressed and staying in character to answer questions about your daily life. This character representation should resemble those of the actors in Colonial Williamsburg whom we saw in the video in class. I have a collection of books that you can use with recipes, games, and sketches of clothing, as well as costume materials.

What happens at the conclusion of this cross-curricular, multi-sensory unit—or, more important, months and years later? The students remember something about the hard work and challenges they faced and the problems they solved. They recall the cornbread and the tug-of-war. Most important, though, they remember that learning and fun went hand in hand, and that they were experts on their topic for that day. They spent a day living in colonial times and sharing that experience with classmates . . . and they loved it!

EXAMPLE 3: WRITING A BOOK FOR YOUNGER STUDENTS

In this lesson, students investigate a topic by creating an illustrated storybook for younger students. This activity works for a unit of study in an upper-elementary inclusion class or in subject-specific inclusion classes in middle and high school, including science, math, history, literature, and the arts. This project builds personal connections between students and the unit of study because students are aware of the responsibility of teaching new information to others and are motivated to learn it. The storybook format eliminates the pressure of using complex vocabulary and sentence structure and makes use of art and creativity. Students who have impairments that prevent them from drawing can download pictures from the Internet or select ones to cut out from magazines. The following example comes from the 8th grade history class of Kevin Schertzer, a teacher at Laguna Blanca School in Santa Barbara, and relates to the War of 1812.

Over the course of the next week, you will be responsible for creating a storybook showing the events of the War of 1812. The storybook will contain pictures you draw showing each of the following events: (1) causes of the war; (2) victories at sea; (3) the fight for Canada; (4) the burning of Washington; (5) the defense of Baltimore; (6) the Battle of New Orleans; and (7) the Peace of Ghent. On the back of each drawing, you will provide a paragraph describing what the picture shows. A good picture will not need much description because it should tell the story of the event on its own. You will be making your storybook for our school's 5th grade students, who are about to start learning about the War of 1812. We are going to send them your storybook as the main source of that learning.

The unexpected follow-up for this project was that the 5th grade students wrote back to the 8th grade book authors about the new things they had learned from their storybooks, the facts they had learned in their own studies of the War of 1812, and additional questions about things they wanted to know more about. Students sustained the correspondence for several weeks, even extending it into cross-grade discussions during lunch.

EXAMPLE 4: GREEK GODS BOOK

In Dominique Smith's 7th grade cultural studies class at Santa Barbara Middle School, students enjoy the opportunity to bring ancient Greek gods and goddesses into the 21st century by creating informational books on them. This multimedia exploration engages all learning styles and uses numerous brain-compatible strategies to motivate students across the academic and developmental spectrum. The unit stimulates personal interests by incorporating teen culture and varied options of study. This investigation also enables gifted students to explore the material more extensively and go beyond the designated requirements to levels of greater challenge and intellectual stimulation.

Students can enter this activity through their dominant learning styles and later increase their experiences in their less-developed intelligences through activities that feel safe because they are so engaging. The more artistic can start with art projects and move out from there with engagement and confidence. The techies can start with Internet research and then, once their interest is stimulated, extend to the other areas of the project. Smith makes sure to recognize talents that do not relate to mainstream academics, modeling respect for students who have gifts outside reading or mathematics. When teachers create learning experiences that incorporate activities making use of student expertise, such as instant messaging, students feel acknowledged by a respected adult and respond with increased confidence. The following steps outline the sections of the project and show where teachers can offer strategic support.

Project introduction. The project introduction should start with the big picture—crucial for global learners—and build interest by suggesting that students will enjoy themselves: "The book that you are about to open is about all the major Greek gods and goddesses. Hopefully by the time you close it, you will have learned many interesting facts and enjoyed yourself in the process."

Connection to the real world. Teachers can stimulate relational memories from the start by using concrete examples about things all students are familiar with. Teachers should call attention to the real-world applications of the knowledge by providing information about what students can "get" from the project. For example, recognizing local business names that are derived from names of Greek gods and goddesses will show students that they already have some familiarity with the topic and help them feel less stressed about the new unit: "Next time you see the Artemis Animal Clinic, use the Atlas Moving Company, learn about arachnids in science, or even send a Valentine's Day card with Cupid on it, you'll know where these names come from and what they refer to."

The project. Students first create books that contain fact sheets about the gods and picture pages representing the imagined forms of these immortals. This open-ended activity lowers students' affective filters because there is no right or wrong way to draw a mythical figure. The final part of the project is a creative writing piece using the information that students learned and making it come alive through their own words and imaginations. Smith offers more than 10 creative writing topics that appeal to the full spectrum of intelligences and interests in an inclusion class. Here are some examples:

- Wise Athena likes to be properly worshipped by mortals. Write a letter to a friend in Rome after attending a festival in Athens in her honor.
- Messenger Hermes is a mischievous god. Write ads to try and imagine how his name and abilities might be used today to promote a product or service.
- Using the language and abbreviations commonly used in modern computer communications, write an e-mail exchange, chat room dialogue, or instant messaging conversation between motherly Demeter and her daughter Persephone.
- Zeus and Hera attend marriage counseling. Using what you know about their behavior, including Zeus's womanizing, write a possible dialogue among Zeus, Hera, and the counselor. (*Note to teachers*: For students challenged by formal writing, the option of writing in dialogue can promote creativity because all students know what conversations sound like. When students are successful in these less-intimidating writing activities, they build skills and confidence that they can apply to subsequent formal writing assignments.)
- Aphrodite writes to the newspaper column "Ask Athena" for advice about her marital problems with Hephaestus and her attraction to Ares. Athena responds. (*Note to teachers*: This choice offers students the opportunity to write at their appropriate level of cognition. Some LD students will set what are reasonable goals for them, such as using an advice column from the daily newspaper as a template and simply modifying the question and answer to fit the era of ancient Greece. Students capable of higher levels of cognition can challenge themselves to write about complex issues with ethical dilemmas. All students can draw from personal experience.)

Concluding summary. Writing a final summary of knowledge gained reinforces students' work and builds self-esteem because they see explicitly what their effort did for them in terms of general knowledge, technical abilities, academic research skills, self-exploration, and planning and prioritizing techniques. Students understand that their goal-directed efforts led them to grow as scholars. Smith writes,

> Much more than being about Greek mythology, here are some other aspects of this whole project that I hope have helped you grow and learn as a student. All these skills will serve you well as you move on to 8th grade and then on to the rest of your academic career. Have you considered that you
>
> • Learned to tackle a long-term project, one step at a time, by sticking to a schedule and meeting regular deadlines along the way?
> • Learned to take notes from reading a book or a Web site and extracting the important facts from each source?
> • Learned to find pictures from various sites on the Internet illustrating your topic? Some of you were great at this even before we started, but others made incredible progress!
> • Learned to use your knowledge of the topic in an original and creative way to write your own fiction and make all these dusty old gods come to life?
> • Learned to accept my comments, corrections, and suggestions and go back to your first drafts and improve on them until they were perfect?
>
> I hope you are very proud of yourself. Did you ever think, when you started the school year, that barely halfway through you would have produced a 40- to 50-page document? Not to mention that to do so, if you count all your rough drafts, you wrote probably another 10 to 15 pages. So give yourself a big pat on the back; you deserve it!

This final acknowledgment reinforces students with authentic, specific recognition of their accomplishments and confirmation of why they should be proud of themselves, showing them the intrinsic reward of learning.

GLOSSARY

acetylcholine: A neurotransmitter that stimulates multiple brain centers, including the hippocampus, the brainstem, and the forebrain (where new learning takes place).

ACTH: A cortisone-releasing hormone that has a positive alerting effect. It is released in response to surprise, novelty, and personal associations. When these feelings are linked to new learning, the released ACTH promotes growth of new dendrites and synaptic connections between neurons. This creates additional circuits and connections among the new information.

affective filter: An emotional state of stress in students during which they are not responsive to processing, learning, and storing new information. This affective filter is represented by objective physical evidence on neuroimaging of the amygdala, which becomes metabolically hyperactive during periods of high stress. In this hyperstimulated state, new information does not pass through the amygdala to reach the information processing centers of the brain.

amygdala: Part of the limbic system in the brain's temporal lobe. It was first believed to function as a brain center for responding only to anxiety and fear. When the amygdala senses threat, it becomes overactivated; PET and fMRI scans show high metabolic activity represented by greatly increased radioactive glucose and oxygen use in the amygdala region. In students, these neuroimaging findings are seen when they feel helpless and anxious. When the amygdala is in this state of stress, fear, or anxiety-induced overactivation, new information coming through the sensory intake areas of the brain cannot pass through the amygdala's affective filter to gain access to the memory circuits.

autonomic nervous system (ANS): The part of the nervous system responsible for regulating the activity of the body's other organs (e.g., skin, muscle, circulatory, digestive, endocrine).

axon: The tiny fibrous extension of the neuron that conducts impulses away from the cell body to other target cells (neurons, muscles, glands).

brain mapping: A neuroscience technique of measuring electrical activity representing brain activation along neural pathways, using electroencephalographic (EEG) response over time. This technique allows scientists to track which parts of the brain are active when a person is processing information at various stages of information intake, patterning, storing, and retrieval. The levels of activation in particular brain regions are associated with the intensity of information processing.

Broca's language center: The brain's language-processing center for the motor control of speech. For more than 90 percent of people, Broca's language center is located in the left frontal lobe, near the hippocampus.

central nervous system: The portion of the nervous system consisting of the spinal cord and the brain.

cerebellar stimulation: A theory proposed for increasing development in the underdeveloped frontal lobes of some people with ADD or AD/HD. The theory holds that physical exercises that call on the balance and coordination centers in the cerebellum in the back of the brain will stimulate the frontal lobes. The theory is based on the finding that almost half of the brain's neurons are found in the cerebellum and many of them have connections with the frontal lobes. It is proposed, although not proven, that increased cerebellar stimulation increases the stimulation and maturation of cortical neurons in the frontal lobes.

cerebellum: A large structure on the top of the brainstem resembling a cauliflower. This structure is very important in motor movement and motor-vestibular memory and learning.

cerebral cortex: The outermost layer of the cerebrum. The cortex mediates all conscious activity, including planning, problem solving, language, and speech. It is also involved in perception and voluntary motor activity.

chunking: A learning strategy enabling students to remember more content more successfully. Because the working memory's capacity for immediate recall is limited to five to nine unrelated items, categorizing and sorting information into that number of chunks rather than trying to memorize many discrete pieces of information helps students internalize the material more effectively.

cognition: The mental process by which we become aware of the world and use that information to solve problems and make sense out of the world. Cognition refers to thinking and all the mental processes related to thinking.

computerized tomography (CT scan, CAT scan): A neuroimaging scan that uses a narrow beam of X-rays to create brain images displayed as a series of brain slices. To produce the image, a computer program estimates how much of the beam is absorbed in small areas within cross sections of the brain.

decoding sensory input: How the brain receives and makes sense of incoming information. Any new information or learning must enter the brain through one or more of the senses (hearing, seeing/visualizing, touching, tasting, smelling, and emotionally feeling). First, the information is decoded by the sense's specific sensory receptors in the body. From there the information travels through the nerves in the skin or body to the spinal cord and up through the reticular activating system to the specialized part of the brain that interprets (decodes) the input from the particular senses.

dendrite food: A nickname for an activity in which students summarize and record new information in their own words. This phrase refers to the fact that new learning, when physically established in the brain, is accompanied by the growth of more connections between nerve cells, called dendrites.

dendrites: Branched protoplasmic extensions that sprout from the arms (axons) or the cell bodies of neurons. Dendrites conduct electrical impulses toward the neighboring neurons. A single nerve may possess many dendrites. Dendrites increase in size and number in response to learned skills, experience, and information storage. New dendrites grow as branches from frequently activated neurons. Proteins called neurotrophins stimulate this dendrite growth.

dopamine: A neurotransmitter most associated with attention, decision making, executive function, and reward-stimulated learning. Neuroimaging has found that dopamine release increases in response to rewards and positive experiences. Scans reveal greater dopamine release while subjects are playing, laughing, exercising, and receiving acknowledgment for achievement.

EEG (electroencephalography): The neurophysiologic measurement of the electrical activity occurring from transmissions between neurons in the cerebral cortex.

endorphins: Peptide hormones that bind to opiate receptors found mainly in the brain. When endorphins activate these receptors, the effect may naturally mimic the opiate (narcotic) effect of reducing the sensation of pain and increasing pleasant emotions. Increased endorphin release is associated with pleasurable activity and exercise.

episodic memory: The "autobiographical" memory; that is, the explicit memory of events such as time, place, and associated emotions that occur together. These are usually associated with single exposures to an experience or life episode that are later recalled in multisensory detail.

event memories: Memories tied to specific emotionally or physically charged events (strong sensory input). Memory theory suggests that memory-provoking or dramatic events can be linked to academic information to increase the emotional significance of the information and thereby increase its memory storage. Recalling the associated emotionally significant event with which academic information is connected may prompt subsequent recollection of the academic material when the event is recalled.

executive function: Cognitive processing of information that takes place in areas in the left frontal lobe and prefrontal cortex that exercise conscious control over one's emotions and thoughts. This control allows patterned information to be used for organizing, analyzing, sorting, connecting, planning, prioritizing, sequencing, self-monitoring, self-correcting, assessment, abstractions, problem solving, attention focusing, and linking information to appropriate actions.

flashbulb memories: Memories of highly significant emotional events that therefore may be recalled in great detail. These personal events result in powerful associative memories, such as what we were doing at the time we heard or saw the event. Critics of this theory contend that flashbulb memories are no more likely to be remembered than ordinary memories but are more vividly recalled because people discuss (review) these significant events more frequently.

frontal lobes: The parts of the brain containing the centers of executive function that organize and arrange information and coordinate the production of language and the focusing of attention.

functional brain imaging (neuroimaging): The use of techniques to directly or indirectly demonstrate the structure, function, or biochemical status of the brain. Whereas *structural* imaging reveals the overall structure of the brain, *functional* neuroimaging provides visualization of the processing of sensory information coming to the brain and of commands going from the brain to the body. This processing is visualized directly as areas of the brain "light up" through increased metabolism, blood flow, oxygen use, or glucose uptake. Functional brain imaging reveals neural activity in particular brain regions as the brain performs discrete cognitive tasks.

functional magnetic resonance imaging (fMRI): A type of functional brain imaging that uses the paramagnetic properties of oxygen-carrying hemoglobin in the blood to demonstrate which brain structures are activated and to what degree during various performance and cognitive activities. Most fMRI research has subjects scanned while they are exposed to visual, auditory, or tactile stimuli and then reveals the brain structures that are activated by these experiences.

glia: Specialized cells that nourish, support, and complement the activity of neurons in the brain. Actrocytes are the most common and appear to play a key role in regulating the amount of neurotransmitter in the synapse by taking up excess neurotransmitter. Oligodendrocytes are glia that specialize to form the myelin sheath around many axonal projections.

gray matter: The nerve cell bodies and dendrites of the brain and spinal cord, which are a brownish-gray color (in contrast to *white matter*, which is primarily composed of supportive tissue).

hippocampus: A ridge in the floor of each lateral ventricle of the brain that consists mainly of gray matter and that has a major role in learning, memory, and emotional regulation. The hippocampus takes sensory inputs and integrates them with relational or associational patterns, thereby binding the separate aspects of the experience into storable patterns of relational memories.

homeostasis: The tendency of a physiological system (i.e., a neuron, a neural system, or the body as a whole) to maintain its internal environment in a stable equilibrium.

hypothalamus: The part of the brain that lies below the thalamus and regulates body temperature, certain metabolic processes, and other autonomic activities that maintain the body at homeostasis (steady physiological state). The hypothalamus consists of a group of important nuclei that mediate many important functions. The hypothalamic nuclei are involved in regulating many of the body's internal organs via hormonal communication. The hypothalamus is a key part of the hypothalamic-pituitary-adrenal (HPA) axis that is so important in the stress response.

limbic system: A group of interconnected deep brain structures involved in olfaction (smell), emotion, motivation, behavior, and various autonomic functions. Included in the limbic system are the thalamus, the amygdala, the hippocampus, and portions of the frontal and temporal lobes. If the limbic system becomes overstimulated by stress-provoking emotion (seen as very high metabolic activity lighting up those brain areas), the information taught at that time will be poorly transmitted or poorly stored in the long-term memory centers.

medial temporal lobe (MTL): The region on the inner side of each temporal lobe that connects with the prefrontal cortex in a circuit. The MTL binds the separate elements of an experience into an integrated memory. This area of the brain includes several areas that are crucial for new memory formation, including the hippocampus.

metabolic hyperstimulation: The increased metabolism (biologic use) of oxygen or glucose to fuel nerve cells. When the limbic system, particularly the amygdala, is hyperstimulated by high stress, it becomes flooded by so much neural metabolic activity that new information cannot pass through it to memory storage and reasoning parts of the brain.

metacognition: Knowledge about one's own information processing and strategies that influence one's learning. After a lesson or an assessment, prompting students to reflect on the successful learning strategies that they used can help reinforce effective strategies and optimize future learning.

myelin: Fat-protein layers of insulation that surround the axons of many neurons. Myelin increases the speed of connections between brain regions, resulting in more efficient information access and retrieval.

neuronal circuits: Electrochemical connections through which neurons send coded communications to one another. When specific patterns of stimulation between the same group of neurons are stimulated repeatedly, their connecting circuit becomes more developed and more accessible to efficient stimulation and response. This is where practice (repeated stimulation of grouped neuronal connections in neuronal circuits) results in more successful recall.

neurons: Specialized cells in the brain and throughout the nervous system that conduct electrical impulses to, from, and within the brain. Neurons are composed of a main cell body, a single axon for outgoing electrical signals, and a varying number of dendrites for incoming signals in electrical form.

neurotransmitters: Brain proteins that transport information across synapses. Neurotransmitters are released by the electrical impulses on one side of the synapse to then float across the synaptic gap carrying the information with them to stimulate the next nerve ending in the pathway. Once the neurotransmitter is taken up by the next nerve ending, the electric impulse is reactivated to travel along to the next nerve. Neurotransmitters in the brain include serotonin, tryptophan, acetylcholine, dopamine, and others. When neurotransmitters are depleted by too much information traveling through a nerve circuit without a break, the speed of transmission along the nerve slows down to a less-efficient level.

neurotrophins (nerve growth factor): Proteins that stimulate growth of nerve cells. During sleep, neurotrophins are released in greater amounts, and there is an associated increase in the formation of new dendrites branching between neurons.

nucleus accumbens: A brain region above the brainstem involved in functions ranging from motivation and reward to feeding and drug addiction.

occipital lobes (visual memory areas): Posterior lobes of the brain that process optical input, among other functions.

parietal lobes: Lobes on each side of the brain that process sensory data, among other functions.

patterning: The process whereby the brain perceives sensory data and generates patterns by relating new with previously learned material or by chunking material into pattern systems that it has used before. Education is about increasing the patterns that students can use, recognize, and communicate. As the ability to see and work with patterns expands, the executive functions are enhanced. Whenever new material is presented in such a way that students see relationships, they can generate greater brain cell activity (formation of new neural connections) and achieve more successful patterns for long-term memory storage and retrieval.

plasticity: The brain's ability to change structurally and functionally as a result of learning and experience. This plasticity results in increased neuronal growth associated with enriched, stimulating environments and activities. Dendrite formation and dendrite and neuron destruction (pruning) allow the brain to reshape and reorganize the networks of dendrite-neuron connections in response to increased or decreased use of these pathways.

positron emission tomography (PET): A neuroimaging technique that produces a three-dimensional image of functional processes in the body based on the detection of radiation from the emission of *positrons* (tiny particles emitted from a radioactive substance administered to the subject in combination with glucose). As the subject engages in various cognitive activities, the scan records the rate at which specific regions of the brain use the glucose. These recordings are used to produce maps of areas of high brain activity with particular cognitive functions. The biggest drawback of PET scanning is that because the radioactivity decays rapidly, it is limited to monitoring short tasks. Newer fMRI technology does not have this same time limitation and has become the preferred functional imaging technique in learning research.

prefrontal cortex: The front part of the brain's frontal lobes. The prefrontal cortex responds to event and memory processing.

pruning: The process of destroying unused neurons. A baby's brain overproduces brain cells (neurons) and connections between brain cells (synapses) and then starts pruning them back around the age of 3. The second wave of synapse formation occurs just before puberty and is followed by another phase of pruning. Pruning allows the brain to consolidate learning by pruning away unused neurons and synapses and wrapping white matter (myelin) around the more frequently used neuronal networks to stabilize and strengthen them.

quantitative electroencephalography (qEEG): A technique that provides brain-mapping data based on the very precise localization of brain wave patterns coming from the parts of the brain actively engaged in the processing of information. Quantitative EEG uses digital technology to record electrical patterns at the surface of the scalp that represent cortical electrical activity or brain waves. "Functional" qEEG testing adds recording to evaluate the brain's responses to reading, listening, math, or other demands and to provide visual summaries in topographic maps.

reinforcement learning theories: Theories based on the assumption that the brain finds some states of stimulation to be more desirable than others and makes associations between specific cues and these desirable states or goals.

relational memory: A form of memory that takes place when students learn something that adds to what they have already mastered; the students engage or expand on "maps" already present in the brain.

reticular activating system (RAS): A lower part of the posterior brain that filters all incoming stimuli and makes the "decision" as to what people attend to or ignore. The RAS alerts the brain to sensory input that sense receptors in the body send up the spinal cord. The main categories that focus the attention of the RAS include physical need, choice, and novelty.

rote memory: A type of memorization that is the most commonly required memory task for students in elementary and secondary school. This type of learning involves memorizing, and soon forgetting, facts that are often of little primary interest or emotional value to the student, such as a list of words. Facts that are memorized by rehearsing them over and over and that don't have obvious or engaging patterns or connections are being processed by rote memory. With nothing to give them context or relationship to one another or to the students' lives, these facts are stored in more remote areas of the brain. These isolated bits are more difficult to locate and retrieve later because there are fewer nerve pathways leading to these remote storage systems.

serotonin: A neurotransmitter used to carry messages between neurons. Too little serotonin may be a cause of depression. Dendritic branching is enhanced by the serotonin secreted by the brain predominantly between the sixth and the eighth hour of sleep (non-REM).

somatosensory cortexes: Areas—one in each parietal brain lobe—where input from each individual sense (hearing, touch, taste, vision, and smell) is ultimately processed.

survival level of attention: The lowest level of attention needed to process and retain information. Too much stress can push students into survival mode—for example, when they feel confused and overwhelmed by a classroom experience to the degree that they cannot connect with, focus on, and create patterns and meaning from a lesson's sensory input data.

synapses: The specialized gaps between two neurons that are involved in information transfer. Neurotransmitters carry information across the space separating the axon extensions of one neuron from the dendrite that leads to the next neuron in the pathway. Before and after crossing the synapse as a chemical message, information is carried in an electrical state when it travels down the nerve.

temporal lobes: Lobes on the sides of the brain that process auditory and verbal input, language and phonetic discrimination, mood stability through projection fibers leading to the limbic system, and learning.

thalamus: The part of the brain that processes sensory input and determines whether it will be kept in the temporary awareness portion of memory or be given more sustained attention. If it is processed as more than transient awareness, sensory input is passed along through the thalamus to the neurons in the amygdala.

working memory: Short-term memory that can hold and manipulate information for use in the immediate future. Information is held in working memory for only about a minute. The memory span of young adults (less in children and older adults) is approximately seven elements for digits, six for letters, and five for words.

zone of proximal development (ZPD): Lev Vygotsky's "zone of readiness," including the actions or topics a student is ready to learn. The zone of proximal development is the gap between a learner's current or actual level of development and his or her potential level of development. This is the set of knowledge that the learner does not yet understand but has the ability to learn with guidance.

BIBLIOGRAPHY

Affleck, J., Madge, S., Adams, A., & Lowenbraun, S. (1988). Integrated class room versus resource model: Academic viability and effectiveness. *Exceptional Children, 54*(4), 339–348.

Anderson, A., & Sobel, N. (2003). Dissociating intensity from valence as sensory inputs into emotion. *Neuron, 39*(4), 581–583.

Anderson, R. C. (1999). Research foundations to support wide reading. In Consortium on Reading Excellence (CORE), *Reading research anthology: The why of reading instruction* (pp. 14–21). Novato, CA: Arena Press.

Arntz, W. (Producer/Director), Chasse, B. (Producer/Director), & Vicente, M. (Director). (2004). *What the bleep do we know!?* [Motion picture]. United States: Lord of the Wind Film.

Ashby, C. R., Thanos, P. K., Katana, J. M., Michaelides, E. L., Gardner, C. A., & Heidbreder, N. D. (1999). The selective dopamine antagonist. *Pharmacology, Biochemistry & Behavior, 81*(1), 190–197.

Baddeley, A. D., & Andrade, J. (2000). Working memory and the vividness of imagery. *Journal of Experimental Psychology: General, 129*(1), 126–145.

Bangert-Drowns, R. L., Kulik, C. C., Kulik, J. A., & Morgan, M. (1991). The instructional effect of feedback in test-like events. *Review of Educational Research, 61*(2), 213–238.

Bartzokis, G., Beckson, M., Lu, P., Nuechterlein, K., Edwards, N., & Mintz, J. (2001). Age-related changes in frontal and temporal lobe volumes in men. *Arch. Gen. Psychiatry, 58*, 461–465.

Baynes, K., Eliassen, J. C., Lutsep, H. L., & Gazzaniga, M. S. (1998). Modular organization of cognitive systems masked by interhemispheric integration. *Science, 280*(5365), 902–905.

Bender, W. N. (2002). *Differentiating instruction for students with learning disabilities.* Thousand Oaks, CA: Corwin Press.

Bennett, C., & Baird, A. (2005). Anatomical changes in the emerging adult brain: A voxel-based morphometry study. *Hum. Brain Mapp., 27*(9), 766–777.

Black, J. E., Isaacs, K. R., Anderson, B. J., Alcantara, A. A., & Greenough, W. T. (1990). Learning causes synaptogenesis in cerebral cortex of adult rats.

Proceedings of the National Academy of Sciences of the United States of America, 87, 5568–5572.

Black, K. J., Hershey, T., Koller, J. M., Videen, T. O., Mintun, M. A., Price, J. L., et al. (2002). A possible substrate for dopamine-related changes in mood and behavior: Prefrontal and limbic effects of a D3-preferring dopamine agonist. *Proceedings of the National Academy of Sciences of the United States of America, 99*(26), 17113–17118.

Bliss, T. V. P., & Collingridge, G. L. (1993). A synaptic model of memory: Long-term potentiation in the hippocampus. *Nature, 361*(6407), 31–39.

Bloom, B. S. (1956). *Taxonomy of educational objectives, handbook I: Cognitive domain.* New York: Longman.

Boggiano, A. (1993). Use of techniques promoting students' self-determination: Effects on students' analytic problem-solving skills. *Motivation and Emotion, 17,* 319–336.

Brembs, B., Lorenzetti, F. D., Reyes, F. D., Baxter, D. A., & Byrne, J. H. (2002). Operant reward learning in *aplysia*: Neuronal correlates and mechanisms. *Science, 296,* 1706–1709.

Brooks, J. G., & Brooks, M. G. (1993). *The case for constructivist classrooms.* Alexandria, VA: Association for Supervision and Curriculum Development.

Brophy, J. (1981). Teacher praise: A functional analysis. *Review of Educational Research, 51,* 5–32.

Bull, B. L., & Wittrock, M. C. (1973). Imagery in the learning of verbal definitions. *British Journal of Educational Psychology, 43,* 289–293.

Caine, R. N., & Caine, G. (1994). *Making connections: Teaching and the human brain.* Menlo Park, CA: Addison-Wesley.

Calonico, J., & Calonico, B. (1972). Classroom interaction: A sociological approach. *Journal of Educational Research, 66*(4), 165–169.

Calvin, W., & Bickerton, D. (2000). *Lingua ex machina: Reconciling Darwin and Chomsky with the human brain.* Cambridge, MA: The MIT Press.

Cameron, J., & Pierce, W. D. (1994). Reinforcement, reward, and intrinsic motivation: A meta-analysis. *Review of Educational Research, 64*(3), 363–433.

Campbell, L., Campbell, B., & Dickinson, D. (1998). *Teaching and learning through multiple intelligences* (2nd ed.). Boston: Allyn and Bacon.

Cardinal, R. N., Winstanley, C. A., Robbins, T. W., & Everitt, B. J. (2004, June). Limbic corticostriatal systems and delayed reinforcement. *Annals of the New York Academy of Sciences, 1021,* 33–50.

Checkley, K. (1997). The first seven . . . and the eighth: A conversation with Howard Gardner. *Educational Leadership, 55*(1), 8–13.

Chomsky, N., & Halle, M. (1991). *The sound pattern of English* (reprint ed.). Cambridge, MA: The MIT Press.

Christianson, S-A. (1992). Emotional stress and eyewitness memory: A critical review. *Psychological Bulletin, 112*(2), 284–309.

Chugani, H. T. (1996). Neuroimaging of developmental nonlinearity and developmental pathologies. In R. W. Thatcher, G. R. Lyon, G. Rumsby, & K. Krasnegor (Eds.), *Developmental neuroimaging: Mapping the development of brain and behavior* (pp. 18/–195). San Diego, CA: Academic Press.

Chugani, H. T. (1998a). Biological basis of emotions: Brain systems and brain development. *Pediatrics, 102*(5), 1225–1229.

Chugani, H. T. (1998b). A critical period of brain development: Studies of cerebral glucose utilization with PET. *Preventive Medicine, 27*(2), 184–188.

Chugani, H. T., & Phelps, M. E. (1991). Imaging human brain development with positron emission tomography. *Journal of Nuclear Medicine, 32*(1), 23–26.

Chugani, H. T., Phelps, M. E., & Mazziotta, J. C. (1987). Positron emission tomography study of human brain function development. *Annals of Neurology, 22,* 487–497.

Cohen, E. G. (1986). *Designing groupwork: Strategies for the heterogeneous classroom.* New York: Teachers College Press.

Cooper, J. R., Bloom, F. E., & Roth, R. H. (1996). *The biochemical basis of neuropharmacology* (7th ed.). New York: Oxford University Press.

Coward, L. A. (1990). *Pattern thinking.* New York: Praeger Publishers.

Depue, R. A., & Collins, P. F. (1999). Neurobiology of the structure of personality: Dopamine, facilitation of incentive motivation, and extraversion. *Behavioral & Brain Sciences, 22*(3), 491–517.

Deschenes, C. (1994). *Adapting curriculum and instruction in inclusive classrooms: A teacher's desk reference.* Bloomington, IN: Institute for the Study of Developmental Disabilities.

Diamond, M., & Hopson, J. (1999). *Magic trees of the mind: How to nurture your child's intelligence, creativity, and healthy emotions from birth through adolescence.* New York: Plume.

Dozier, R. W., Jr. (1998). *Fear itself: The origin and nature of the powerful emotion that shapes our lives and our world.* New York: Thomas Dunne Books.

Draganski, B., Gaser, C., Busch, V., & Schuierer, G. (2004). Neuroplasticity: Changes in grey matter induced by training. *Nature, 427,* 311–312.

Dunston, P. J. (1992). A critique of graphic organizer research. *Reading Research and Instruction, 31*(2), 57–65.

Eich, E. (1995). Searching for mood dependent memory. *Psychological Science, 6*(2), 67–75.

Eliassen, J., Souza, T., & Sanes, J. (2003). Experience-dependent activation patterns in human brain during visual-motor associative learning. *The Journal of Neuroscience, 23*(33), 10540–10547.

Epstein, H. (1978). Growth spurts during brain development: Implications for educational policy and practice. In J. Chall & A. W. Mirsky (Eds.), *Education and the brain* (pp. 343–370). Chicago: University of Chicago Press.

Fiedorowicz, C. (1999, November). Neurobiological basis of learning disabilities: An overview. *Linking Research to Policy and Practice: Second Canadian Forum.*

Proceedings of the Canadian Child Care Federation and Canadian School Boards Association's Second Canadian Forum, Ottawa, Canada.

Fuchs, J. L., Montemayor, M., & Greenough, W. T. (1990). Effect of environmental complexity on size of the superior colliculus. *Behavioral and Neural Biology, 54*(2), 198–203.

Gabriel, J. (2001, August). New terrain: Mapping the human brain. Available: www.brainconnection.com/content/158_1

Galvan, A., Hare, T., Parra, C., Penn, J., Voss, H., Glover, G., et al. (2006). Earlier development of the accumbens relative to orbitofrontal cortex might underlie risk-taking behavior in adolescents. *J. Neurosci., 26*(25), 6885–6892.

Gardner, H. (1991). *The unschooled mind: How children think and how schools should teach.* New York: BasicBooks.

Gardner, H. (1999). *Intelligence reframed: Multiple intelligences for the 21st century.* New York: BasicBooks.

Gerlic, I., & Jausovec, N. (1999). Multimedia: Differences in cognitive processes observed with EEG. *Educational Technology Research and Development, 47*(3), 5–14.

Giedd, J. N., Blumenthal, J., Jeffries, N. O., Castellanos, F. X., Liu, H., Zijdenbos, A., et al. (1999). Brain development during childhood and adolescence: A longitudinal MRI study. *Nature Neuroscience, 2*(10), 861–863.

Gogtay, N., Giedd, J. N., Lusk, L., Hayashi, K. M., Greenstein, D., Vaituzis, A. C., et al. (2004). Dynamic mapping of human cortical development during childhood through early adulthood. *Proceedings of the National Academy of Sciences of the United States of America, 101*(21), 8174–8179.

Goldberg, R., Higgins, E., & Herman, K. (2003). Predictors of success in individuals with learning disability: Results from a twenty-year longitudinal study. *Learning Disabilities Research & Practice, 18*(4), 222–236.

Goleman, D. (1995). *Emotional intelligence.* New York: Bantam Books.

Grabowski, T. J., Damasio, H., & Damasio, A. R. (1998). Premotor and prefrontal correlates of category-related lexical retrieval. *NeuroImage, 7*(3), 232–243.

Greenough, W. T., & Anderson, B. J. (1991). Cerebellar synaptic plasticity—Relation to learning versus neural activity. *Annals of the New York Academy of Sciences, 627,* 231–247.

Greenough, W. T., Withers, G., & Anderson, B. J. (1992). Experience-dependent synaptogenesis as a plausible memory mechanism. In I. Gormezano & E. A. Wasserman (Eds.), *Learning and memory: The behavioral and biological substrates* (pp. 209–229). Hillsdale, NJ: Lawrence Erlbaum Associates.

Hart, J., Jr., & Gordon, B. (1992). Neural subsystems for object knowledge. *Nature, 359*(6390), 60–64.

Hewson, M. G., & Hewson, P. W. (1983). Effect of instruction using students' prior knowledge and conceptual change strategies on science learning. *Journal of Research in Science Teaching, 20,* 721–743.

Hoyert, D., Heron, M., Murphy, S., & Kung, H. (2006). Deaths: Final data for 2003. *Natl Vital Stat Rep., 54*(13), 1–120.

Huttenlocher, P. R., & Dabholkar, A. S. (1997). Regional differences in synaptogenesis in human cerebral cortex. *Journal of Comparative Neurology, 387,* 167–178.

Iidaka, T., Anderson, N., Kapur, S., Cabeza, R., & Craik F. (2000). The effect of divided attention on encoding and retrieval in episodic memory revealed by positron emission tomography. *Journal of Cognitive Neuroscience, 12*(2), 267–280.

Introini-Collison, I. B., McGaugh, J. L., Nagahara, A. H., Cahill, L., Brioni, J. D., & Castellano, C. (1990). Involvement of the amygdala in neuromodulatory influences on memory storage. *Neuroscience and Biobehavioral Reviews, 14*(4), 425–431.

Introini-Collison, I. B., Miyazaki, B., & McGaugh, J. L. (1991). Involvement of the amygdala in the memory-enhancing effects of clenbuterol. *Psychopharmacology, 104*(4), 541–544.

Jeffries, K. J., Fritz, J. B., & Braun, A. R. (2003). Words in melody: An H2150 PET study of brain activation during singing and speaking. *NeuroReport, 14*(5), 749–754.

Jenkins, R. (2001). *Churchill: A biography.* New York: Farrar, Straus and Giroux.

Jensen, E. (1998). *Teaching with the brain in mind.* Alexandria, VA: Association for Supervision and Curriculum Development.

Jernigan, T. L., & Tallal, P. (1990). Late childhood changes in brain morphology observable with MRI. *Developmental Medicine and Child Neurology, 32*(5), 379–385.

Johnson, D., & Johnson, R. (1989). Cooperative learning: What special educators need to know. *The Pointer, 33,* 5–10.

Johnson D., & Johnson, R. (1992). Encouraging thinking through constructive controversy. In N. Davidson & T. Worsham (Eds.), *Enhancing thinking through cooperative learning* (pp. 120–137). New York: Teachers College Press.

Kagan, S., & Kagan, M. (1998). *Multiple intelligences: The complete MI book.* San Clemente, CA: Kagan Cooperative Learning.

Katz, L., & Smith, M. (1974). Laterality and reading proficiency. *Neuropsychologia, 12,* 131–139.

Kempermann, G., & Kuhn, H. G. (1997). More hippocampal neurons in adult mice living in an enriched environment. *Nature, 386*(6624), 493–495.

Kinomura, L., Larsson, J., Gulyas, A., & Roland, L. (1996). Activation by attention of the human reticular formation and thalamic intralaminar nuclei. *Science, 271*(5248), 512–514.

Kohn, A. (2004, Sept. 15). The cult of rigor and the loss of joy. *Education Week,* pp. 6–8.

Krashen, S. D. (1987). *Principles and practice in second language acquisition.* London: Prentice-Hall International.

Kumar, D. D. (1991). A meta-analysis of the relationship between science instruction and student engagement. *Educational Review, 43*(1), 40–66.

Leopold, W. (1949). *Speech development of a bilingual child, a linguist's record (Vol. 4).* Evanston, IL: Northwestern University Press.

Luna, B., Thulborn, K., Munoz, D., Merriam, E., Garver, K., Minshew, N., et al. (2001). Maturation of widely distributed brain function subserves cognitive development. *Neuroimage, 13*(5), 786–793.

Malone, T. (1981). What makes computer games fun? *ACM SIGSOC Bulletin, 13*(2–3), 143.

Marcason, W. (2005). Can dietary intervention play a part in the treatment of attention deficit and hyperactivity disorder? *Journal of the American Dietetic Association, 105*(7), 1161–1162.

Margalit, M., & Idan, O. (2004). Resilience and hope theory: An expanded paradigm for learning disabilities research. *Thalamus, 22*(1), 58–65.

Marshall, J., Caplan, D., & Holmes, J. (1975). The measure of laterality. *Neuropsychologia, 13*, 315–321.

Martin, R. C. (1993). Short-term memory and sentence processing: Evidence from neuropsychology. *Memory and Cognition, 21*(2), 173–183.

Martin, S. J., & Morris, R. G. M. (2002). New life in an old idea: The synaptic plasticity and memory hypothesis revisited. *Hippocampus, 12*, 609–636.

McClure, S., Yoir, M., & Montague, P. (2004). The neural substrates of reward processing in humans: The modern role of fMRI. *Neuroscientist, 10*(3), 260–268.

McCourt, F. (2005). *Teacher man: A memoir.* New York: Scribner.

McGregor, G., & Vogelsberg, R. (1998). *Inclusive schooling practices pedagogical and research foundations: A synthesis of the literature that informs best practices about inclusive schooling.* Baltimore: Paul H. Brookes Publishing.

McGuire, J. M. (1998). Educational accommodations: A university administrator's view. In M. Gordon & S. Keiser (Eds.), *Accommodations in higher education under the Americans with Disabilities Act (ADA)* (pp. 20–45). New York: Guilford Press.

Meece, J. L., Wigfield, A., & Eccles, J. S. (1990). Predictors of math anxiety and its influence on young adolescents' course enrollment intentions and performance in mathematics. *Journal of Educational Psychology, 8*, 60–70.

Meltzer, L., Reddy, R., Pollica, L. S., Roditi, B., Sayer, J., & Theokas, C. (2004). Positive and negative self-perceptions: Is there a cyclical relationship between teachers' and students' perceptions of effort, strategy use, and academic performance? *Learning Disabilities Research & Practice, 19*(1), 33–44.

Meltzer, L. J., Roditi, B., & Stein, J. (2002, January). Preserving process learning in the era of high-stakes testing: Research-based strategies for teaching test-taking. *MASCD Review*, 23–30.

Montague, P., Hyman, S., & Cohen, J. (2004). Computational roles for dopamine in behavioral control. *Nature, 431*, 760–767.

Nader, M. A., Daunais, J. B., Moore, T., Nader, S. H., Moore, R. J., Smith, H. R., et al. (2002). Effects of cocaine self-administration on striatal dopamine systems in rhesus monkeys: Initial and chronic exposure. *Neuropsychopharmacology, 27*(1), 35–46.

Nunley, K. F. (2002). Active research leads to active classrooms. *Principal Leadership, 2*(7), 53–61.

Nuthall, G. (1999). The way students learn: Acquiring knowledge from an integrated science and social studies unit. *Elementary School Journal, 99*(4), 303–341.

O'Grady, W., Dobrovolsky, M., & Aronoff, M. (Eds.). (1997). *Contemporary linguistics: An introduction* (3rd ed.). New York: St. Martin's Press.

Ojemann, G. A. (1991). Cortical organization of language and verbal memory based on intraoperative investigation. In D. Ottoson, *Progress in sensory physiology* (Vol. 12) (pp. 193–230). New York: Springer-Verlag.

Olds, J. (1992). Mapping the mind onto the brain. In F. Worden, J. Swazcy, & G. Adelman, *The neurosciences, paths of discovery* (pp. 61–65). Boston: Birkhauser.

Olff, M. (1999). Stress, depression and immunity: The role of defense and coping styles. *Psychiatry Research, 85*(1), 7–15.

Olsen, K. (1995). *Science continuum of concepts for grades K–6.* Kent, WA: Center for the Future of Public Education.

Olton, D. S. (1984). Comparative analysis of episodic memory. *Behavioral & Brain Sciences, 7,* 250–251.

Olwocki, G., & Goodman, Y. (2002). *Kidwatching: Documenting children's literacy development.* Portsmouth, NH: Heinemann.

Pastor, P. N., & Reuben, C. A. (2002, May). Attention deficit disorder and learning disability: United States, 1997–98. National Center for Health Statistics. *Vital and Heath Statistics, 10*(206). Available: www.cdc.gov/nchs/data/series /sr_10/sr10_206.pdf

Patrick, B. C., Skinner, E. A., & Connell, J. P. (1993). What motivates children's behavior and emotion? Joint effects of perceived control and autonomy in the academic domain. *Journal of Personality and Social Psychology, 65,* 781–791.

Pawlak, R., Magarinos, A. M., Melchor, J., McEwen, B., & Strickland, S. (2003, February). Tissue plasminogen activator in the amygdala is critical for stress-induced anxiety-like behavior. *Nature Neuroscience, 6*(2), 168–174.

Perry, B. D., Pollard, R. A., Blakley, T. L., Baker, W. L., & Vigilante, D. (1995). Childhood trauma, the neurobiology of adaptation, and "use-dependent" development of the brain: How "states" become "traits." *Infant Mental Health Journal, 16*(4), 271–291.

Piaget, J. (1971). *Biology and knowledge.* Chicago: University of Chicago Press.

Poldrack, R., Clark, J., Pare-Blagoev, E., Shohamy, D., Myano, J., Myers, C., et al. (2001). Interactive memory systems in the human brain. *Nature, 414,* 546–550.

Pressley, M., McDaniel, M. A., Turner, J. E., Wood, E., & Maheen, A. (1987). Generation and precision of elaboration: Effects on intentional and incidental learning. *Journal of Experimental Psychology/Learning, Memory, and Cognition, 13*(2), 291–300.

Pressley, M., Symons, S., McDaniel, M., Snyder, B. L., & Turnure, J. E. (1988). Elaborative interrogation facilitates acquisition of confusing facts. *Journal of Educational Psychology, 80*(3), 268–278.

Pressley, M., Wood, E., Woloshyn, V., Martin, V., King, A., & Menke, D. (1992). Encouraging mindful use of prior knowledge: Attempting to construct explanatory answers facilitates learning. *Educational Psychologist, 27*(1), 91–109.

Pryor, M. L. (2003). *Effects of online inclusive teacher training on the attitudes and self-efficacy beliefs of general education teachers towards students with learning disabilities.* Dissertation, Columbia University Teachers College. Available: http://digitalcommons.libraries.columbia.edu/dissertations/AAI3080071/

Pulvirenti, L. (1992). Neural plasticity and memory: Towards an integrated view. *Functional Neurology, 7*(6), 481–490.

Ramey, C. (1996, Feb. 19). Your child's brain. *Newsweek,* p. 61.

Raskind, M., Goldberg, R., Higgins, E., & Herman, L. (1999). Patterns of change and predictors of success in individuals with learning disabilities: Results from a twenty-year longitudinal study. *Learning Disabilities Research & Practice, 14*(1), 37–49.

Redfield, D. L., & Rousseau, E. W. (1981). A meta-analysis of experimental research on teacher questioning behavior. *Review of Educational Research, 51*(2), 237–245.

Reeve, J. (1996). The interest-enjoyment distinction in intrinsic motivation. *Motivation and Emotion, 13,* 83–103.

Reeve, J., & Bolt, E. (1999, September). Student-centered classrooms and the teaching styles they exhibit. *The Journal of Educational Psychology, 91*(3), 537–548.

Robinson, D. H., & Kiewra, K. A. (1996). Visual argument: Graphic organizers are superior to outlines in improving learning from text. *Journal of Educational Psychology, 87*(3), 455–467.

Rossi, E. L., & Nimmons, D. (1991). *The 20-minute break: Reduce stress, maximize performance, and improve health and emotional well-being using the new science of ultradian rhythms.* Los Angeles: Tarcher.

Routman, R. (2000). *Conversations: Strategies for teaching, learning, and evaluating.* Portsmouth, NH: Heinemann.

Schmuck, R. A., & Schmuck, P. A. (1983). *Group processes in the classroom.* Dubuque, IA: William C. Brown.

Schneider, W. (1993). Varieties of working memory as seen in biology and in connectionist/control architectures. *Memory and Cognition, 21*(2), 184–192.

Schneider, W., & Chein, J. M. (2003). Controlled and automatic processing: Behavior, theory, and biological mechanisms. *Cognitive Science, 27,* 525–559.

Seeman, P. (1999). Images in neuroscience. Brain development, X: Pruning during development. *American Journal of Psychiatry, 156,* 168.

Sethi, A., & Mischel, W. (2000). The role of strategic attention deployment in development of self-regulation: Predicting preschoolers' delay of gratification from mother-toddler interactions. *Developmental Psychology, 36*(6), 767–777.

Shadmehr, R., & Holcomb, H. H. (1997). Neural correlates of motor memory consolidation. *Science, 277*(5327), 821–825.

Shanahan, T. (1997). Reading-writing relationships, thematic units, inquiry learning: In pursuit of effective integrated instruction. *The Reading Teacher, 51*, 12–19.

Shaw, P., Greenstein, D., Lerch, J., Clasen, L., Lenroot, R., Gogtay, N., et al. (2006). Intellectual ability and cortical development in children and adolescents. *Nature, 440*(30), 676–679.

Sirevaag, A. M., & Greenough, W. T. (1991). Plasticity of GFAP-immunoreactive astrocyte size and number in visual cortex of rats reared in complex environments. *Brain Research, 540*(1–2), 273–278.

Sousa, D. (2000). *How the brain learns: A classroom teacher's guide.* Thousand Oaks, CA: Corwin Press.

Sowell, E. R., Peterson, B. S., & Thompson, P. M. (2003). Mapping cortical change across the human life span. *Nature Neuroscience 6*(3), 309–315.

Squire, L. R. (1992). Memory and the hippocampus: A synthesis from findings with rats, monkeys, and humans. *Psychological Review, 99*(2), 195–231.

Stahl, N. A., Simpson, M. L., & Hayes, C. G. (1992). Ten recommendations from research for teaching high-risk college students. *Journal of Developmental Education, 16*(1), 2–10.

Stainback, W., & Stainback, S. (1991). A rationale for integration and restructuring: A synopsis. In J. W. Lloyd, N. N. Singh, & A. C. Repp (Eds.), *The regular education initiative: Alternative perspectives on concepts, issues, and models* (pp. 225–239). Belmont, CA: Thomson Brooks/Cole.

Stainback, S., Stainback, W., & Forest, M. (1989). *Educating all students in the mainstream of regular education.* Baltimore: Paul H. Brookes Publishing.

Stein, J., & Talcott, J. (1999). Impaired neuronal timing in developmental dyslexia—The magnocellular hypothesis. *Dyslexia, 5*, 59–77.

Thesen, T., Jonas, V., Calvert, G., & Österbauer, R. (2004). Neuroimaging of multisensory processing in vision, audition, touch, and olfaction. *Cognitive Processing, 5*(2), 84–93.

Thompson, M., Vidal, C., Giedd, J., Dagger, P., Blumenthal, J., Niccolson, R., et al. (2001). Mapping adolescent brain change reveals dynamic wave of accelerated gray matter loss in very early-onset schizophrenia. *PNAS, 98*(20), 11650–11655.

Vallerand, R. J., Fortier, M. S., & Guay, F. (1997). Self-determination and persistence in a real-life setting: Toward a motivational model of high school dropout. *Journal of Personality and Social Psychology, 72*, 1161–1176.

Van Overwalle, F., & De Metsenaere, M. (1990). The effects of attribution-based intervention and study strategy training on academic achievement in college freshmen. *British Journal of Educational Psychology, 60*, 299–311.

Vermetten, Y. J., Vermunt, J. D., & Lodewijks, H. G. (1999). A longitudinal perspective on learning strategies in higher education: Different viewpoints towards development. *British Journal of Educational Psychology, 69,* 221–242.

Virtamo, J., Pietinen, P., Huttunen, J., Korhonen, P., Malila, N., Virtanen, M., et al. (2003). Incidence of cancer and mortality following alpha-tocopherol and beta-carotene supplementation: A postintervention follow-up. *Journal of the American Medical Association, 290*(4), 476–485.

Wagner, A., Schacter, D., Rotte, M., Koutstaal, W., Maril, A., Dale, A. M., et al. (1998). Building memories: Remembering and forgetting of verbal experiences as predicted by brain activity. *Science, 281,* 1185–1190.

Webb, D., & Webb, T. (1990). *Accelerated learning with music.* Norcross, GA: Accelerated Learning Systems.

Werner, E., & Smith, R. (1989). *Vulnerable but invincible: A longitudinal study of resilient children and youth.* New York: Adams, Bannister, and Cox.

Wiersma, U. J. C. (1992). The effects of extrinsic reward on intrinsic motivation: A meta-analysis. *Journal of Occupational and Organizational Psychology, 65,* 101–110.

Willis, J. (2006). *Research-based strategies to ignite student learning.* Alexandria, VA: Association for Supervision and Curriculum Development.

Wong, B., & Jones, W. (1982). Increasing metacomprehension in learning disabled and normally achieving students through self-questioning training. *Learning Disability Quarterly, 5,* 409–414.

Wunderlich, K., Bell, A., & Ford, A. (2005). Improving learning through understanding of brain science research. *Learning Abstracts, 8*(1), 41–43.

INDEX

Abecedarian Project, 108
abilities
  diversity of
    accommodating. *See* accommodations
    building acceptance of. *See* community building
    as normal, 6, 12–13
    and peer perception of LD students, 13, 34
    respect for, as hallmark of good teacher, 11–13
  identification of, 52–53
academic priming (lesson previewing), 29, 74
academic success, stereotypical, limited perspective of, 13
accommodations
  in assessments, 49
  discussing with students, 38
  physical, 22
  for report writing, 179, 182, 185–186
  for tests, 165, 168–169
acetylcholine, 71, 169
acting out, as stress reaction, 44
ADD (attention deficit disorder), definition of, 62. *See also* attention difficulties; attention disorders
AD/HD (attention deficit/hyperactivity disorder)
  attention-focusing devices, 69–70
  brain research on, 63–64, 69, 88–89
  definition of, 62, 63

goal-directed behavior. *See* goal-directed behavior
  growing brain pathways and, 68, 73, 103
  medications for, 105–106
  patterning for brain network alignment, 68–70
  self-concept, improving, 92–93
  and stress, 67, 69, 88
  and substance abuse, 76–77, 78, 103
  teaching strategies. *See* AD/HD teaching strategies
  in teenagers, 75–79
  therapies for, 103–106
AD/HD teaching strategies
  adapting whole-class lessons, 93–101
  class discussions, 98–100
  cooperative work groups, 86–88, 99–100
  dramatization, 100
  inclusiveness, 96–98
  interests of students, engaging, 81–83, 86–87, 96–100
  lesson assessment checklist, 101–102
  metacognition skills, 79, 83, 84
  motivational strategies
    positive reinforcement, 64–66, 68
    relevance, 67–68
  organizational skills, teaching, 85–86
  overview, 63–64
  patterning for brain network alignment, 68–70
  personalization, 100–101

AD/HD teaching strategies (*continued*)
   physical movement, 94–95
   presentations, 97
   promise of desired activity, 99
   to promote dopamine release, 73–75
   to promote goal-directed behavior,
      81–84
   to provoke interest, 67–68
   raising empathy for AD/HD students,
      88–93
   respect, 64–65
   sample lesson, 98–100
   sensory stimuli, 97–98
   success, building on, 68, 72, 79, 83,
      84–86, 106–107
   surprise and novelty, 71–72, 95–96, 98
   for teenagers, 78–79
   visualization, 100–101
affective filter. *See* information pathway in
   brain; limbic system
ALEKS (Assessment and Learning in
   Knowledge Spaces), 70, 163
Americana Experience (sample culminating activity), 145–146
American Colonial Settlements sample
   lesson plan, 98–100
amygdala
   in brain information pathway, 17–18,
      72
   disequilibrium-prompted curiosity
      and, 24
   emotional states and, 6, 18–19
   limbic system and, 18
   memory and, 116
   response to appropriate challenge,
      44–45
   reward behavior and, 71
   stress and, 43
analysis skills, teaching, 164–165
analytical learners. *See* sequential (analytical) learners
Assessment and Learning in Knowledge
   Spaces. *See* ALEKS
assessments
   accommodation of diversity in, 49
   of AD/HD students, 64–66
   of dramatizations, 133

   explaining to parents, 49
   formative, 31–32, 118–119
   of group work, 87
   rubric-based, 31
   in student-centered lessons, 129
   student participation in, 32
   teacher self-evaluations
      criteria for, 50, 174–175
      lesson success, 101–102
attention
   attention-focusing devices, 69–70,
      74–75
   levels of, 66–68
   nature of, 66
attention deficit disorder. *See* ADD
attention deficit/hyperactivity disorder.
   See AD/HD
attention difficulties
   physical accommodations for, 22
   as stress reaction, 44
attention disorders. *See also* ADD (attention deficit disorder); AD/HD (attention deficit/hyperactivity disorder)
   medications for, 105–106
   prevalence, 62
   therapies for, 103–105
auditory learners, review and reinforcement for, 156
automatic memory, 115–116
axons, 3, 19

Bake Sale (sample culminating activity),
   146–147
Black Star, Bright Dawn (novel), 139
bodily-kinesthetic intelligence, 55, 56,
   156
boredom, as stress reaction, 44
brain
   anatomy, 3
   information pathway in, 2–3, 17–20,
      60, 72
   pruning in, 20, 76, 152
   unconscious selection process for sen-
      sory input, 66
brain research. *See also* functional brain
   imaging
   on AD/HD, 63–64, 69, 88–89

brain hemisphere differentiation, 112–113

brain maturation, 76–77
on enrichment activities, 108–109
future directions in, 173–174
growing brain pathways, 20, 68, 73, 103, 108–109, 111, 151–152
importance of utilizing, 173–174
informing parents about, 47–48
and learning styles, 60
movement and learning, 94
overview of, 172–173
plasticity of brain, 80–81, 108–109, 152
teacher resources needed to study, 60–61
and teaching practice, impact on, 3, 5–6, 20, 60–61
teenage brain, 76–77
visualization, benefits of, 83

breaks
for AD/HD students, 74
and stress reduction, 45

bullying, strategies to combat, 41, 42

calculators, 162
California Standards for the Teaching Profession, 59
card parties, 120
CAT scan. *See* computerized axial tomography

cerebellum
automatic memory, 115–116
procedural memory and, 115
stimulation of, for attention disorders, 103

cerebral cortex
brain information pathway and, 2, 3
maturation of, 76–77

challenges. *See also* goal setting
amygdala response to, 44–45
as inclusive teaching strategy, 24–25
as motivational strategy
avoiding frustration, 24–25
overcoming past discouragement, 28–29
partial participation and, 28–29
parental feedback on level of, 48

choice
as AD/HD teaching strategy, 73
enrichment activities and, 109
as inclusive teaching strategy, 27–28
learning logs and, 30
vs. learning objectives, 28
as motivation, 27–28
as multisensory teaching strategy, 117–118
vs. structure, 73

Choosing Sides activity, 95
Chugani, Harry, 4–5
chunking, as brain function, 2
Churchill, Winston, 78
class discussion, student-centered questions, 125–128
class expert charts, 35–36
class interest graphs, for community building, 35, 41
class meetings, for community building, 36
ClassPad (alternative calculator), 162
classrooms. *See also* inclusion classrooms
learning-conducive, characteristics of, 8
supportive, need for, 51, 64
cliques, strategies to combat, 41
Cody (student), 65, 106–107
Colony Day sample activity, 187–190
Comets for Every Student sample lesson plan, 121–125
community building
classroom strategies, 35–36
cross-curricular learning and, 137
feedback as, 39
grades 4–6, 39
raising empathy for AD/HD students, 88–93
teacher modeling and, 36–38
community learning, benefits of, 13
community service requirements, validating for students, 137
computer feedback systems, 161
computer games, appeal of, 25
computerized axial tomography (CT/CAT scan), 1
computer review systems, 162–163
concrete operational stage, 33

confidence
    cross-curricular learning and, 135
    essay tests and, 167
    inclusion classrooms and, 41
    metacognition and, 154–155
    stress reduction and, 44
cooperative learning, benefits of, 13
cooperative work groups, as AD/HD
    teaching strategy, 86–88, 99–100
coping strategies, importance of learning,
    17
cross-curricular learning, 133–139
    academic benefits, 133–137
    definition of, 134
    nonacademic benefits, 137–138
    parents and, 137–138
    sample lesson plans, 139–144,
        183–184
    speakers for, 136, 138
CT scan. See computerized axial tomogra-
    phy
cues, as AD/HD teaching strategy,
    74–75
culminating activities
    overview, 144–145
    sample activities, 145–147, 187–190
curiosity, as motivation, 24–25
curriculum, standardized, as counterpro-
    ductive, 9, 51, 59–60. See also stan-
    dardized tests
curriculum sales departments, misuse of
    medical data, 4

decision-making skills. See executive func-
    tions
delayed gratification. See goal-directed
    behavior
dendrites, 3, 19
developmental level
    identification of, 52–53
    and lesson planning, 32–33
diet, AD/HD and, 104
discouragement, overcoming, 33–34. See
    also frustration
discovery, as AD/HD teaching strategy, 73
disequilibrium, curiosity prompted by,
    24–25

diversity of abilities
    accommodating. See accommodations
    building acceptance of. See community
        building
    as normal, 6, 12–13
    and peer perception of LD students,
        13, 34
    respect for, as hallmark of good
        teacher, 11–13
Dominocielo-Ho, Victor, 138
dopamine
    brain centers of, 71
    and brain information pathway, 72
    and brain reward response, 26, 71–73,
        103
    class discussion and, 126
    low levels in AD/HD students, 63
    stimulant medications and, 64
    stimulating release of, 71–73, 103–104
    teaching strategies to promote release
        of, 73–75
    teenagers and, 75–79
dramatization
    as AD/HD teaching strategy, 100
    benefits of, 129
    as enrichment teaching strategy,
        129–133
    sample activity, 188–189
    social studies skit activity, 130–133

EEG biofeedback therapy, for AD/HD,
    104–105
elementary school
    culminating activity samples, 145–146,
        187–190
    dramatization sample activity,
        130–133
    inclusive teaching strategies, 38–39,
        39–40
e-mail response technology, 161–162
emotional intelligence, 53
emotional memory, 116
emotions. See also limbic system
    coping strategies, importance of learn-
        ing, 17
    limbic system response to, 6, 18–19
    and memory, 114–116

and neuronal pathway activation, 19–20
endorphins, 169
engagement
    importance of, 8
    as multisensory teaching strategy, 118
enrichment activities. *See also* cross-curricular learning; culminating activities; dramatization; learning centers; multisensory teaching strategies; student-centered activities
    benefits of, 108–109
    overview of, 109–110
    preventive, 173
epileptic children, glucose metabolism in, 4–5
episodic (event) memory, 114–115
essay tests, preparation strategies, 167–168
event (episodic) memory, 114–115
executive function process centers, stimulating memory utilization by, 20
executive functions. *See also* goal-directed behavior; goal setting; judgment skills; organizational skills; prioritization skills; study skills; time management skills
    AD/HD and, 64, 68
    benefits of instruction in, 6–7
    functions included in, 6–7
    reward behavior and, 71
    stimulant medications and, 64
    teaching of, 164–165
    in teenagers, 75–76
    test preparation and, 164–165
exercise, as AD/HD therapy, 103–104
exploratory learners, inclusive teaching strategies for, 58–59
Explorer sample lesson plan, 176–184

familiarity, and patterning for brain network alignment, 68–70
feedback
    computer feedback systems, 161
    computer review systems, 162–163
    formative assessment, 31–32, 118–119
    as inclusive teaching strategy, 31–32
    motivation and, 31–32
    rubric-based (pre-feedback), 31
    student participation in, 32
    summaries of knowledge gained, 192–193
    supporting LD students through, 39
fMRI (functional magnetic resonance imaging)
    how it works, 1–2
    reward behavior studies, 71–72
focus time, reporting of, 48
formative assessment, 31–32, 118–119
frontal lobes
    AD/HD and, 63–64, 68, 103, 104
    brain information pathway and, 3, 60
    limbic system and, 18
    reward behavior and, 71
    in teenagers, 75–76
    test preparation and, 164–165
frustration. *See also* stress
    in high school students, 43
    strategies for overcoming, 29–30, 33–34, 37–38, 38–39
functional brain imaging
    AD/HD, 63–64, 69, 88–89
    on diversity of abilities, 12
    dopamine release stimulation, 71
    engagement, 118
    experiential learning, 116
    imaging technology, 1–2
    misuse and misinterpretation of, 3–4
    multisensory learning, 111
    and neurobiological basis of learning disabilities, 5
    patterning for brain network alignment, 69
    reward behavior
        in general, 71–72
        in teenagers, 77, 78
functional magnetic resonance imaging (fMRI). *See* fMRI

Gamboa, Judy, 15–16
games
    computer, appeal of, 25
    memory, during attendance-taking, 99
    movement-oriented, 94–95
    for review and reinforcement, 160

Gardner, Howard, 53, 173
gifted students
    reassuring parents of, 47
    review and reinforcement for, 156
global learners, inclusive teaching strategies for, 58
glucose metabolism, and learning potential, 4–5
goal-directed behavior, 79–86
    benefits of, 79–80, 84
    teaching strategies to encourage, 81–84
goal planners, 26
goals, supporting students who fail to reach, 27
goal setting. *See also* challenges
    for discouraged students, 34
    importance of, for success, 17
    as inclusive teaching strategy, 26–27
    motivation and, 26–27
    process of, 26–27
grade levels
    culminating activity samples
        elementary through high school, 187–190
        grades 4–8, 145–146
    dramatization, grades 4–8, 130–133
    inclusive teaching strategies
        grades 4–6, 39–40
        grades K–3, 38–39
        middle school, 40–42
    multisensory lesson samples
        grades 4–7, 120–121
        grades K–3, 121–125
    writing project samples
        elementary through high school, 184–194
        grades 5–8, 176–184
grades, as predictor of life success, 17
grading. *See* assessments
grammar lessons
    metacognition in, 153–154
    tying to cross-curricular units, 139
graphic organizers, 119, 185
gray matter. *See* cerebral cortex
Greek Gods Book sample lesson plan, 191–194
groups. *See* partners and groups

height check, as teaching tool, 94
high school
    culminating activity samples, 187–190
    inclusive teaching strategies, 42–43
    writing project samples, 184–194
hippocampus
    disequilibrium-prompted curiosity and, 24–25
    dopamine release and, 71
    limbic system and, 18
    semantic memory and, 114
homework
    advising parents on, 47–48
    e-mail response technology and, 161–162
    parental feedback on, 48
    relevance and meaning of, 45–46
    starting in class, 30–31
Hot Potato activity, 159–160
Hunter, Madeline, 151
hyperactivity
    in adults, 75
    brain studies, 64
hyperkinetic behavior, brain studies, 64

IDEA. *See* Individuals with Disabilities Education Act
Iditarod sample lesson plan, 139–144
IEP. *See* individualized education program
imaging. *See* functional brain imaging
inclusion classrooms
    benefits and advantages of, 16
    continuum of abilities in, 6
    decoration of, 96, 109
    seating arrangements, 109, 115
    teacher concerns, 16
    true inclusiveness in, 14
inclusiveness
    as AD/HD teaching strategy, 96–98
    language of, 37, 59
inclusive teaching strategies, 20–34. *See also* AD/HD teaching strategies; cross-curricular learning; culminating activities; dramatization; motivational strategies; multisensory teaching strategies; student-centered activities

academic priming (lesson previewing), 29, 74
benefits of, 14–16, 40–41
challenges. *See* challenges
choice. *See* choice
cross-curricular learning as, 135
developmentally appropriate lesson planning, 32–33
discouragement, overcoming, 33–34
disequilibrium-prompted curiosity, 24–25
for exploratory learners, 58–59
feedback, 31–32
for global learners, 58
goal setting. *See* goal setting
grades 4–6, 39–40
grades K–3, 38–39
high school and beyond, 42–43
importance of employing, 59–61
individualized instruction, incremental approach to, 21, 49
learning logs, 30
manipulation and application of information, 109
meetings with individual students, 147
middle school, 40–42
multiple intelligences and, 55–56
observation, 21–22
organizational skills instruction. *See* organizational skills
overview of, 13
partial participation, 28–29
physical accommodations, 22
professional feedback on, 49–50
relevance and meaning. *See* relevance and meaning
for sequential (analytical) learners, 57
suitability for all students, 6–7, 52
teacher enthusiasm, 24
independent work, in learning centers, 147–149
individualized education program (IEP), IDEA requirements for, 13–14
individualized instruction
e-mail response technology and, 161–162
incremental approach to, 21, 49

regular meetings with students, 147
Individuals with Disabilities Education Act (IDEA), 13–14
information pathway in brain
strengthening of neuronal pathways in, 20, 68, 73, 103, 108–109, 111, 151–152
structure and function of, 2–3, 17–20, 60, 72 (*See also* brain research)
interest mode, in AD/HD students, 67–68
interests. *See also* relevance and meaning
class interest graphs, for community building, 35, 41
connecting less-interesting material to, 135–136
connecting to, as teaching strategy, 41, 67–68, 81–83, 86–87, 96–97
International Consortium for Brain Mapping, 173
Internet, as source for relevance-creating strategies, 45
interpersonal intelligence, 22, 55
intrapersonal intelligence, 55
introduction for report, sample assignment, 180
IQ, as predictor of life success, 17

James (student), 85–86
Journal of the American Dietetic Association, 104
judgment skills. *See also* executive functions
teaching, 164
in teenagers, 76–78

kidwatching. *See* observation of children
Koch, Ron, 97
K-W-L charts, 119, 129, 139, 143

language of inclusiveness, 37, 59
LD. *See* learning disability
learning centers, 147–149
Learning Disabilities Association of Arizona, 15–16
learning disability (LD)
definition of, 11–12, 52
diagnosis of, 52–53
neurobiological basis of, 5

learning disability (LD) (*continued*)
  prevalence, 62
  preventive diagnosis of, 173
  as temporary condition, 5, 15
learning logs, 30, 149
learning strategies, effective, student self-awareness of, 154–155
learning styles. *See also* multiple intelligences; multisensory teaching strategies
  definition of, 52
  enrichment activities and, 109
  and essay test preparation, 167
  exploratory learners, 58–59
  global learners, 58
  and goal setting, 34
  helping parents understand, 47
  identification of, 52–53, 56
  national and state standards' recognition of, 59
  physical accommodations for, 22
  in review and reinforcement, 119–120, 155–156
  sequential (analytical) learners, 57
  technological review aids and, 160–161
lessons
  planning, developmental appropriateness in, 32–33
  sample. *See* sample lesson plans
  student-centered, 128–129
Life in Colonial America sample lesson plan, 184–190
life-skills discussions, 41
limbic system. *See also* amygdala
  AD/HD and, 63–64
  brain information pathway and, 2
  components of, 18
  emotional states and, 6, 18
listening, and community building, 36
logical-mathematical intelligence, 54

Magnetism sample lesson plan, 120–121
mainstreaming, *vs.* full inclusion, 14
manipulation and application of information, importance of, 109
Margalit, Malka, 40–41
Marshmallow Test, 79–80

math lessons, tying to cross-curricular units, 139–140
Mazziotta, John, 4–5, 173
McCourt, Frank, 36–37
meaning. *See* relevance and meaning
medial temporal lobe, limbic system and, 18
meetings, with individual students, 147
memory. *See also* review and reinforcement; tests, preparation strategies
  as brain function, 2, 3
  brain information pathway and, 17–18
  cross-curricular learning and, 134–135
  effective strategies for, 22–23
  emotion and, 114–116
  growth of neuronal pathways, 20
  memory systems, overview of, 113–116
  multisensory learning and, 111, 116–120
  personalization and, 117, 118
  reward and, 45
  strategies to improve, by memory type, 114–116
metacognition
  review and reinforcement with, 152–155
  teaching to AD/HD students, 79, 83, 84
middle school
  culminating activity samples, 145–146, 187–190
  dramatization sample activity, 130–133
  inclusive teaching strategies, 40–42
  multisensory lesson samples, 120–121
  writing project samples, 176–194
Mischel, Walter, 79–80
modeling
  by students, of poor behavior, in community building, 42
  by teacher, in community building, 36–38
motivation
  importance of, 8
  limbic system response to, 18

motivational strategies
  academic priming (lesson previewing),
    29, 74
  for AD/HD students
    positive reinforcement, 64–66, 68
    relevance, 67–68
  challenges. *See* challenges
  choice. *See* choice
  class meetings, 36
  discouragement, overcoming, 33–34
  disequilibrium-prompted curiosity,
    24–25
  feedback. *See* feedback
  frustration, overcoming, 29–30,
    33–34, 37–38, 38 39
  goal setting. *See* goal setting
  learning logs, 30
  partial participation, 28 29
  positive reinforcement. *See* positive
    reinforcement
  prediction of test items, 165
  relevance and meaning. *See* relevance
    and meaning
  success as, 38, 68, 72, 79, 83, 84–86
    (*See also* positive reinforcement)
  teacher enthusiasm, 24
MRIs, brain development studies, 76–77
multiple intelligences, 53–56. *See also*
  diversity of abilities; learning styles;
  multisensory teaching strategies
  activities to stimulate, 119–120
  broader categories of, 57–59
  and inclusive teaching strategies,
    55–56
  national and state standards' recogni-
    tion of, 59
  shift in prevalence of types, in U.S., 56
  uncovering, through inclusive strate-
    gies, 15–16
multisensory teaching strategies
  assessments, formative, 118–119
  benefits of, 110–113
  choice, 117–118
  engagement, 118
  learning centers, 147–149
  memory stimulation via, 111, 116–120
  multiple media usage, 117

review and reinforcement, 119,
    155–156
  sample lesson plans, 120–125, 182–183
music, as attention-focusing device, 70
musical-rhythmic intelligence, 54–55

narrative lessons, and student motivation,
  23
Narrative Sequencing activity, 94–95
National Center for Health Statistics, 62
naturalist intelligence, 53, 55
neuronal pathways. *See also* brain research
  activating factors, 19–20
  strengthening of, 20, 68, 73, 103,
    108–109, 111, 151–152
neurons, 3, 17
neurotransmitters
  AD/HD and, 63–64
  role of, 19
norepinepherine
  AD/HD and, 63–64
  exercise and, 103–104
note taking
  as review and reinforcement strategy,
    157
  sample assignment, 181
  teaching, 157–159
novelty. *See* surprise and novelty
nucleus accumbens, reward behavior and,
  71, 77

observation of children
  in challenge design, 29
  and individualized instruction design,
    49
  as teaching strategy, 21–22
obsessive-compulsive disorder (OCD), 63
OCD. *See* obsessive-compulsive disorder
organizational skills, 30–31. *See also* executive functions
  to AD/HD students, 85–86
  sample assignment, 178–179
  in studying, 164
outlines
  in essay test preparation, 167
  reports presented as, 185–186
  sample assignment, 181

ownership, as AD/HD teaching strategy, 73–74

papers
    teacher comments on, ensuring that students read, 32
    writing project samples, 176–194
parents
    cross-curricular programs and, 137–138
    discussing rewards with, 49
    explaining assessments to, 49
    homework advice for, 47–48
    homework feedback from, 48
    involvement of, as natural, 47
    pressure on teachers from, 47
partial participation, as motivational strategy, 28–29
partners and groups. See also culminating activities; dramatization
    as AD/HD teaching strategy, 86–88, 99–100
    benefits of, 146
    community building through, 41–42
    enrichment activities and, 109
    partner pair-shares, 139
    prediction of test items, 165
    team review activities, 159–160
patterning, for brain network alignment, 68–70
peer editing, in essay test preparation, 167
peer interviews
    for community building, 35
    sample assignment, 177
peer support, 40–41. See also community building
perseverance, importance of, 17
personalization
    as AD/HD teaching strategies, 100–101
    and memory retention, 117, 118
PET (positron emission tomography) scans
    engagement, 118
    experiential learning, 116
    growing brain pathways, 108
    how it works, 1–2

misuse/misinterpretation of, 4–5
    and preventive diagnosis, 173
Phelps, Michael, 4–5
physical accommodations, 22
physical movement, as AD/HD teaching strategy, 94–95
Piaget, Jean, 32–33
Pinon, Mona, 23
play, teenagers and, 78
positive reinforcement
    as AD/HD teaching strategy, 74, 78–79
    class discussion and, 127
    limbic system response to, 18
    as motivational strategy, 64–66, 68
    and release of dopamine, 71–73
positron emission tomography (PET) scans. See PET scans
prediction, of test items, as test preparation strategy, 165–166
pre-feedback (rubric-based feedback), 31
prefrontal cortex, working memory and, 114
preoperational stage, 33
presentations, as AD/HD teaching strategy, 97
previewing of material (academic priming), 29, 74
prioritization skills, 164–165. See also executive functions
proactive approach to life, importance of, 17
procedural memory, 115
progress
    praising. See positive reinforcement
    in time management, reviewing, 27
project-based learning, benefits of, 13

qEEG (quantitative electroencephalogram), 1–2, 105
quantitative electroencephalogram. See qEEG
questions, student-centered, 125–128
quiz games, for review and reinforcement, 160

RAS. See reticular activating system
realia, and student motivation, 23

reinforcement. *See* review and reinforcement
reinforcement learning theory, 71–73
relational connection, and memory retention, 117, 118
relational memory, 116
relevance and meaning. *See also* cross-curricular learning; interests
    for AD/HD students, 67–68
    cross-curricular learning and, 133–137
    of homework, 45–46
    as inclusive teaching strategy, 22–23
    learning logs and, 30
    as motivational strategy, 22–23
    sample assignment, 178, 192
    strategies for creating, 45
    stress and, 45
report-writing process, sample assignment, 179–181, 186–187
resident expert charts, 35–36
respect, as teaching strategy, 64–65
reticular activating system (RAS)
    AD/HD and, 63–64
    in brain information pathway, 18
    emotion and, 18–19
    response to appropriate challenge, 45
    response to stress, 43
review and reinforcement. *See also* study skills; tests, preparation strategies
    and brain structure, 151–152
    importance of, 151–152
    as multisensory teaching strategy, 119
    strategies for, 119–120, 155–160
        graphic organizers, 119, 185
        K-W-L charts, 119
        metacognition, 152–155
        multisensory review, 119–120, 155–156
        note taking, 157–159
        presentations and projects, 119
        team review activities, 159–160
    summaries of knowledge gained, 192–193
    technologies for, 160–163
rewards
    discussing with parents, 49
    and learning ability, 45

reward behavior studies
    in general, 71–72
    in teenagers, 77, 78
Ritalin, 64
role-playing activities, in community building, 42
rubric-based feedback (pre-feedback), 31

sample lesson plans
    for AD/HD students, 98–100
    Americana Experience, 145–146
    American Colonial Settlements, 98–100
    for attention disorder students, 98–100
    Bake Sale, 146–147
    Choosing Sides activity, 95
    Comets for Every Student, 121–125
    for cross-curricular learning, 139–144, 183–184
    culminating activities, 145–147, 187–190
    Explorer Report, 176–184
    Greek Gods Book, 191–194
    Iditarod, 139–144
    Life in Colonial America, 184–190
    Magnetism, 120–121
    for multisensory learning, 120–125
    reports and writing, 176–194
    Writing a Book for Younger Students, 190–191
Sandy (student), 85
Schertzer, Kevin, 190–191
scientific principles, modeling with movement, 95
selective mode, in AD/HD students, 68
self-concept, positive
    importance of, 17
    overcoming LD stereotypes, 34–35
self-discipline. *See* goal-directed behavior
self-monitoring. *See* goal-directed behavior
semantic memory, 114
sensory input
    patterning for brain network alignment, 68–70
    unconscious selection process for, 66

sequential (analytical) learners
    inclusive teaching strategies for, 57
    review and reinforcement for, 156
Smith, Dominique, 191–194
social adjustment, inclusion classrooms
    and, 14–15, 40–41
social exclusion, strategies to combat, 41,
    42
social studies skit activity, 130–133
special education classes, common prob-
    lems in, 15
sports, organized, AD/HD students and,
    103–104
standardized curriculum, as counterpro-
    ductive, 9, 51, 59–60
standardized tests
    explaining to children, 49
    limitations of, 168
    and pressure to standardize curricu-
        lum, 59–60
    teaching mandated content, 135
standards, national and state, on learning
    styles/multiple intelligences, 59
stimulant medications, AD/HD and, 64
stories, and student motivation, 23
stress
    in AD/HD students, 67, 69, 88
    indicators of, 44
    limbic system response to, 18
    praise and, 78
    RAS response to, 43
    reduction strategies
        for classroom, 43–46
        for tests, 46–47
    supportive classroom, need for, 51, 64
    tests and, 46–47, 166, 167, 169–170
structure, *vs.* choice, 73
student-centered activities, 125–129
    lessons, 128–129
    overview of, 125
    questions, 125–128
study skills. *See also* review and reinforce-
    ment; tests, preparation strategies
    executive functions and, 164–165
    importance of learning, 152–153
substance abuse, AD/HD and, 76–77, 78,
    103

success
    attributes leading to, 17
    components of, 16–17
    five critical conditions of, 17–20
    as motivational strategy, 38, 68, 72,
        79, 83, 84–86, 106–107 (*See also*
        positive reinforcement)
    visualizing, benefits of, 83
support. *See also* community building
    feedback and, 39
    peer, 40–41
    for students who fail to reach goals, 27
    systems, importance of, 17
supportive classrooms, need for, 51, 64
surprise and novelty
    and memory, 115
    as teaching strategy, 71–72, 95–96, 98
survival mode, in AD/HD students, 66–67
synapses, 4–5, 19
synthesis of information, executive func-
    tion process centers and, 20

tapping, in AD/HD students, 70
Teacher Man (McCourt), 36–37
teacher-researcher partnership, future of,
    172–174
teachers
    benefits of cross-curricular learning for,
        138
    and brain research
        benefits of understanding, 7–8
        time and resources needed to study,
            60–61
    impact of inclusion classroom on, 16
    modeling by, in community building,
        36–38
    passion of, as student motivation, 24
    professional feedback for, 49–50
    professional growth
        time and resources needed for,
            60–61
        value of, 8
    self-evaluation by
        criteria for, 50, 174–175
        lesson success, 101–102
teaching strategies. *See also* AD/HD
    teaching strategies; cross-curricular

learning; dramatization; inclusive
    teaching strategies; motivational strate-
    gies; multisensory teaching strategies;
    student-centered activities
    and brain research. *See* brain research
    effective, core concepts underlying, 8,
        174
technology
    brain imaging technology, 1–2
    and multiple intelligence types, 56
    for review and reinforcement, 160–163
teenagers
    AD/HD teaching strategies, 78–79
    brain structure, 76–77
    and dopamine, 75–79
    executive functions in, 75–76
    judgment skills in, 76–78
temporal lobes, 114
tests
    accommodations, 165, 168–169
    executive functions and, 164–165
    instructions, verifying understanding
        of, 170
    open-note, to encourage note taking,
        158
    post-test routines, 170–171
    preparation strategies, 165–171
        essay tests, 167–168
        explicit strategy instruction, 168
        prediction of test items, 165–166
        preparation guides, personal,
            166–167
        student feedback on test expecta-
            tions, 166–167
        study guides, 169
        on test day, 169–170
    reviewing results of, 170–171
    and stress, 46–47, 166, 167, 169–170
    stress reduction strategies, 46–47

teacher comments on, ensuring that
        students read, 32, 171
    value of, 163–164
thalamus, 18
thumbs up/down, as teaching tool, 94
time, allowing additional, as AD/HD
        teaching strategy, 74
time management skills. *See also* executive
        functions
    vs. goal-directed behavior skills, 83
    helping AD/HD students with, 74
    helping report writers with, 182
    prediction exercises, 27
    progress, monitoring, 27
    for tests, 170
treasure charts (goal planners), 26
trip planners (goal planners), 26

verbal-linguistic intelligence, 54, 56
visualization, as AD/HD teaching strategy,
        100–101
visual-spatial intelligence, 54

What the Bleep Do We Know!? (film), 69
white matter, in brain anatomy, 3
"Why?" (Willis), v–vi
Willis, Judy, v–vi
Willis, Malana, 8, 21
withdrawn students, physical accommo-
        dations for, 22
wizard plans (goal planners), 26
working memory, 114
Writing a Book for Younger Students
        sample lesson plan, 190–191
writing project samples, 176–194

Yeager, Beth, 145

zone of proximal development, 29

ABOUT THE AUTHOR

Dr. Judy Willis, a board-certified neurologist and middle school teacher in Santa Barbara, California, has combined her training in neuroscience and neuroimaging with her teacher education training and years of classroom experience. She has become an authority in the field of learning-centered brain research and classroom strategies derived from this research.

After graduating Phi Beta Kappa as the first woman graduate of Williams College, Willis attended UCLA School of Medicine, where she remained as a resident and was ultimately Chief Resident in Neurology. She was in private practice for 15 years, and then received a credential and master's degree in education from the University of California, Santa Barbara. She has taught in elementary, middle, and graduate schools; was a fellow in the National Writing Project; and currently teaches at Santa Barbara Middle School. Her articles about the neurology of learning have been published in many educational journals, and she is a speaker at state and national professional educator conferences. She is also the author of the ASCD book *Research-Based Strategies to Ignite Student Learning* (2006).

Willis is also a regular contributor to wine literature and writes wine columns for two newspapers. Her 2005 article in *Decanter* magazine described the impact of the film *Sideways* on California Pinot Noir sales. She can be reached by e-mail at jwillisneuro@aol.com.

RELATED ASCD RESOURCES:
THE BRAIN AND LEARNING IN INCLUSION CLASSROOMS

At the time of publication, the following ASCD resources were available (ASCD stock numbers appear in parentheses). For up-to-date information about ASCD resources, go to www.ascd.org.

AUDIO

Building an Inclusion Learning Environment at the Secondary Level by Susanne Flatley, Kathleen Pilla, and Sandra Weinman (#504361)

Differentiation for ALL Students in Inclusive, Urban Classrooms by Jacki Anderson, Ann Halvorsen, and Linda Lee (#504308)

Early Childhood Inclusion: Positive Approach to a Successful Classroom by Laura Micko (#505270)

Inclusion: From the Eyes of Students and Teachers After Implementation by Pamela Musick (#505286)

Surviving Inclusion: Helpful Strategies and Assistive Technologies for Teachers by Kay Lehmann (#203149)

MULTIMEDIA

The Human Brain Professional Inquiry Kit by Bonnie Benesh (#999003)

NETWORKS

Visit the ASCD Web site (www.ascd.org) and search for "networks" for information about professional educators who have formed groups around various topics, including "Brain-Compatible Learning" and "Multiple Intelligences." Look in the "Network Directory" for current facilitators' addresses and phone numbers.

ONLINE COURSES

Go to ASCD's Home Page (www.ascd.org) and click on professional development to find the following ASCD Professional Development Online Courses: *The Brain: Memory and Learning Strategies*; *The Brain: Understanding the Mind*; *The Brain: Understanding the Physical Brain*; *The Inclusive Classroom*; and *Our Multiple Intelligences*.

PRINT PRODUCTS

Brain Matters: Translating Research into Classroom Practice by Patricia Wolfe (#101004)

Teaching to the Brain's Natural Learning Systems by Barbara K. Given (#101075)

Teaching with the Brain in Mind, 2nd edition by Eric Jensen (#104013)

Creating an Inclusive School, 2nd edition by Richard A. Villa and Jacqueline S. Thousand (#105019)

Inclusive Schools in Action: Making Differences Ordinary by James McLeskey and Nancy Waldron (#100210)

Educational Leadership October 2003 Teaching All Students (#103386)

VIDEOTAPES

The Brain and Learning Series (#498062)

The Brain and Mathematics Series (#400237)

The Brain and Reading Series (#499207)

For more information, visit us on the World Wide Web (http://www.ascd.org); send an e-mail message to member@ascd.org; call the ASCD Service Center (1-800-933-ASCD or 703-578-9600, then press 2); send a fax to 703-575-5400; or write to Information Services, ASCD, 1703 N. Beauregard St., Alexandria, VA 22311-1714 USA.